Driv'n by Fortune

Driv'n by Fortune

The Scots' March to
Modernity in America, 1745–1812

SAM ALLISON

With a Foreword
by Richard W. Pound

DUNDURN
TORONTO

Editor: Allison Hirst
Copy editor: Michael Melgaard
Design: Laura Boyle
Cover design: Laura Boyle
Front cover image adapted from John H. MacNaughton, *The 78th Fraser Highlanders* (around 1880)
Back cover image courtesy of the Art Gallery of Ontario, *Landing Craft* AGOID.106297=SML053-05103
Printer: Webcom

Library and Archives Canada Cataloguing in Publication

Allison, Sam, 1943-, author
        Driv'n by fortune : the Scots' march to modernity in America, 1745–1812 / Sam Allison; foreword by Richard W. Pound.

Includes bibliographical references and index.
Issued in print and electronic formats.
ISBN 978-1-4597-2203-3 (pbk.).--ISBN 978-1-4597-2204-0 (pdf).-- ISBN 978-1-4597-2205-7 (epub)

1. Great Britain. Army. Fraser's Highlanders--History. 2. Canada--History, Military. 3. United States--History, Military. I. Title. II. Title: Driv'n by fortune.

UA652.F7A45 2015   356'.10941   C2014-906764-X
                                                      C2014-906765-8

1   2   3   4   5   19   18   17   16   15

Conseil des Arts du Canada   Canada Council for the Arts   Canada   ONTARIO ARTS COUNCIL CONSEIL DES ARTS DE L'ONTARIO an Ontario government agency un organisme du gouvernement de l'Ontario

We acknowledge the support of the **Canada Council for the Arts** and the **Ontario Arts Council** for our publishing program. We also acknowledge the financial support of the **Government of Canada** through the **Canada Book Fund** and **Livres Canada Books,** and the **Government of Ontario** through the **Ontario Book Publishing Tax Credit** and the **Ontario Media Development Corporation.**

Care has been taken to trace the ownership of copyright material used in this book. The author and the publisher welcome any information enabling them to rectify any references or credits in subsequent editions.

— *J. Kirk Howard, President*

The publisher is not responsible for websites or their content unless they are owned by the publisher.

VISIT US AT
Dundurn.com | @dundurnpress | Facebook.com/dundurnpress | Pinterest.com/dundurnpress

Dundurn
3 Church Street, Suite 500
Toronto, Ontario, Canada
M5E 1M2

Contents

List of Maps

List of Tables

Foreword

by Richard W. Pound

Sam Allison was as skillful setting the hook for my modest contribution to his book as he was in the identification of the principle theses of this work. While my family name, Pound, is about as English as can be imagined, he knew that my mother's family were Highland Scots, with a full line of Frasers. Added to that background is the fact that there were (as I understand the family lore) several members of the family who were part of the 78th Fraser's Highlanders regiment, serving, *inter alia,* at Louisbourg, Quebec, and Montreal. Fraser is a name held by one of my sisters, by one of my children, and, of course, my kilt is Ancient Fraser. It was child's play for him to dangle the bait of writing a foreword for the book, bait that proved to be irresistible.

There are several features of this work that will give it a well-deserved place in Canadian history. The first is its ability to establish the context for the involvement of the Scots in warfare in Europe and the Americas. Although it is not often commented upon (especially by the Scots themselves), the fact of the matter is that they, especially the Highlanders,

were well -sought-after mercenaries. Part of the reason was circumstan-
tial — a combination of birth rates, lack of other employ, natural strength
derived from the harsh living conditions, and their shared language and
culture. The Highlanders proved to be capable, adaptable, and serially
loyal to those who paid their wages. Many stayed where they served and
became part of those communities, both in Europe and, as it is relevant
to the Canadian aspects of the work, in North America.

The second feature is the exposure and debunking of several myths,
romantic and otherwise, about the Highlanders in general and the Frasers
in particular. The Battle of Culloden had been, to be sure, an important
and humiliating defeat for some of the Scots. However, they recovered
and prospered soon after, and did little to contradict the beneficial effects
of the new view the English held of them. Allison uses Mark Twain's
apt description of what he called "Sir Walter's disease," the hopelessly
romantic view of the Highlanders in Sir Walter Scott's immensely popular series of novels. The real context of the Fraser's Highlanders was
not Culloden, but the Scottish Enlightenment, which had an enormous
impact on almost every aspect of life in the eighteenth and nineteenth
centuries. As Allison points out, the Scots had a major impact on economics, trade, shipping, science, medicine, religion, governance, and
politics that continues to this day.

A third feature of importance to Canadian, British, and United States
history is Allison's examination of the battle for Quebec on the Plains of
Abraham. A great deal of inaccurate and romanticized stories of that battle have long plagued the reality of what actually happened and why. It is
true that General James Wolfe was anxious, indeed desperate, to conquer
Quebec, a stronghold that effectively controlled access to North America
— not because North America was particularly important to the British,
but rather as a part of an ongoing, larger European conflict between
the French and the British. It was this context that made the victory at
Quebec so important, and Wolfe such a hero (especially after he was
killed in the process), despite the fact that it was thousands of miles away
from the main conflict and that the battle lasted less than half an hour.
Often overlooked is that Wolfe had with him, in the Fraser's as well as in

other units, very well-seasoned and disciplined troops, excellent sailors who could manage the tidal aspects of the St. Lawrence River at Quebec, and soldiers who, because of their service in continental Europe, could speak French, an attribute that proved essential, perhaps even decisive, when the final plan to capture Quebec was launched. The arrangements for the attack are described in a manner that brings the battle alive and that debunks the much-propagated myth that undisciplined Highlanders threw down their muskets and, in some sort of bloodlust, charged with their claymores. In fact, the charge (against the exposed flank of an exhausted enemy that was forced to come out from the fortified town of Quebec to do battle on difficult ground) was a pre-considered part of the plan of battle and succeeded precisely as Wolfe intended.

These are among the many well-considered exposures of historical inaccuracies and uncritical examinations of conventional conclusions that Allison identifies. It is refreshing to see such observations and one can only hope that, with this example, historians of the future will be willing to challenge existing accounts that are based less on fact and more on convenience or a perceived need to conform to some national or political agenda. As the work demonstrates, one Canadian history did not end and 1759 and another begin in 1760; there is a continuum and the Scots were an important part of making that continuum function for both sides of the earlier conflict. Allison observes that the influence and persistence of the Scots kept potential conflict from becoming racist, reducing it instead to the level of a manageable political issue. The presence of the Scots in Quebec contributed to the lack of support for the independence struggle in the colonies to the south. Those Scots in the Thirteen Colonies with military experience were, in fact, decidedly loyal to the Crown, which, once independence was established, led to their subsequent persecution and expulsion, and the arrival of large numbers of displaced Loyalists in Canada. There are some trenchant conclusions on the post-revolutionary America that deemed it white, male, and "Patriot," a political and practical reality far different from the flowery language often used by Americans to describe the outcome of their conflict with the British.

Allison makes a compelling argument that the impact of the Scots in Canada was greater after the fall of Quebec than during the conquest itself. An extraordinarily high percentage of the Highlanders who returned to Scotland when the 78th was disbanded came back to North America with their families, and often with other recruits. They were driven by ambition, not by poverty or starvation. Land was free for the veterans, or cheap for others, and ownership of property was an important measure of success and influence. Suffrage was then based on owning property; the concept of universal suffrage was generations in the future and was believed at the time to be a path to anarchy. The frontier experience gained through military experience — for many, a seven-year stint during which they mastered the means of clearing dense forests, transport by land and water, and experimented with crops and shelter — accounted for the high rate of re-migration of members of the regiment back to Canada. The conditions in the new world held no fears for them and their survival. The kilt and the red jacket led to them becoming landowners and prominent members of their communities. Scots in general were in the intellectual vanguard of North American modernity.

If there is any disappointment that results from reviewing the work, it is the apparent reluctance in recent histories to recognize the particular importance to Quebec and Canada of those Scottish contributions, starting with the Fraser's Highlanders, perhaps as a matter of perceived political correctness; a failing that genuine scholars should both regret and overcome. The facts are evident enough. Pretending they do not exist can be neither explained nor condoned.

— Richard W. Pound, C.C., O.Q., Q.C.
Chancellor Emeritus of McGill University,
former Chairman of Canada's National History Society
Hon. Colonel of the Canadian Grenadier Guards

Acknowledgements

Encouragement and advice about this book came from professors Brian Young of McGill and John Dickenson of the Université de Montréal. The late Hugh MacMillan of Ottawa, as well as Sandy Campbell of Glengarry; Barbara Rogers of Vancouver; Bruce Bolton, former colonel of the Black Watch of Canada; Neil Fraser, chief of the Clan Fraser, Canada; and Marie Fraser (editor of the Clan Fraser Society newsletter Canadian Explorer) made an invaluable contribution. Historians Paul Goodman, Earle Chapman, Ben Walsh, and Christopher Culpin (formerly of the Schools History Project of Trinity and All Saints College, Leeds, England), clarified many of the subjects discussed.

The librarians of the Burlington Public Library in Vermont, the North Carolina State Archives, the Mount Allison University and Library Archives, and the Provincial Archives of New Brunswick opened many intellectual doors about eighteenth-century Scottish migration patterns. The Royal Bank of Scotland Group Archives provided the data that linked banking to militarism, migration, and modernity.

Dr. Fiona Watson and Mairi Stuart of the University of Stirling in Scotland provided environmental information and invaluable prints of the Scots timber industry. Dr. Ted Harvey of the University of Glasgow was a mine of information on the Scottish Enlightenment and Scots soldiers in Canada. As well, over the years, the superb McGill University Library and Rare Book Collection, particularly through the support of now-retired librarian Mrs. Nellie Reis, provided the evidence that fleshed out this book.

Much appreciation goes to Barry Penhale, publisher emeritus at Dundurn, and to editors Jane Gibson and Allison Hirst, for their dedicated interest and support, and for the attention given to detail throughout the manuscript. And to Richard W. Pound, for providing the foreword.

I owe an enormous debt to my wife, Heather Allison, who prepared my manuscript with patience, cheerfulness, and accuracy, and to my two adult children, Lindsay and Meredith, both of whom lived with and contributed intellectually to this book for over a decade. Responsibility for any errors, misinterpretation, or bias lies firmly with me as the author.

Introduction

I drew into service a hardy and intrepid race of men ...
[who] served with fidelity as they fought with
valour and conquered ... in every part of the world.
— Pitt the Elder on "Highlanders," House of Commons, January 14, 1766

At 2:00 a.m., the 78th Fraser's Highlanders, as part of Major General James Wolfe's army, sped twenty-two kilometres (fourteen miles) down the turbulent St. Lawrence River. Captain Simon Fraser in the lead landing craft misled several French sentries stationed along the riverside by ordering them, in French, to be quiet. The force landed at the chosen unguarded cove at about 4:00 a.m., and Captain Donald MacDonald led eight Highlanders approximately ninety metres east of the path that went up the treed cliff. On the clifftop, MacDonald walked back to the path and again barked misleading orders in French. The Highlanders completely overwhelmed the confused sentries and drove off their sleeping companions. Then, General Wolfe's contingent climbed the path, which placed them on the Plains of Abraham, one and a half kilometres from Quebec City's walls.

By about 8:30 a.m., the 78th and the rest of the British Army were sleeping in a thin red line across the Plains, waiting for Louis-Joseph de Montcalm's army to muster. The "Battle for a Continent" on September

13, 1759, "measured by results … was one of the great battles of the world."[1] Yet, the actual fight was no dramatic tooth-and-nail struggle. It lasted approximately from 10:00 a.m. to 10:15 a.m. This short but murderous rout brought great acclaim to the 78th, partly because "Wolfe's victory at Quebec and the subsequent expulsion of the French from North America was a world-historical moment."[2] The battle led to the biggest land transfer in history — the transfer of New France to Britain and Spain. In turn, this transfer sparked a series of events that converted the Thirteen Colonies and New France into the United States and Canada. This battle was a global turning point, ensuring "that English, not French, would become the world language."[3] The generals of both armies were killed, an epic touch that immortalized Wolfe, Montcalm, and the battle itself.

After the fall of New France, the 78th patrolled the frontier near New England until the end of the Seven Years' War in 1763. The Fraser's Highlanders, raised in 1757, were then disbanded.

Why write biographies of men in such a short-lived Highland unit? Well, unlike many eighteenth-century immigrants, we can track these men with some certainty through their later military organizations during the American Revolution and through their land patents in New York, Vermont, and Canada. They are also interesting people who participated in critical events in world history. The officers who spoke French fluently enough to fool Montcalm's sentries were products of the Scots mercenary tradition. Some had served with the French Royal Scots and others had come from the Scots Brigade in the Netherlands after serving in South America. The 78th's military and migratory lives were more extensive and cosmopolitan than many people currently think.

The importance of the events the Highlanders witnessed from 1745 to 1812 meant that an unusual number of the 78th's letters, diaries, memoirs, and lists were saved on both sides of the Atlantic. This book shows what these Highlanders wrote, and what contemporary authors, such as Boswell and Samuel Johnson, wrote about them. These men made their mark on the literature of the time as well as the battles they fought in from 1745 to 1812 both in Europe and North America.

Scots soldiers played a role in forging Britain, Canada, and the United States into nation states. However, many important bits of the 78th's story did not travel well over time because of nationalistic perspectives in the history books of Canada, England, and the United States. "Nations are built on a shared view of the past — and that shared view is often wrong.... They [nationalist historians] leave out the bits where different people share histories."[4] Observations from prominent, award-winning historians have been selected to illustrate the way bias has been written into these national histories.

Nineteenth- and twentieth-century historical fiction also influenced the story of these Highlanders: "Walter Scott shaped readers' sense of the past with a force ... no scholarly article could approach."[5] Men in this regiment had a huge impact upon a historical fiction that *did* travel well over time. For instance, Colonel Simon Fraser, prosecutor in the Appin murder case, appears in Robert Louis Stevenson's *Kidnapped* and *Catriona*, stories still popularized by screen and television. However, "popularizing a fact through fiction can sometimes involve fictionalizing a fact."[6] Nineteenth-century fiction smudged twenty-first-century facts about these Highland Scots in America.

Our Approach: "The Big Questions"

The 1745 Jacobite Rebellion, the Seven Years' War, the Scottish Enlightenment, and the American Revolution are among the more analyzed and fictionalized episodes in history. These events are impossible to include thoroughly within the confines of one book. Consequently, I will focus on the "big questions" that directly involved these Highland soldier-settlers. While none of these chapters claim to reveal new truths, history is treated as a debate, and this book discusses arguments about past issues over which intelligent people may differ. This is part of a timeless conversation about eighteenth-century relationships. In the process, this book repudiates many of the conventional assumptions about Scotland and the birth of the United States and Canada. Aspects of eighteenth- and nineteenth-century life are connected in ways that will perhaps surprise the reader. The following summary of events provides a brief historical and geographical background.

Shifting Allegiances and Transformations

In the 1745 Jacobite Rebellion, the Clan Fraser regiment, led by the chief's son, Simon Fraser, fought for Bonnie Prince Charlie, son of the Catholic King James Stuart.[7] The Jacobites were trying to regain the Crown from the Protestant King George II; they were crushed in 1746 at the Battle of Culloden by Scottish and English troops loyal to the ruling Hanoverians.

In the Seven Years' War (1756–63), eleven years after he was defeated at Culloden, Simon Fraser, now the clan chief, raised a regiment from men who had fought for *both* sides at Culloden. Labelled the 78th Fraser's Highlanders, they now served King George against France. This conflict, fought over five continents, was not just the "French and Indian War," as it is known in the United States. The shortage of manpower to wage this huge conflict led British prime minister William Pitt to arm Highlanders in unprecedented large numbers soon after the 1745 Rebellion. Thousands of Highland Scots served in the British forces in North America in addition to the three Highland regiments: 42nd (Black Watch), 77th (Montgomerie's Highlanders), and the 78th Fraser's. After the Seven Years' War, veterans of the 78th took up free land alongside relatives who had served in other regiments, the artillery, marines, and navy. Approximately forty thousand Scots emigrated between 1763 and 1776.[8] Indeed, "mass emigration from Scotland to the Americas dates from the second half of the eighteenth century."[9]

These Highlanders came from a modernizing Scotland. After the 1745 Rebellion, the Fraser and other rebel estates were taken over by the Crown and forced into many changes. In the Highlands, the new way of life "stressed the need to replace traditional relationships with modern (commercial) ones … this change would free the Gaels (Highlanders) from … their chiefs."[10] Scotland was in the midst of the Scottish Enlightenment (peak years circa 1750–1800), and pioneered intellectual and practical technological advances. Scotland's great achievements transformed Europe as well as the Scots themselves.

The Scottish Enlightenment influenced the veterans of the Fraser's Highlanders in the New World to oppose the American Revolution of 1776–83 and caused them to re-migrate to Canada after. However, conventional wisdom in many history books asserts that the Highland Scots opposed the Revolution because they were reactionary and culturally medieval.

Supporters of the American Revolution, including Benjamin Franklin and Thomas Jefferson, were also influenced by the Scottish Enlightenment.[11] Lowland Scots intellectuals in the Thirteen Colonies, but not in Scotland, supported that Revolution, too. In addition, many 78th veterans who had returned to Scotland joined new Highland regiments to again fight in America. Some of these men also took up land in Canada. As a consequence, a "second period of military settlement began with the end of the American Revolution."[12]

The American Revolution was more than a struggle between Britain and its Thirteen Colonies (the future United States). It was also a European war, a war of ideals, and a civil war among the peoples in colonial America. For example, the Ulster Scots Protestants were one of "the core cultures of rebellion" against the Crown.[13] Part of the intent of this work is to show that the military experience and cultural ideals of the Scots Highlanders made them one of the core cultures of Loyalism, which explains why "Scots came to be so reviled by the Colonial Patriots."[14]

The thirteen separate colonies became a free republic of thirteen United States partly through the help of autocratic France. Yet, these thirteen militantly Protestant colonies had initiated the Seven Years' War against a militantly Catholic France. Highland Scots Jacobites fought in the 1745 Rebellion with the help of France, but fought *against* France in the Seven Years' and American Revolutionary Wars. Allegiances and loyalties shifted dramatically between 1745 and 1812. Explanations are offered for "an intriguing paradox" that has long puzzled the students of American history: "Why did the Highlanders, bitter foes of the House of Hanover in the first half of the eighteenth century, rally to the unpopular cause of Hanoverian George III thirty years after their defeat and humiliation in the Forty-Five?"[15]

The United States declared war on Canada and Britain in 1812. The Highland Scots continued to support the Crown during this conflict. By then, Scots "regiments became the back bone of the British Army; their gentlemen served as colonial governors; and their merchants exploited the colonial trade."[16] Indeed, Scots became the capitalist backbone of the Canadian economy. This is no historical accident. This book shows that Scots militarism, migration, and capitalistic modernity were all connected. In addition, the 1812 war ended the practice of Scots military-migratory settlement: "The last military settlements established in Canada were those in the Bathurst District of Upper Canada following the War of 1812." As far as I know, this is the first book to track the soldiers of a British regiment before they joined and after they served in that regiment.

Who Was Who?

As the *Dictionary of Canadian Biography* states, "Untangling the several Alexander Frasers who served with the 78th Foot in the campaigns of the Seven Years' War has been a perennial problem."[18] There were seventeen Alexander Frasers, and many similar names held the same rank in the 78th Fraser's Highlanders. The 78th Fraser's Highlanders fought in the Seven Years' War, and the 71st Regiment, also called Fraser's Highlanders, fought in the American Revolutionary War. Different men, such as "Lieutenant John Nairne," appear with the same name and rank in *both* regiments, and the same name appears with a different rank in the same regiment — there is both a Lieutenant and Captain Nairne of the 78th.

Even more bewildering, the same men were given different names. Donald MacDonald, who spoke French to the sentries, is often labelled Donald McDonnell by historians.[19] The same Lieutenant Allan Stewart is also called Allan Steuart and Allen Stuart in the different lists recording him from 1745 to 1790.[20]

There is a Highland tradition of naming male children after the paternal grandfather, and female children after the maternal grandmother. Consequently, contemporary Scots had difficulties with similar names.[21] During the Revolutionary War some men unintentionally twice received the stipulated three pound bonus for enlisting, while others of the same name received nothing. Settlement records of the 78th in North America are also plagued by problems arising from similar names.[22]

Captain Simon Fraser, who spoke French to the Quebec sentries from his position on the British landing crafts, was accompanied by at least five other Simon Frasers.[23] However, Colonel Simon Fraser could *not* climb the cliffs *nor* command during the actual battle, since he had been wounded. Yet, Colonel Fraser is shown as one of the figures in West's famous painting *The Death of* Wolfe[24] and some scholars even have him saying things that he could not possibly have said in the battle.[25] To add to this confusion, there are a great many other Simon Frasers prominent among the early Scots in North America.[26]

The most common surname in the regiment was "Fraser," followed by variations of "MacDonald." Similar names make it impossible to track individuals through Scotland, the Netherlands, France, Canada, and the Thirteen Colonies with complete accuracy. These men often shifted into other regiments and then claimed land as members of their new regiment. It is difficult to know for certain which veterans of the 78th served in other regiments. References are often only to "Mr. Fraser of the 78th Regiment." Documents written after the conquest by Quebec's French-speaking notaries were so confusing and full of misspellings that they were impossible to decipher. "Macaille de Dondy" in Quebec legal contracts may be "Mackay from Dundee," but "MacLenine de Lebarat en Écosse" could be MacLean, MacKinnon, MacNeil, MacNichol, or MacQueen, all of whom were in the 78th.

No matter the names of its members, the 78th prospered. Its soldiers were neither the first nor the most numerous to cross the Atlantic. However, it is no historical accident that their children were the first to cross the continent. The 78th Fraser's Highlanders, driven by fortune, settled far beyond their country to make an impact far beyond their times. This is their story.

1

Mercenary Migration
Through Europe

Rats, lice and Scotsmen, you find them the world over.
— Medieval French proverb

From the 1200s to the 1700s, thousands of Scots mercenary soldiers served European monarchs and principalities. I have organized their stories into different eras: a *Buildup* when the foundations for mercenary traditions were laid, a *Take-Off* that expanded military activity throughout Europe, and finally a *Globalization*, which took the mercenaries into the colonial empires of the Dutch, French, Spanish, Swedish, Russian, and Turks. Mercenary activity rose and fell with economic conditions in Scotland and the scale of wars abroad. I will focus on some of the obvious impacts such military service had on Scotland and the host countries that employed them. For example, these men worked for pay, which was often in the form of land or similar recompense, rather than money. Consequently, many stayed on their new land in the host country, and then attracted fellow Scots to that country. The Scots' encounter with Europe from the 1200s to the 1700s often involved a military-migratory land relationship. This is not to underestimate Scottish trade with Europe, but it indicates a side to Scotland that is often ignored.

Buildup 1250–1550

France, medieval Europe's greatest and richest country, was the largest employer of Scottish soldiers in the three hundred years of Buildup between 1250 and 1550. The *Gens d'armes écossais* (Scots Guards), formed in 1425[1] to guard the King, was composed of men with surnames such as Fraser, MacLeod, and Ramsay. This unit is the most famous example of Scottish mercenary activity that took place during this period. William Wallace (c. 1270-1305), Hollywood's *Braveheart* and King Robert the Bruce (1274–1329) established trade and treaties between France and Scotland.[2] France and Scotland formed the "Auld Alliance" to protect themselves from England. France funded Scottish soldiers to defend its interests, and so military traffic was mostly one way, from the smaller and poorer Scotland. This Auld Alliance lasted until the Reformation of the 1500s, at which point Protestant Scotland moved away from Catholic France toward Protestant England.

Table 1: Scottish Military-Migratory Activity		
1250+ Buildup	1550+ Take-Off	1700+ Globalization
Fraser aristocrats in French Scots Guards.	**Fraser Clan Unit** fights for Sweden in Poland (1656+).	78th (1756–63) and 71st **Fraser's Highlanders** (1776–83) in North America.
FRANCE, largest employer of Scots soldiers (15,000 in 1400s). Hugh Kennedy, major supporter of Joan of Arc. Captain of Scots Guards in 1559 accidentally kills King Henry II in a jousting accident. **GERMANY**, the fragmented nature of its principalities makes it difficult to trace the Scots. Willy Douglas killed by English mercenaries.	**FRANCE** Scots in colonies of Brazil and New France, but drift away from France (Jean Stuart becomes Hans Stuart in Sweden). **SWEDEN** Largest employer of Scots (Thirty Years War): approximately 25,000 Scots in their army. Scots enlist for Sweden in 1573, 1610, 1618–48. Some claim that 20% of Scots males fought in Thirty Years' War and sometimes changed sides.	**CHINA** Colin Campbell is ambassador for Sweden 1734–38. **INDIA** Scots and Franco-Scots, such as the nephew of John Law the financier, fight for French. **DUTCH GUIANA (Suriname)** Scots Brigade in the Netherlands served here. Gabriel Stedman (1744–97) writes an anti-slavery book about his experiences.

IRELAND, probably the earliest area (1259) for Scots mercenaries; "Gallowglass," form a hereditary military caste and localize their names hold land in return for military service.

AUSTRIA Some Scots fight for Austria in the Thirty Years' War, but most fight against them.

Count Walter Leslie (1606–67) helps murder Wallenstein becomes a major landowner and converts to Catholicism.

IRELAND MacDonnells of Antrim separate from MacDonalds of Scotland in 1558.

Scots army of 1643 bond to make themselves independent of anyone except their paymasters.

20–30,000 Scots settle Ireland 1600–1650.

POLAND Approximately 30,000 Scots here in 1600 and then 30,000–40,000 more migrate here 1600-50.

RUSSIA Scots aristocrats settle in Russia include: Carmichael, Carr, Barclay, Ogilvy, Bruce, Douglas, Gordon.

Patrick Gordon (1635–99) close adviser to Peter the Great.

NETHERLANDS Scots Brigade in Netherlands from 1500s to 1783 (American Revolution).

John Nairne (1731–1802) serves in 1740s, then joined the 78th and dies owning a seigneurie in Lower Canada.

NEW FRANCE Jacobites, Douglas (Languedoc Reg), and Johnstone fight at Culloden, then on Plains of Abraham for France.

Alan Breck Stewart (hero in *Kidnapped*) possibly serves here.

NORTH AMERICA 1763– 75 Scots soldier settlers trigger first mass migration (approx. 45,000) to 13 colonies, (NY/Vermont/ N.C).

Thousands re-migrate to Canada after American Revolution 1783+.

Soldier-settlements by regiments in Revolutionary and 1812 wars.

In the 1400s the French hired many nations to fight for them. Medieval armies are notoriously difficult to count, but the fifteen thousand mercenary Scots in France made up approximately 10 to 20 percent of the French army.[3] About 5 percent of Scotland's male population served there,[4] and John Stewart had his six thousand Scottish soldiers help him

MAP 1: SCOTTISH MERCENARY ACTIVITY
1250-1783

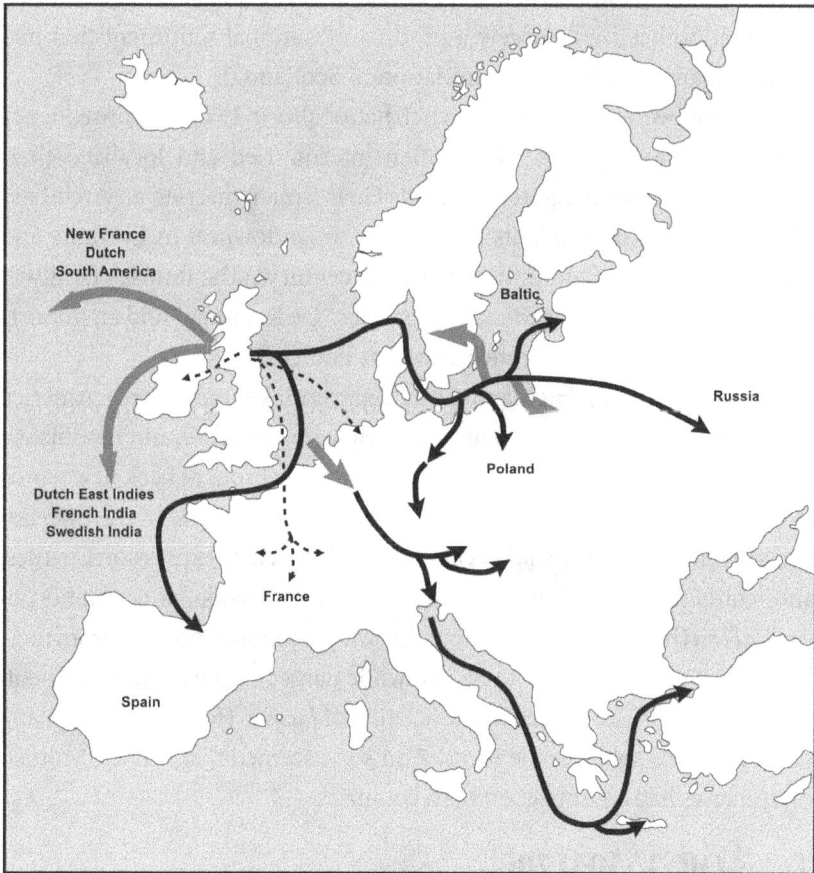

Origins ------▶	1250 – 1550 +	Ireland, France, Germany
Take-off ━━━▶	1550 – 1700 +	Baltic, Netherlands, Central Europe
Maturity ▰▰▰▶	1700 – 1783 +	Europe, European Empires

become the Constable (head of the King's household) of France. However, it is only "in the last decade or so scholars have recognized the importance of Scotland's medieval migration heritage."[5] In the 1990s, when Scotland's future was seen to lie in Europe, historians began uncovering its old European past to connect to its new European future.[6]

While some writers romanticize the era of the Auld Alliance, medieval French and Scots alike saw it in a very different light.[7] A French proverb of the time claimed that "Rats, lice and Scotsmen, you find them the world over."[8]After a period of French military presence in the late 1500s, Scotland was swept by anti-French feeling, and "the Scottish Reformation itself was largely a product of national sentiment that had formed against the French domination of Scotland."[9]

The Scots were granted joint French nationality in 1513 as a consequence of their military service.[10] They often intermarried and localized their names. Ann Fraser, daughter of a Scots Guardsman, married an Archibald MacLeod. Their descendants became major landowners in Lorraine and survived as "Maclot" until the nineteenth century.[11] The Ramsay family in the Scots Guards became the much grander "De Ramezay," and an important noble family in New France as well as France.[12]

The 78th Fraser's Highlanders in eighteenth-century North America brought back new words such as *canoe*, *wigwam*, *moccasin*, and new plants. In the nineteenth century, British soldiers in India brought back new words like *bungalow*, *khaki*, and *caravan*, and foods such as curry. In the fifteenth and sixteenth centuries, soldiers also brought back new expressions, names, and words to Scotland. Housewives shouted "gardy-loo," a corruption of *gardez l'eau* (beware of water) before throwing night soil and slops from their windows. Stewart changed to Stuart, while names such as Pettigrew (petit, little) evolved. [13] The French pronunciation of *Jacques* (Jock) is still the slang name for Scots soldiers: the Jocks. And so, it seemed that Franco-Scottish mercenaries had an impact on both countries.

Take-Off, 1550–1700

The Take-Off of the Scottish mercenary relationship to Europe between 1550 and 1700 occurred because European warfare changed dramatically.

Monarchs taxed the emerging commercial classes and financed a military revolution of larger armies, navies, forts, and guns. In addition, the Little Ice Age in the seventeenth century created famine conditions that encouraged thousands of Scots to emigrate.[14] Geoffrey Parker's *Global Crisis* also outlines how climate change generated wars at this time.

The discovery of trade routes to the New World and India had changed the economy, ship design, and firearms. Scottish mercenary activity reflected such changes, and large numbers of Scots flowed to more places. For example, in 1555 Scots bodyguards played a major role in the story of the Chevalier de Villegagnon, who led the failed French attempts to colonize Brazil in an early instance of mercenary globalization.[15]

However, the relationship between Scottish soldiers and the French monarchy changed at this time. King Henry II (1519–59) ordered Captain Montgomery, the commander of his Scots Guards, to compete in a jousting tournament against him. Montgomery accidentally wounded his royal employer, who later died from the resultant infection.[16] After this tragic accident, only Franco-Scots, rather than native Scots, were recruited for the Guards that served at the Louvre Palace. The king's regiment of assimilated Scots continued as an institution, with the use of Scots passwords and customs, up until the time of the French Revolution of 1789.[17]

During the French Wars of Religion (1562–98), Scots mercenaries played a major role in helping Henry IV (1553–1610) win the French throne and found the Bourbon line of kings, which lasted until the French Revolution. Joint French-Scots nationality was then renewed in 1599 by a grateful Henry IV, possibly the greatest and certainly the most beloved of the French kings. New France was founded in 1608 with his backing, and it is no historical anomaly that one of New France's earliest settlers was Abraham Martin, *dit l'écossais* (named the Scotsman), for whom the Plains of Abraham would later be named. Martin's wife may also have been Scottish, and together they welcomed one of the first colonial births in New France.

The Protestant Reformation also changed the relationship of Scots mercenaries to France. Henry IV was a Huguenot (Protestant) who converted to Catholicism and granted freedoms to Protestants. However, the

In folchem Habit Gehen die 800 In Stettin angekommen Irrlander oder Irren.

SCOTTISH SOLDIERS IN SERVICE OF GUSTAVUS ADOLPHUS, 1631.
Contemporary German Broadside in British Museum.

This early German print of Scots mercenaries serving in seventeenth-century Sweden and Poland labels them as "Irish." Gaelic speakers were often assumed to be Irish. (Picture Collection, The New York Public Library, Astor, Lenox, and Tilden Foundations.)

King was assassinated by a Catholic fanatic in 1610. Cardinal Richelieu, who was immortalized as the villain in the fictitious *Three Musketeers*, then restricted religious freedoms and banned Protestant traders, including the Kirkes, or Kers, from New France. France became a militantly Catholic country, while the formerly Catholic Scotland became militantly Protestant. The trickle of Franco-Scots leaving France for religious reasons became a flood.

The Kirke brothers, born in Dieppe, France, held joint French-Scots nationality. Jean Rotz (Ross), the mapmaker for King Francis I and then for Henry VIII of England, was also a Franco-Scot from Dieppe. The Kirkes were Huguenot traders expelled by Cardinal Richelieu. This explains their hostility to the Catholic-only New France. The brothers, as Scottish aristocrats, had important connections to the King of Scotland and England, Charles I. As a young man, the future

Charles I had set off with friends from Dover "where a Scot named Kirk joined them and they set sail for Dieppe."[18]

The seafaring Kirke brothers joined Sir William Alexander and started Scots settlement in Nova Scotia (New Scotland). However, the French destroyed these early Scottish settlements, so the Kirkes used their connection to Charles I as King of Scotland and England to obtain letters of marque as privateers to attack New France. In 1629, the Kirkes captured Quebec City in the names of *both* Scotland and England and the brothers were burnt in effigy in Paris. They later adopted English nationality and one became a governor of Newfoundland. Only the name Nova Scotia survived as a record of their contest with France for possession of the New World. New France was handed back in 1632 and the Kirkes lost their historical importance.

After the Union of the Crowns of Scotland and England in 1603, there was a drift of Scots away from France. Nevertheless, Scots enlisted in French armies up to the time of the Fraser's Highlanders.

Jean Stuart was born in France. His father and grandfather were members of the Scots Guards in Paris. Jean became a devout Huguenot and left France for Scotland, probably because Protestants were being murdered and driven abroad during the French Wars of Religion. In Scotland he was known as John Stewart. He left after a short while to become a soldier in Danzig (now Gdańsk, Poland)[19] but joined the Swedish army and became the Swedish quartermaster general. [20] In 1626, when Gustavus Adolphus II (1594–1632) decided to reorganize the aristocracy and number them, Jean/John had become Hans Stuart, whose aristocratic family number was eighty-six. Sweden had replaced France as the major employer of Scottish soldiers by the 1600s.

Migration changed Jean Stuart to John Stewart, then to Hans Stuart. Scots were transformed because they transferred cultural loyalty to other countries. Aristocrats of Scots descent maintained ties to Scotland, and yet transferred among diverse European countries. The Scots mercenary tradition became institutionalized at home yet aristocratically connected throughout Europe. This raises questions. Was Hans/Jean Stuart, whose grandfather *may* have been born in Scotland, really a Scot? And if so, when did these migrants stop being counted as Scots?

In 1656, James Fraser, son of the fourteenth chief of the Clan Fraser (1591–1645), raised forty-three Frasers to fight for the Swedes in Poland.[21] In return for raising the men, James Fraser was given a captain's commission, and a man named Hugh Fraser was commissioned a lieutenant. Only Hugh Fraser returned to Scotland. The others chose to settle in Poland, where they had been granted land. Later, there are references to a prominent merchant in Poland, a William Fraser, who had a son born in 1670, also named William.[22] Scottish mercenaries moved eastward to Europe for a better future. The Poles had become rich with the export of grain, and could hire mercenaries to protect their interests because several countries fought with Poland to obtain its wealth. Scots Protestants and Catholics were awarded land by several of the warring sides in a Catholic but tolerant Poland. There were about thirty thousand Scots settled in Poland in 1600.[23] By 1603 there was a Scottish Brotherhood that helped needy Scots, and the Polish government commissioned an officer from one of the Polish Scots regiments to write a report on his countrymen.[24]

Scots militarism and migration were closely related.

Table 2: Scottish Migration, 1600–50		
Destination	Minimum	Maximum
Ireland	20,000	30,000
Poland	30,000	40,000
Scandinavia	25,000	30,000
Elsewhere	10,000	15,000
Rough Numbers	85,000	115,000

* see endnote 26

One of the fears expressed in England at the Union of the Crowns in 1603 was that England would become, like Poland, overrun with Scots.[25] Scottish historians estimate that a further thirty to forty thousand Scots migrated to Poland from 1600 to 1650.[26] Poland and its Scots community there were destroyed by wars with Prussia and Russia, although Scots settlement eastward continued until the late 1700s.

The ordinary Scottish foot soldiers adapted to the country they soldiered in. These soldiers were immersed in the local economy because they were often living with, working for, and buying their supplies from locals. They were mobile when most people were not. Life was often harsh, especially for the wounded and sick. Sometimes they were integrated by marriage and disbanded in the host country. The Scottish peddler became a familiar figure, even in central and eastern Europe:[27] "The vast majority were packmen, plying their trade on horseback, selling cheap household wares into the remotest part of the country.... In straightened times ... they exchanged the role of professional trader for that of professional soldier."[28] Scots had their fares paid to soldier in Poland and often stayed on as petty traders rather than return home.

The Take-Off era from 1550 to 1700 saw Scots establishing themselves within the aristocratic elites of France, Austria, Sweden, Poland, Prussia, Russia, and the German Principalities. In Russia, from the 1570s onward, we find records of Carmichaels, Carrs, Barclays, Ogilvies, Douglases, and Gordons.[29] Patrick Gordon, a personal friend of Peter the Great and the most famous Scots mercenary to serve in Russia, was only one of many who elbowed their way into the Russian aristocracy by virtue of their military service.[30] Their descendants became prominent in Russian life and even had places named after them. Brusovski Street in Moscow commemorated the Bruces. Prince Michael Barclay de Toille (1761–1818), born in Estonia and the grandson of a Scots mercenary, became governor-general of Finland, Russian minister of war in 1812, then commander-in-chief of the Russian army that fought against Napoleon in 1813. The name, "de Toille" commemorates Towie, the ancestral home of the Barclays. In Austria, a man by the name of Walter Leslie (1606–67) penetrated the very highest levels of aristocracy during the Take-Off period.

Walter Leslie, a Protestant, changed his allegiances several times before joining the "Catholic" Austrian Habsburg side in the Thirty Years' War (1618–48). In 1638, Leslie helped free the imprisoned Prince Rupert, who gained fame fighting Oliver Cromwell in the English Civil War. Rupert became the first chairman of the Hudson's Bay Company, and Rupert's Land in Canada is named after him.[31]

Leslie and another Scottish Protestant, John Gordon, arranged the murder of their friend and former leader, Wallenstein, the great mercenary general for the Austrian Habsburgs. The Emperor of Austria rightly feared that Wallenstein was going to defect to the Swedish side of the Thirty Years' War and richly rewarded the now-Catholic Leslie with land, titles, and diplomatic positions. James Leslie, Walter Leslie's Scottish heir and nephew, also became a count[32] and gained fame for defending Vienna from the Turks.

The Leslies were unashamed professional soldiers on the make.[33] During the Take-Off period, the huge numbers of Scottish mercenaries deeply influenced the outcome of the civil war in Britain between Parliament and King Charles I (1600–49). In order to defeat the King, the Scottish Covenanters, extreme Presbyterian Protestants, had raised a formidable army, many of whom had been mercenaries who returned from Swedish service. In 1643, after months of unpaid wages, this army signed a bond of "mutual assistance to make themselves independent of anyone except their paymasters,"[34] meaning that they would not disband until they were paid what they were owed by the Covenanters. In order to pay their army, the Covenanters used the two hundred thousand pounds from the sale of King Charles I to Cromwell. The King had surrendered to them, believing himself safe. The Roundheads, or Parliamentary forces under Cromwell, of course, subsequently tried, then beheaded Charles.

Scottish mercenaries were at the cusp of the many military developments during this period in history. One of the largest employers of Scottish soldiers, Gustavus Adolphus, was also one of the great military innovators in European history. Soldiers from the Scots Brigade in the Netherlands elsewhere transferred military tactics and ideas to Sweden. It was in Sweden that Scots perfected the system of platoon volley firing by the odd numbers while the even numbers reloaded and General Hugh McKay of Scourie (c.1640–92) experimented with fixed bayonets on the outside of the gun barrel, later perfecting it in Scotland.[35] Robert Monro's (c.1590–1680) book, *Monro, His Expedition with the Worthy Scots Regiment Called Mac-Keys* is one of the important studies of warfare at this time.[36] The true significance of Scottish mercenaries "lies in their invention and dissemination of revolutionary military hardware and tactics to the armies of the rest of Europe."[37]

There is great dispute about the number of Scots involved in migratory and mercenary activity at this time. The Scottish historian Steve Murdoch writes that estimates of the numbers of Scots who fought in the Thirty Years' War (1618–48) range from twenty-five thousand to fifty thousand.[38] A study by Scottish historians Smout, Landsman, and Devine claims that from 1600 to 1650 "it is likely that almost twenty percent of young men left Scotland ..."[39] While this study is a valuable guide to the scale and geographic diversity of migration, this claim is difficult to prove. Even if fifty thousand Scots emigrated over the thirty years of war, that is fewer than two thousand men per annum out of a Scottish population of approximately 1.1 million, somewhere around 5 percent of the young men. The study should have excluded those thousands of young males who did not leave Scotland but were born into the large Scottish communities abroad. As well, the study fails to calculate those who re-migrated back to Scotland, such as the thousands who returned to fight in the British Civil Wars of the 1640s. Mercenary service was sometimes only a temporary move. The very nature of mercenary regiments and Scottish emigrants makes it difficult to provide accurate figures. Mercenary units were built on a flow of recruits, deaths, desertions, and amalgamations with other units. Scots immigrants in seventeenth-century Poland, for instance, were classed with the Jews and Gypsies precisely because the Scots were also wanderers.

Elusive and imprecise data about migration and mercenary activity make it difficult for historians to count mercenary migrants, let alone make generalizations about them. Historians such as A. Grosjean believe that the Scots fought for Sweden because this was "a cause they saw as their own in the army of an ally."[40] However, at that time, Scottish officers in Swedish armies often crossed the lines before a battle to meet relatives and friends on the other side. Contemporary Scottish writer and soldier, Sir Thomas Urquhart (1611–60) claimed that "the Scots are an unconquered people; for whenever, in any great battle, in the Thirty Years' War, they are beaten on one side, they must, for that very reason have been victorious on the other."[41]

The ambiguity and complexity of Scottish mercenary migrants make it impossible to assign a national identity to them at that time. As was said earlier, Patrick Gordon started off as a Catholic, changed sides three times, and died soldiering for Orthodox Russia. The Protestant Walter Leslie also changed allegiances several times and died as a loyal Austrian Catholic. Jean/John/Hans Stewart adopted several identities, and the descendants of most Scottish soldiers assimilated into their new country, language, and religion.

Cambridge University historian Tim Blanning suggests that "historians would do well to look beyond social divisions and even ideology and culture, to hardnosed economic interests."[42] In turn, my research explains the Take-Off of Scottish mercenary activity as a response to the economic conditions in Europe at the time. According to University of California professor Brian Fagan, during the Little Ice Age Finland lost about one-third of its population in the famine of 1696–97, the Thames in London froze over, and "the Arctic ice pack extended so far south that Eskimos took to landing their kayaks in Scotland."[43] The cold weather resulted in a much shorter growing season, which meant that crop yields fell. The push from the Scotland of the seventeenth century was similar to the push from Ireland in the Great Famine of the nineteenth.

Montreal's oldest house, the Château Ramezay, was built by an aristocratic family of New France. Their ancestors were originally called Ramsay and served as Scots guards around the French kings. Indicators of a Scots mercenary presence dot Europe and its colonies. (Photograph by Sam Allison.)

Scots were pushed to the Swedish, rather than the Habsburg, side of the Thirty Years' War because it was faster, easier, and cheaper to sail to Sweden than to travel to the Habsburg side in central Europe. The Swedes reportedly paid more generously and more regularly than the Habsburgs. However, huge amounts of land changed hands in the seventeenth century because the victors expropriated the lands of the losers and awarded it to their supporters. Consequently, hungry Scottish mercenaries were also pulled to Europe by both sides at the prospect of gaining land.

Globalization, 1700–1783

The final period of Scottish mercenary activity from 1700–83 can be labelled Globalization because soldiers and their descendants can be found in the colonial empires of France, Sweden, the Netherlands, Spain, and Russia. The Dutch Empire in North America had the Livingstones, Scots traders who migrated from the Scottish colony in the Netherlands and became a prominent family in New York after the English captured the colony. Gabriel Stedman (1744–97),[44] a former officer in the Scots Brigade in the Netherlands, wrote an important anti-slavery book about his soldiering adventures in Dutch Guiana (Suriname). John Nairne, who later joined the 78th Fraser's Highlanders, also served in Dutch Guiana. New Sweden in North America had Scots soldiers too. The Swedish East India Company employed Scots, and their first ambassador to China was a man named Colin Campbell. A Jean Law, nephew to the Scottish economist John Law (1671–1729), fought in India for the French in the 1750s to the 1760s.

Records show more Scots in New France than in any other European colony, perhaps because it was conquered by the British, who recorded their presence there. Many bizarre situations arose because Scots fought Scots in New France. James Johnstone (1719–91) from Edinburgh, who served as Montcalm's aide-de-camp on the Plains of Abraham, recorded that he met his nephew from the British side after the French surrendered. There were a Colonel Ross, possibly Alan Breck Stuart, and several rank and file soldiers of Scots origin in New France. Douglas of the Languedoc regiment was in command of the sentries guarding the cliffs that General Wolfe's men climbed. This Douglas, who may have been a Scot, fought for the Jacobites at Culloden and was captured with another Douglas. A British officer wrote, in 1746, "I must again renew my request to Your Grace that they be allow'd to go home upon their paroles…. I received civilities from their relations in France…. Their names are Douglas, Capitaine dans le regiment de Languedoc and Douglas, Capitaine dans le regiment de Drummond du Royal Ecossais, but they are both Frenchmen. Morton."[45] The Seven Years' War (1756–63) was the last war where the Scots mercenary tradition placed Scottish soldiers on both sides of a war.

The number of Scots serving foreign countries seems to have dropped considerably with the creation of the British Army in 1707. The Union of Parliaments united Scotland with England, and the new British Parliament financed both Scottish and English regiments so that the prospect of regular pay probably diverted many rank and file Scots soldiers into British rather than mercenary service. The Scottish officer class still migrated to foreign service in some numbers until the disbandment of the Scots Brigade in the Netherlands during the American Revolution (1776–83).

Gabriel Stedman served in the last Scots mercenary regiment, which brutally suppressed a slave revolt in Dutch South America. The regiment was dissolved during the American Revolution when the Dutch fought against Britain. Stedman grew to loathe slavery, and his memoirs, printed in the 1790s, helped turn British public opinion against the slave trade. (Manuscripts, Archives and Rare Books Division, Schomburg Center for Research in Black Culture, The New York Public Library, Astor, Lenox and Tilden Foundations.)

Stedman married Joanna, a slave girl, and offered payment for her freedom. Her owner refused, and Stedman, along with their son, was forced to return to Europe without her, never to see her again. Their tragic story continues to be a powerful indictment of slavery. (New York Public Library 125628.)

Much of the mercenary story during the Globalization period has been overshadowed by the attention paid to exiled Scottish Jacobites following the 1715 and 1745 Rebellions. James Keith (1696–1758) was only one Jacobite from the 1715 rebellion who exemplifies many of the characteristics of the typical professional soldier, as he went on to fight for Spain, Russia, and Prussia.[46] Lord MacLeod (1727–89), a Jacobite in the 1745 rebellion, fled to Sweden, where his military service led to his becoming a Swedish count. He then decided to return to Scotland and restore his social position there by raising the Highland Light Infantry, one of the most famous regiments in British history. Military activity transformed many rebels into heroes, and often turned heroes into rebels, throughout Scotland's long and storied history. The exodus of approximately five thousand Jacobites to Europe and seven hundred to North

America is portrayed by historians, novelists, and Scottish folk songs as unusual and massive. A later chapter deals with historical distortions, but Scottish Jacobites were only travelling a well-worn path. For instance, the Scots Brigade in the Netherlands alone had recruited several thousand soldiers during the eighteenth century. Mercenary migration has been more or less absent from British history books and popular memory.

Scottish mercenaries were honoured in foreign places far more than the exiled Jacobites. In Vienna, for example, a section of the city walls was named the Schoten Tor (Scots Gate). Today, the Schoten Gymnasium (Scots College) educates the Austrian secondary school elite on the Schoten Gasse (Scots Street). The Douglas Gate in Danzig, Brusovsky Street in Moscow, and the Château Ramezay in Montreal are signposts to the Scottish mercenary past, not to a Jacobite one. The Keithstrasse in Berlin remembered James Keith, not because he was a Jacobite, but because he died in Prussian service. However, this is not to disparage Jacobite mercenaries such as James Johnstone at Quebec; they had an impact on a wider world history, rather than just British, Canadian, or United States history.

This brings us to the idea that Scottish soldiers serving in the eighteenth-century North American colonies (1756–1812) can also be placed within the context of Scottish mercenary activity. As said, there were Scots on both sides during the Seven Years' War, and those in the British Army such as Colonel Fraser and Captain MacDonald of the 78th had fought against the British Army at Culloden. Many of the soldiers in the Fraser's Highlanders had relatives scattered throughout European armies and a few even had relatives fighting for the French.[47] It is impossible to accurately calculate how many of the 78th Fraser's had been mercenaries or who shifted back to mercenary service in Europe at the end of the Seven Years' War. Similar names and false names (wanted Jacobites) are a problem and it is difficult to be sure, for example, that the James Murray who wanted to enlist in the 78th from Prussia is, in fact, the same man who did enlist. Approximately fifteen officers were recruited directly from the Dutch and French armies, but there were several officers, such as James MacQueen, who transferred to the 78th from the Black Watch, but had served previously with the Dutch. Therefore, in total, almost a third of the 78th officers who served from 1756–63 had seen mercenary service. This is probably a conservative estimate because a surprising number of Scots officers including General James Murray, the first British Governor of Canada, had served as young boys in foreign regiments. Some of the privates in the 60th regiment in North America were Scots who had enlisted from Germany.[48] Some eighteenth-century Scots had a surprisingly cosmopolitan background.

A comment one reads frequently in Canadian history books is that a roll call of the Battle on the Plains of Abraham in Quebec (1759) reads like a list of the Highland clans at Culloden (1746). The British side at Quebec had Frasers, Murrays, and Montgomeries, while the French side had Douglases, Rosses, and Johnstones. Seventeenth-century battles in Poland also contained Frasers, Murrays, and Montgomeries.[49] There was even a Polish Johnstone, though he was labelled Major General Count Von Johnstone, similar to the Ramsay who was labelled the King's Lieutenant Jean-Baptiste-Nicholas-Roch de Ramezay.

Emigration has led some historians to claim seventeenth-century Poland was "Scotland's America." T.C. Smout, the Historiographer Royal of Scotland, wrote, "What twentieth-century historians partly fail to grasp themselves and fail totally to convey to the outside world, was the scale and significance of the early Scots movement abroad."[50] Indeed, Clan Fraser soldiers fought in Poland under the son of their clan chief in the 1650s, and then some of the 78th were Frasers who fought in North America under their clan chief of the 1750s.

Mercenary employment was different from service in the British Army abroad. British regiments returned home after fighting in Europe or the Empire, but as has been said, Scots in regiments raised under European colours often married and retired in the host country or its colonies. Soldiering under foreign flags enabled Scots to flow out of Scotland in large numbers. Migration could involve a relatively short distance to Ireland or long distance moves to places like Russia. The time spent abroad could be short for some, but usually involved more long term or permanent settlement. Sometimes these soldiers emigrated of their own accord, but most were driven to the ranks by poverty and were shipped out as part of a military unit.

The methods of officially recruiting Scots for foreign service changed over time, but by the eighteenth century, military service was a unique form of "chain migration" helped by previous migrants. Military service involved a migratory network that paid the soldiers' passage to other countries. This Scottish network was extended over time and across Europe. By the mid-1700s when the Fraser's Highlanders were recruited, young Highlanders were, in many ways, "migrants in waiting," in limbo until a military network recruited them.

Foreign service was a bridge that carried Scots into societies across the Europe and the New World. Such militarism kicked civic and economic gates open for adventurous Scots. Scottish soldiers were not just "in" a country, they rapidly became "of" that country in terms of work and land ownership. This military service transformed people and transferred innovations throughout much of Europe. Migrating Scots soldiers were military and cultural magpies, collecting and distributing knowledge and techniques in the days before mass printing and literacy. Not surprisingly, this pattern of behaviour continued as the 78th Fraser's soldiered and settled in North America. I argue in later chapters that this regiment was not just a valuable military asset, but like their mercenary predecessors, adapted to the conditions they found, and were also important innovators in the social, economic, and political life of the Americas.

2

Explaining the Scots' Highland and Mercenary Traditions

Enlist, bonnie laddie, and come awa' wi' me.
— Scottish folk song

The men of the 78th Fraser's Highlanders were shaped by several factors: geography, the Highland society of the time, the Clan Fraser itself, the mercenary tradition, and contemporary events such as the modernization of the region following the Jacobite Rebellion. In this chapter I will discuss these factors and also explain how enlistment in the 78th helped bring an end to Scottish mercenary service by the 1780s.

Scottish Geography

The Highlands and islands of Scotland include a series of mountains cut by deep valleys, fast-flowing rivers, *firths* (fjords), and large *lochs* (lakes). The terrain of the area divided and isolated the Highland region as well as its residents.[1] Consequently, Scotland "was a country of regions rather than of centralized government" until the 1700s.[2]

This isolation and division led to the growth of distinct, cohesive Highland clans. The thin soils and rocky wet hills created an economy based on the raising of cattle. The Highlanders herded their cattle for miles as they wandered over unfenced mountains in search of pasture. The men, usually carrying only oatmeal, could navigate or track their animals for days using only the sun and the stars as their compass. Compared to the Lowland Scots or English urban poor, who subsisted on oats or wheat, the Highlander was comparatively well fed on milk, beef, fish, and game hunted in the then-wooded parts of the Highlands.[3] Good nutrition gave them the physical ability to out-march their opponents and overwhelm them with a sword charge.

The Highlands were also cut off socially, culturally, and linguistically from the rest of eighteenth-century Britain. Economically, except for cattle exports, Highland agriculture and trade were tiny compared to the rest of Scotland. However, the sheer geographic size of this area, which contained about 40 percent of Scotland and 13 percent of Britain, meant that the Highlands could not be ignored. Most important, this region posed a military threat, which was made very apparent during the Jacobite unrest of 1715, 1719, and 1745. The 1745 Rebellion, when thousands of Highlanders marched into England, was the most famous of a long series of Highland raids.

Rustling cattle is often viewed today in a humorous fashion, but in the eighteenth century it was a highly organized crime involving armed gangs, blackmail, murder, and illicit exports worth thousands of pounds. Highlanders partook in this activity, and, not surprisingly, both the Highlands and its residents were widely disliked by the victims of raids and rebellions in the rest of Scotland and England.

Eighteenth century travellers, such as the Irishman Edmund Burke, wrote that the huge, naked rocks, being just above the heath, produced the disagreeable appearance of a scabbed head.[4] The great English playwright Oliver Goldsmith complained that the hills and rocks "interrupted every prospect."[5] Indeed, it was not until the writings of Sir Walter Scott appeared in the early 1800s that the Highlands began to be appreciated for their wild beauty. And, as for the residents of the area, according to King James VI, Highlanders were divided into two groups: one was barbarous, the other exceedingly barbarous.[6]

Demographically, the north of Scotland was far more important in the eighteenth century than it is today. Even as late as 1801, there were 1.6 million people living in Scotland, with 740,000 resident in the north, 180,000 in the south, and 670,000 in the central lowland zone.[7] The demographic size of the north helps to explain the vast number of Highland regiments that were raised and operated in the latter part of the eighteenth century. Indeed, until 1800, England had a smaller population than the joint Celtic nations of Scotland, Ireland, and Wales.

Highland Society

Besides the kilts and bagpipes, the most obvious feature of eighteenth-century Highland life was the clan system:

> What distinguished Highland clansmen was their relationship to the chief. The word *clann* means children, and the Highland clan was, above all things, a family, a family in which everybody believed that they were all, from chief to blacksmith, descendants of one founder … the mountains and tortuous nature of the country lent itself to a great many little, distinct groups of people.[8]

Not all clans held lands, so Scottish kings had to deal with landlords and clan spheres of influence. For instance, in 1587, King James VI operated with one list of 105 landlords and another list of thirty-four clans and their chiefs for the same area of the Highlands.[9] The clan system did not have a "legal and substantive" existence,[10] partly because "new clans could be spawned with remarkable speed."[11] Large clans, such as the Frasers of Lovat, who lived in definite areas, were economic units and sometimes had their own regiments headed by their chiefs. Between the chief who controlled the land, and the clansmen who rented it, were the *tacksmen*. The latter group rented the land from the chief and then sublet it to the people.

There was great pride in belonging to a clan, and great social identification with the clan name (even though some had adopted the name). Clan names identified a man's history, allegiance, and origin. Scottish kings outlawed names such as MacGregor and Graham in an attempt to destroy undesirable groups. The eldest son of the 6th Chief of the outlawed MacGregors, for example, enlisted as a lieutenant in the 78th Fraser's Highlanders under the name of "John Murray" because the name MacGregor was illegal until 1785.[12] Modern historians have often decried the outlawing of names, but it was part of the government's efforts to curb criminal activity in the Highlands. The most conspicuous feature of Scots names is the use of *Mac*, *Mc*, or *M'*, which all mean "son of" in the Gaelic language.

The Clan Fraser

The Frasers have been an integral part of Scottish history for more than eight hundred years. The name likely originated in Anjou, France[13] — the French word for strawberry is *fraise*, and growers were called "fraisiers." The Frasers first appeared in Scotland around 1160 in East Lothian. They moved into Tweeddale, in southeastern Scotland, during the twelfth and thirteenth centuries, and from there into the counties of Stirling, Angus, Inverness, and Aberdeen. About five generations later, Sir Simon Fraser (the Patriot) was captured fighting for Robert the Bruce, and in 1306, like William Wallace before him, was executed with great cruelty by King Edward I. This Simon Fraser's family line ended because he had no male heirs to pass on his name. The senior line, the Frasers of Philorth, is descended from Sir Alexander Fraser, who took part in the victory at Bannockburn in 1314 under Robert the Bruce and was appointed Chamberlain of Scotland in 1319. The Frasers of Lovat (*lovat* means "swampy plain" in Gaelic) are descended from a younger brother of the Chamberlain, Sir Simon Fraser. Lovat chiefs are called *MacShimidh*, meaning "son of Simon." Many of the Lovat Frasers who settled in Inverness-shire were given the personal name of Simon, although this naming pattern was not always followed until the present line of Lovat chiefs who are all named Simon.

The eleventh Lord Lovat (who would later be known as Simon the Fox) obtained a commission in the Black Watch, the first Highland regiment raised for the British Army. However, Lord Lovat became a Jacobite, lost his Black Watch commission, and rallied his clansmen in support of Bonnie Prince Charlie's rebellion in 1745.

During the 1745 Rebellion, Highland clans fought one another. Lowland Scots fought Highland Scots, and a few Englishmen and Irishmen fought for Bonnie Prince Charlie, the son of James Stuart. It was not, as many believe, an Anglo-Scottish conflict. While the Hanoverians were unpopular in Britain, the Catholic Stuarts were even less popular and managed their various uprisings only with the help of France and Spain. The 1745 Rebellion has been interpreted as a romantic but futile effort. However, it nearly plunged Britain into a devastating civil war, and there was little sympathy for Lord Lovat, who was beheaded for treason at the Tower of London in 1747. The Crown confiscated Lord Lovat's title and estates and imprisoned his son.

The British regiment, the 78th Fraser's Highlanders, was created by the same Simon Fraser of Lovat (1726–82) who led the Clan Fraser regiment in rebellion. The Fraser's Highlanders regiment was the first in British service built around a clan chief. Officially, it was named Fraser's Highlanders because Simon was a British colonel, *not* because he was clan chief.

In both the Jacobite and British regiments of Frasers, a man's place was determined by his place in the clan. The nineteenth clan chief of the Frasers of Lovat was the lieutenant-colonel of the 78th Regiment of Foot. Sons of chiefs, such as Donald MacDonald of Clanranald, who spoke French to the sentries at Quebec, were the captains; tacksmen, or "tenants" of the chief were the lieutenants, as the word suggests; and the clansmen were the foot soldiers. I will discuss the British military traditions that also contributed to the shaping of this regiment in chapter 3.

Simon Fraser was appointed lieutenant-colonel of the 78th Regiment of Foot and accompanied his men to North America. Later, in 1775, he raised the 71st Fraser's Highlanders to fight in the American Revolution, although he did not accompany the latter regiment overseas. In 1772, in an effort to regain his position in the Hanoverian state, Simon Fraser petitioned to have the confiscated Lovat title and lands restored to him. Consequently, in 1774, a special Act of Parliament granted the confiscated Lovat estate to Fraser in recognition of his military service. This act required that a payment of £20,978 be made. He paid, but, as a former rebel, Simon Fraser never regained the Lovat title and became known as "General

Simon Fraser." He married, died without issue in 1782, and then his younger half-brother, Archibald Campbell Fraser (1736–1815), succeeded him in
the Lovat estates and as the Member of Parliament for Inverness.

The Highlands of 1750–1812

Powerful new economic currents from North America drastically altered Scotland in the years between 1745 and 1812. However, within Scotland, the Highlands were changing because of a series of Acts
of Parliament that imposed a new legal, economic, and social ethos.
Clanship had already been in decline long before the 1745 Rebellion,
but by 1746, the rest of Britain had had enough of Highland uprisings, and the British government, with strong approval from Lowland
Scotland, was determined to destroy clanship. The ruling Whigs attacked the social system in the Highlands and the Islands, believing
the clan system to lie at the root of a region "disaffected to government,
averse to labour, and impatient of all lawful subordination.[14]

The Whigs believed clan chiefs behaved like "feudal tyrants" so they
stressed the need to replace clan relationships with modern commercial
ones.[15] Clansmen were to be freed from their chiefs by placing them in a
capitalist relationship with one another. The central British government
had the will, means, and political support to integrate Highlanders more
closely into the wider British society and economy. Kilts were banned, as
it was thought kilts contributed to backwardness. Under the Disarming
Acts, bagpipes were forbidden as "instruments of war," for clan pipers
were an integral part of clan regiments and clan life — in 1743, Lord
Lovat bonded with William Fraser and sent him to Skye for seven paid
years to be perfected as "a Highland Pyper."[16] The passing of the Heritable
Jurisdictions Act saw the great clan chiefs stripped of their feudal-like
powers, including military rights over their clansmen. No longer could
the chief of the MacDonalds of Keppoch answer, when asked what his
income was, "I can call out and command 500 men."[17]

Clan chiefs became landlords, not warlords. Land previously held in
common by the chiefs and their clansmen reverted to the chiefs, not to
the clansmen. However, Lord Lovat's lands, mostly in Inverness-shire,

had been acquired by special grant from the King, or through marriage, and were never held in common with his Fraser clansmen. As a consequence, the entire Lovat Estate and those of many other rebels were seized by the Crown.

The *Scottish Forfeited Estate Papers* (henceforth referred to as *SFEP*) are records showing the scope and pace of the changes on the Lovat Estate, one of the many administered by a Board of Commissioners for the Annexed Estates after 1745. The commissioners were mandated to use the rents from the estates for the public good, so they were required by the British government to keep a careful account of the lands under their supervision. The *Lovat Estate Papers* are extensive, "possibly because Simon, Lord Lovat, had an inveterate objection to paying his debts, and the claims on his estate were therefore numerous."[18] The inventory of Lovat lands in the *SFEP* taken right after the failed rebellion reads that "the inhabitants are strangers to the right method of Agriculture, Manufactures and Industry ... the common people are generally lazy, ignorant and addicted to drinking."[19]

Unlike today, the cost of modernizing the Lovat Estate came from farm rents, not from British government tax money. The rent collected from the Fraser clansmen, instead of going to benefit Lord Lovat, now paid for the Estate's "improvement." According to the *SFEP*, "indirectly the unsuccessful Rising did more for the welfare of Scotland than might have resulted from the Restoration of the Stuart dynasty."[20] In other words, the destruction of the clan system brought more benefits than the status quo.

In this new regime, the Fraser clansmen learned to enclose lands, build bridges, afforest moors with young trees, drain lochs and marshes, improve salmon fishing, start boat building, and experiment with new agricultural methods. Presbyterian churches and ministers were established to reform "the nest of papists" claimed to be on Lovat lands. Schools to teach English and practical skills such as knitting, spinning, and linen-making were also established. The mission of the commissioners was "cultural as well as economic and political in nature."[21]

The Lovat papers also cast light upon the 78th Fraser's Highlanders in the 1750s–60s. In return for the promise of a land lease, tenants were

encouraged to join the 78th. According to the papers, the commissioners tried to absorb the soldiers who returned from North America by
building "King's Cottages," planting apple trees, and hiring 140 of them
to work on the estate.[22] However, the veteran soldiers were not good
workers, and kept taking time off to visit friends and relatives.[23] Both
the officers and men of the former 78th competed for leases, which
drove up rents.[24] There are various complaints about rent increases and
other charges throughout the *SFEP*. Lieutenant McTavish of the 78th,
for example, complained about paying ten pounds toward "altering and
widening the Dee river channel."[25]

The commissioners took action against the fifteen or so whisky stills
on the Lovat estate, not only because the inhabitants "employ most of
their time distilling spirits," but because they were using up valuable timber resources. Ex-soldiers were employed in the timber trade. There was
at least one sawmill on the estate, which made over two hundred pounds
per annum.[26]

The people and the land were to be made more productive and "cultural values were imported from the Lowlands and England."[27] These
new moral principles "spilled over ... penetrating what recent historians call the 'mentalities'; the 'habits of the mind' and the 'habits of the
heart' that make up 'the whole moral and intellectual state of a people'."[28]
Highland culture's shared values, and dispositions changed dramatically and by 1812, Highlanders were seen as loyal, law-abiding, and very
Presbyterian in outlook.

Yet, the *SFEP* fails to record the unhappiness and problems that persisted in the Highlands. The area experienced a population explosion
between 1745 and 1812, probably as a result of the warming climate, important agricultural improvements, and vaccination against smallpox.
Despite "improvements" to the forfeited and other estates, the infertile
Highlands could not support the increase in population and became
even more poverty-stricken. The Welsh traveller, Pennant, wrote of the
Highlands as a place where "the people are torpid with idleness and most
wretched. Their hovels are most miserable; made of poles wattled and covered with sods. Till the famine pinches, they will not bestir themselves."[29]

Urbanization and industrialization in the Lowlands absorbed the sharp increase in Scottish population numbers. However, this did not happen in the Highlands where, as we have said, the many Highland regiments formed from the 1750s to 1812 absorbed much of the surplus of young men. It is no historical accident that mass Highland emigration to North America started in the 1760s when the Fraser's and other Highland soldiers returned home to tell of the many opportunities there.

Highland Soldiers

The rugged terrain of the Highlands ensured that local herdsmen were extremely fit, and these superb physical specimens became remarkably efficient soldiers. As I mentioned earlier, a cattle-based rural society meant that the Highlanders were usually better fed than the Lowland or English urban poor. Whatever the reason, there was no contest between Highland and other regiments when it came to physical endurance. Much of the military success of Bonnie Prince Charlie in 1745 lay in the ability of his troops to outmarch their opponents. I think that good nutrition played a major part, but some eighteenth- and nineteenth-century historians have attributed the great marching ability of Bonnie Prince Charlie's Highland troops only to the fact that they did not carry baggage. The Marquis of Montrose, for example, led an army of Highlanders that marched sixty miles in one day — and fought at the end of it — a feat they repeated several times.[30] Highland soldiers were on a par with the Zulu soldiers encountered by the British in Africa in the nineteenth century. Hard lands produce hard soldiers.

The Highland Scots soldiers were also disciplined, cohesive, and composed. They were savage fighters on the battlefield but self-controlled and contained when not fighting. Restrained, directed violence characterized Prince Charlie's Highland soldiers. Travellers were often safer in the Highlands than in the rest of Britain.[31] Highland society before the Rebellion can be described as a military society. Young men were routinely taught to kill and, more important, when *not* to kill.[32] Highland males did not use their fists like the English or sticks like the Irish, but instead wielded dirks (daggers) or even swords. Custom conceded victory to the first man to draw blood and so Highland honour was satisfied without killing. The famed outlaw Rob Roy MacGregor, for instance, fought twenty-two duels, none of which ended in death, though he did kill several people in battle.[33] Highland regiments, unlike Lowland, English, or Irish regiments, were much less likely to brawl among themselves and were highly valued by the British Army.

Mercenary Tradition

At a time when most countries were poor and backward, medieval Scotland was conspicuously so. Consequently, Scotland developed a different socioeconomic structure to the rest of Europe. Napoleon said that poverty was the best military school, which partly explains why Scotland was a first-rate producer of soldiers from 1250 to 1783. The great French historian, Fernand Braudel, said that, as a general rule, internal European migration was from the mountains to the lowlands. There was then a constant incentive for Scots, in such a mountainous country, to migrate to the richer lowland parts of Europe, and mercenary work was the path many took. As a result, a migratory military culture flourished.

Scotland did not experience the drastic centralization and modernization that England did after the Norman Conquest of 1066. In France and England, feudal society was built around the land. The king, as owner of the land, was at the top of a social and military structure that extended down through the nobles to the serfs or slaves at the bottom. Nobles paid homage to the king for land, while serfs or slaves were tied to and sold with the land.

Scotland was geographically too divided for the medieval kings to impose uniformity. Consequently, the Scots had different socio-political arrangements to the English and French. The monarch was the King of Scots, not King of Scot*land*. Even Robert the Bruce, one of the great warrior kings of Europe, was King of Scots. We speak of Mary, Queen of Scots, and Elizabeth of England. This is not a semantic quibble, but reflects Scotland's unusual political structure. The Scots had a king of the people not of the land. This is exemplified in the Declaration of Arbroath, dated April 6, 1320, which states: "But if our King were to abandon the cause by being ready to make us, or our kingdom, subject to the King of England or the English, we would at once do our utmost to expel him as our enemy and the betrayer of his own rights and ours, and should choose some other man to be our king, who would be ready to defend us."[34]

There was nothing like the Scottish Declaration of Arbroath until the American and French Revolutions of the late 1700s: "After the French Revolution every monarch had, sooner or later, to learn to change from the national equivalent of 'King of France' to 'King of the French,' that is, to establish a direct relation to the collectivity of his or her subjects, however lowly."[35]

The disadvantage of a collectivist monarchy was that the French then joined the Scots to rebel and depose their governments to an unusual degree after 1789. One scandalized Victorian English critic claimed that the Scots were not burdened by an excessive attachment to their princes.[36] Weak, central authority in Scotland led to rebellions, which, in turn, led to the losers becoming available or being required to go to foreign wars in Europe.

Bonds of Manrent

The relationships that medieval Scots developed encouraged migratory and military activity, especially among the lower orders of society. The Wars of Independence against England, led by William Wallace, often involved the Scots destroying their own castles, towns, and farms to starve out the English invaders, which forced the Scots to move elsewhere as well. A serfdom based only on tying the poor to the land had to be abandoned, as the land itself was abandoned. As a result, Scotland abolished serfdom long before other European countries. However, in order to maintain economic and other relationships, a unique type of bondage for serfs arose. Bonds of manrent, which maintained social cohesion between chiefs or lords and the clansmen, were critical in a mobile, illiterate, and insecure society: "Scotsmen produced what was to all intents and purposes a new word — *manrent* — one of the strongest social bonds known in the feudal era."[37]

Some bonds of manrent extended over time and across the Atlantic: "[A]lliance between the Frasers of Foyers and the MacTavishes of

Stratherrick was reflected later in the North West Company of Canada."[38] An excerpt from this 1721 bond reads: "[T]he said family of Foyers and their respective servants and followers on the one part ... and Clan McTavish on the other part, faithfully engage, bind, and oblige themselves to live in the strictest amenity ... and to maintain, defend and assist one another in all actions, causes, pleas and controversies."[39] W. Stewart Wallace, a Canadian historian, wrote that the Frasers entered the NWC "due chiefly to the clannishness of Simon McTavish, based on ties of friendship and kinship that went back to the treaty of peace ... in 1721."[40]

After 1745, the existence of bonds of manrent, which integrated outsiders into the clans, was used by the British government to justify the denial of ordinary clansmens' claims to land. The Duke of Argyll said that clans were of a "lawless, arbitrary, turbulent and dangerous character,"[41] and that clans existed "by mere enlistment — by Bonds of Manrent entered into with strangers — by the adoption of children of slaughtered foes — by the absorption of the broken remnants of other Septs."[42] This ideological assault on the clan system by the British government would ultimately prove successful. The ties that bound the chief to his clan vanished, as did the ties that bound clansmen to the land. The chiefs then replaced the people with sheep during the Highland clearances.

Bonding and Society

The Scots habit of bonding with each other entered into their national life, as well.[43] The Protestant Reformation took a quick and almost universal hold in Scotland because John Knox, the major figure behind the Protestant Reformation in Scotland, adapted the new Protestant idea to the old Scots idea of manrent. Knox touched a deep chord in his countrymen by declaring that those who bonded for Protestantism were connecting with God as well as with one another. Knox called them "Covenanters" (after the Ark of the Covenant in the Bible), and created a huge wave of religious enthusiasm that effectively swept Catholicism out of Scotland.

Freemasons, a secret brotherhood bound by various ceremonies and signs, are another example of social bonding in Scotland. The Scots introduced Freemasonry to countries such as France and Russia. Scottish

Masons were also influential in North America: Colonel Simon Fraser of the 78th Fraser's Highlanders was the second Provincial Grand Master in Canada, and Sergeant James Thompson, also of the 78th, was a Masonic member.

Scottish people had contractual relationships between chiefs and clansmen, lords and peasants, political plotters, religious enthusiasts, and military adventurers. Bonds of manrent faded with the rise of literacy and written legal documents. However, as I will explore in chapter 6, a unique feature of eighteenth-century Scots migrants to North America was their habit of bonding with one another rather than becoming indentured to North Americans.

Bonding and Mercenaries

Contracts bonding eighteenth-century Scots for military service abroad were not that different to bonds of manrent linking clans together. Historians have often explained the united fury of Scottish soldiers to clan and family ties, but it went deeper than that. Entire regiments of free-enterprise mercenary Scots had been shifting from country to country and side to side since the seventeenth century.

By the 1750s, Scottish mercenary activity had adapted to war, the most extensive industry in Europe, although Scotland was only one of many nations that filled the ranks of mercenaries who fought across the continent. However, few European nations provided so many soldiers over such a long period and for such a range of employers and destinations. Part of the reason for this was the geographic location of Scotland. The Scots could easily sail to many places, whereas the Swiss, for example, would have had to march long distances to reach such destinations.

Before the development of European national states in the late eighteenth century, there was always great demand for mercenaries across the continent. The European peasantry was generally not interested in fighting wars: Thomas More's *Utopia* argues that "the common folk do not go to war of their own accord, but are driven to it by the madness of princes."

European armies prior to the eighteenth century could not take to the field for long, nor could they suffer heavy casualties without serious domestic repercussions. However, there were always adventurous Scottish aristocrats willing to seek their fortunes abroad, and hungry masses anxious to follow for coin. Furthermore, Scots professional soldiers were acquainted with the latest military ideas, and often represented the nearest thing to a professional fighting force that a monarch could get. The Scottish nobility was a warrior aristocracy accustomed to bonding followers for domestic battles. It was quite easy to progress to bonding followers for international battles. There were occasions when the poor were kidnapped and pressed into mercenary service. Yet the Scots could also be said to have led and followed one another with an adventurous enthusiasm for mercenary money.

Scotland produced excellent soldiers. The Scots had to fight the English many times to retain their independence, but even when there was peace with England, the Scottish countryside was rife with violence caused by regional rivalries, endless retaliatory raids, or timeless clan feuds. All this fighting was good training. In addition, Scotland was too poor to maintain a large national army, except at very rare times in history. Therefore, their fighters became soldiers abroad.

Scots soldiers were paid under contract and operated as free-enterprise professionals, not as state-sponsored conscripts. A particularly savage or untrustworthy mercenary colonel would find that his supply of recruits dried up quickly, or he might even be killed, because he did not have the power of the national state to protect him.[44] There are sufficient incidents throughout the sparse material on Scots mercenary history to suggest that such regiments were not based on a brutal top-down relationship from officers to men. Discipline may have been less savage than that experienced by their contemporaries in English regiments, where the lash was endemic. Certainly, eighteenth-century regiments such as the 78th Fraser's Highlanders made far less use of the lash than their English counterparts. Arguably, the absence of the lash had much to do with the Scots mercenary tradition.

The old Scots mercenary idea that soldiering was a contractual relationship or bond applicable to both parties came into conflict with the new British idea that soldiers were the subordinate subjects of their own national state. Thus, soldiers in eighteenth-century Scotland, now part of

Britain, began to be thought of as agents of the national state rather than as individual actors in their own right. This shift away from freely contracted professional soldiers did not come easily, and conflicts often arose:

> When the Highlanders entered the King's service they considered themselves as a contracting party in the agreements made with the government, from whom they naturally expected the same punctual performance of their engagement ... when they found ... the terms which had been expressly stipulated with His Majesty's officers violated, the Highlander ... warmly resented such unexpected treatment.[45]

There were several famous mutinies by eighteenth-century Highland regiments due to the fact that Highlanders saw themselves simply as professional soldiers with the British state as their employer, rather like their forebears in regiments throughout Europe. The new British Army Code, which saw soldiers as subjects of the nation state, conflicted with the old mercenary code, which allowed soldiers to transfer their allegiance elsewhere if their contracts were broken. Mutinies were common in British Highland regiments precisely because the Highlanders had their own tradition of professional soldiering.

The propensity of Highlanders to mutiny against their officers contradicts the idea that Highland regiments were mostly clan levies officered by their chiefs. Money was the chief attraction for officers and men to join British Highland regiments in the last half of the eighteenth century. Enlistment helped them to gain "access to the British fiscal state's material resources"[46] and paid for Highland military-migration across the North Atlantic.

Whether viewed in medieval times, Renaissance times, or the Enlightenment of the eighteenth century, Scots mercenary service flourished. The mercenaries were originally Catholic, but continued on as Presbyterian Protestants after the Reformation had converted most of them. Before and after the Union of the Crowns with England in 1603, and of Parliaments in 1707, Scottish soldiers trooped into Europe. Before and after the gunpowder revolution and the creation of standing armies, the Scots were mercenaries. The Scots tradition of professional soldiering transcended many of the major changes in European history.

The powerful mercenary tradition finally came to an end because of radical political and economic changes taking place in the eighteenth century. Politically, by joining England during the Seven Years' War (1756–63), Scotland became a player in European life and was no longer a neutral bystander from which mercenaries could be drawn. Many European states were alarmed by the huge increase in British wealth, power, and influence after 1763. Consequently, while the British were involved in the American Revolutionary War (1776–83), the Dutch, French, and Spanish took the opportunity to declare war against Scotland and England. The Dutch disbanded their Scots Brigade in the early 1780s, ending the demand for Scots mercenaries in that country.

The wars in America from 1756–1812 made it more profitable for professional soldiers to serve in British rather than foreign regiments. Consequently, the supply of mercenaries to Europe was defeated by a new, more powerful, economic attraction: free land in North America, obtained by wearing a red coat and a kilt.

I believe that eighteenth-century Highland modernity deserves more prominence today. Historians have always emphasized the terrible brutality of the Jacobite Rebellion (1745–46), but have ignored that "sheer pacification has been of enormous benefit whenever it has occurred, whether in the Scottish Highlands or [elsewhere]."[47] The eighteenth-century "improvements" in the Highlands have been overshadowed by the Enlightenment in the Lowlands. I argue a doubly revisionist view of that Scottish Enlightenment by presenting it as more Scottish by including Highlanders, and more international by including Canada within its orbit.

The sociologist Anthony Giddens states that modernity is a complex idea that involves bringing people up to date with a pace and scope of change that sweeps away the old order. Inherent in the idea of modernity is a contrast with tradition.[48] The Highlands of 1745 offer a huge contrast to the Highlands of 1812. The clan tribalism of 1745 was transformed into an impersonal harsh capitalism that converted often Catholic or Episcopalian rebels into the poor but hard working Presbyterian loyalists that lived in the Highlands of 1812.

Giddens also claims that socio-economic actions in modern life are constantly examined and reformed in the light of incoming information about those actions.[49] For example, in the early 1750s, the survey in the *Lovat Estate Papers* does not mention the potato as a major crop, but suggests that "planting potatoes would ... be an Excellent Method to Cultivate Wild and Barren Soil."[50] By the 1780s, the *Statistical Account of Scotland* showed that not only had potatoes become the dominant crop on the Lovat Estates, farmers were constantly experimenting to improve their quality.[51] It is not surprising then that in 1763, Governor James Murray, at the behest of the Highland soldier-settlers, held field trials to determine which of the tubers grew best in the wild and barren forests of the New World.

Simon McTavish (1750–1804) was reputedly the wealthiest man in Canada in his era. He modernized the fur trade and created North America's first transcontinental organization, the North West Company. The Company's pioneering explorations laid the geographical foundations of modern Canada. (Library and Archives Canada, Mikan 283377 c092920k.)

And finally, Giddens believes that "the emergent social order of modernity is capitalistic"[52] and "one of the fundamental consequences of modernity ... is globalization."[53] The Fraser-McTavish bond of man-rent mentioned previously characterized Highlanders in 1721, and the Canadian fur trade characterized them by 1812. John McTavish, a rebel in 1745, became a 78th lieutenant in North America, and his son, Simon McTavish, then emigrated there to claim his father's land. By the 1800s, Simon was a major capitalist in the NWC exporting furs from the Pacific and Arctic across the Atlantic to his cousin in London, John Fraser of McTavish, Fraser and Company.[54] The Fraser-McTavish story demonstrates that thanks to service in the 78th the clan tribalism of 1721 evolved into the Canadian global capitalism of 1812.

3

The Eighteenth-Century British Military Machine in America

Handle well your fuzee [musket], your sword, your pen and your books.
— Captain John Nairne, 78th Fraser's Highlanders, "John Nairne"

The 78th served only in North America, so in this chapter I will explore how the military machine in the New World shaped the men of this regiment. British officers disliked overseas service in North America because of "hardships due to scanty provisions for lodging and having to pay high prices for all necessities of life."[1] Disease was also an implacable enemy, and the "hospital" loomed large in the life of these men. Colonel Fraser of the 78th wrote soon after landing in Nova Scotia: "In this Camp in less than a fortnight the 2 field officers, 6 Captains, seventeen subalterns and above 300 men were down with the flux.... I have lost 20 men and there are about 200 still ill."[2] While I deal with Highlanders' adaptation to North America in chapters 7 and 9, it is perhaps important to keep in mind that these men went through winters, hot summers, and disease on the frontiers of North America.

Organization

The eighteenth-century British military machine that shaped the 78th Fraser's and other regiments contained a host of overlapping jurisdictions with no centre of responsibility. There was a degree of rationale to this because British society was fearful of a powerful standing force that might be employed by a particular interest group.[3] Indeed, the army was not particularly loved by any section of British society at the start of the Seven Years' War. Eighteenth-century armies were, by and large, grim organizations that contemporaries viewed with disdain, if not fear. Often composed of the impoverished and the criminal, regiments were governed with iron discipline.

In Britain, a mixture of private and public monies funded the army.[4] For example, the banks received a substantial commission from the government for paying the soldiers and for purchasing supplies in North America. Colonel Simon Fraser drew funds deposited by the government into the John Coutts Bank of Edinburgh to pay for the 78th's wages, food, clothing, and shelter. The government issued arms, but officers met the regiment's other needs by using funds from Coutts Bank.

The basic unit of the British Army was the regiment, which was subdivided into companies. The grenadier companies acted as shock troops, specially trained for assault, while the companies of light infantrymen provided a specialized tactical role. There were about one hundred Frasers in each of twelve companies, totalling approximately twelve hundred men, which made them Major General James Wolfe's largest regiment. Each company within the regiment was led by a captain, and was further divided into platoons each led by a lieutenant.

The Regiment as a Social Unit

The 78th Fraser's *Orderly Book*, written by Captain John Nairne (1731–1802) from May to December 1762, is an eyewitness account of the 78th's time in New France. Nairne's account of regimental life should be viewed with caution, as it is difficult to obtain corroboration of the incidents mentioned.[5] While Nairne probably did not write untruths, he almost certainly put a "spin" on the official record. For instance, he shows cases where members of the Fraser's Highlanders were charged with criminal activity, but does not tell us the results of those charges. Reading between the lines, we get the sense that Nairne was trying to prove that the 78th was a first-rate military unit.

During the 1750s, Sergeant MacLeod enlisted in the 78th at the age of seventy. Incredibly, he also fought in the American Revolution in the 1770s. He was one of the many 78th soldiers who left letters, memoirs, or books about their lives. (Courtesy of Earl Chapman Archives.)

This Highland regiment employed men, drummer boys, and even wives (who were hired to wash, cook, clean, and nurse subject to military discipline). There were a small number of surprisingly old soldiers, as well. For example, the uniquely experienced Sergeant MacLeod was enlisted even though he was seventy years old. Nairne's *Orderly Book* asks officers to mount a guard "to be composed of the old men and those who are any ways Disabled."[6]

There were limited pensions for older soldiers, and there were limited places where wounded older soldiers (Chelsea Pensioners) could be supported. Consequently, some veterans were kept by the Fraser's as charity cases because of conspicuous service.[7]

The 78th sometimes managed to pass on its charity cases to other regiments when it was disbanded. John MacKenzie, a severely wounded veteran of the 78th, enlisted in the West Fencible Regiment (Argyll Western Fencibles) until he was discharged at the age of seventy-two.[8] Captain Hugh Montgomerie, a 78th veteran who had become colonel of the West Fencible Regiment, perhaps took pity on MacKenzie and signed him up.[9] There were fifty-three invalids on the Fraser's muster rolls when the regiment

Private of the 78th, by D. Anderson. (Permission from Macdonald-Stewart Foundation.)

was disbanded, and fewer than twenty were admitted to become Chelsea Pensioners,[10] who received help of five pennies per day.[11] The Pensioners lived at subsistence levels and the other invalids had to beg in the streets.

Training the 78th

The Fraser's Highlanders, according to Nairne's *Orderly Book*, drilled incessantly. Drilling — exercising in eighteenth-century language — was conducted primarily in companies, and consisted of five principal parts: the manual exercise, the platoon exercise, the evolutions, the firings, and the manoeuvres.

The manual exercises were movements covering the loading of a weapon, swordsmanship, and ceremonial duties such as saluting with a weapon.

Platoons formed the basic firing unit for discharging muskets following voice or drum commands. The regiment fired by platoon, not as one unit. Platoons were grouped in threes. Each one of the three platoons would discharge its weapons in a volley depending on its place in the firing line. At Quebec in 1759, General Wolfe's plan of alternate firing consisted of platoon volleys fanning out in different directions. The firing along the regimental line could start alternately with the platoons on the left, then with those on the right, and finally with those in the centre. This was apparently most effective, but the system required a high degree of discipline and training.

The evolutions were short, precise movements on foot performed when in rank and file: turning, about-turning, and opening and closing the rank and file.

Finally, manoeuvres were large-scale exercises involving the infantry, artillery, and cavalry in planned moves.

In the spring,[12] the Frasers' daily training started at 5:00 a.m., with "each company to be exercised twice a day Sundays excepted in two squads, one Composed of those who can Exercise Best the other of the most awkward, that by Sergts. and Corporals who … are not out of humour with Clouns."[13] Allowances were made for the inept. However, when the regiment was labouring to rebuild Quebec City during the summer heat, the increased workload led to a change in routine and the men exercised only once a day.[14]

The sergeants and corporals drilled the men to operate with a military bearing and were instructed, according to Nairne's *Orderly Book*, to "use the men kindly but not with familiarity." In other words, sergeants had to be strict but not bullies, and were to be helpful but keep a social distance from the men. The officers had to ensure that the men were clean, well-housed, and looked after if sick or wounded. This kilted regiment expected "every soldier whether he is on duty or not to have his face, hands and knees well wash'd — his hair well com'd [combed] cut short on the top of his head, and his locks short."[15]

Until recently, the view of many historians was that "most of the British officers, quite unperturbed by their lack of experience in forest warfare, clung to their narrow class prejudices."[16] This idea that British officers were prejudiced against Aboriginal peoples and colonial soldiers to a degree that harmed their ability to adapt and fight in the forests is a myth. In fact, the eighteenth-century British Army did adjust its training and tactics to the terrain in summer and winter and found a way to wage war successfully in North America.[17] For example, travel by river was so important in this new land that the troops had to know their way around canoes and boats. Captain Nairne canoed around various parts of his future seigneury while still in the army. Various units from the 78th canoed to upstate New York on military business. Sergeant Thompson recorded many anecdotes about longboats, and it is obvious that the 78th spent a great deal of time travelling on lakes and rivers.[18]

New France was a frontier society geared to warfare, and the military abilities of the French-Canadian coureurs du bois — fur traders— were greater than those of the colonial troops raised in British North America.[19] French Canadians were raised from childhood to be wilderness soldiers and incomparable fighters.[20] However, the Highland soldiers learned to match the coureurs du bois in military efficiency.

When the French Canadians were besieging British-held Quebec City during the winter of 1759–60, the 78th had to adapt to winter conditions unfamiliar to them in order to attack the French lines around the city. General James Murray, in charge of the defence, and Sergeant Thompson of the 78th both mention the bilingual Captain MacDonald's success in leading his men on snowshoes against the French. MacDonald was the negotiator for the British in dealings with the French enemy, and Murray sent him to arrange prisoner exchanges so that "he might have an opportunity to take a view of their posts."[21] Having spied out the French lines, MacDonald then successfully attacked them at night on snowshoes. Highland soldiers learned to carry themselves with "self possession" in the winter and summer, and on both the land and waters of North America.

Officer Training

The only military education many new officers had was via the army's guidebook, so training took place on the job. In the Fraser's, a good number of the officer corps had soldiered in France, Holland, Prussia, or Austria. Many had fought for the Jacobites or for the Hanoverians in the 1745 Rebellion, and part of the military success of the Fraser's can be attributed to their experienced officers. While Colonel Simon Fraser had limited military experience, he had highly professional officers to advise him. Major General Wolfe wrote that the 78th had "the manliest corps of officers I ever saw."[22]

John Nairne wrote a memorandum to his Canadian son, and Malcolm Fraser, another 78th veteran, wrote to Nairne's second son about army life.[23] Nairne advised against smoking because it was a "Dutch habit" (Nairne served with the Scots Brigade in the Netherlands). He also says to "handle well your fuzee [fusil / gun] your sword, your pen and your books" and "know every man by name and know their several characters and Dispositions."

Nairne believed that the British officer should be a highly professional figure, adept at handling weapons, people, ideas, and writing.[24] Malcolm Fraser notes that soldiering is a social contract, to the death if necessary: "I would also recommend to you to read useful books ... and to acquire a competent knowledge of History, both Ancient and Modern, especially that of the country in whose service you are engaged ..."[25] Fraser is not advising the young Nairne to read about Canada or Britain, but about the "country in whose service you are engaged," a mercenary mindset that persisted, in this case, until the War of 1812. Fraser advised the young officer to keep his men obedient, but to never forget that "the Private Man who serves in the ranks, is your fellow soldier and fellowman, and that you are bound to show him every attention and humanity in your power."

Historians usually describe the eighteenth-century British Army in a very different light: "Most of their officers treated them like animals. The men were flogged mercilessly for the slightest breach of discipline."[26] The brutal top-down pattern of discipline often used to describe the eighteenth-century British military machine does not seem to be applicable to the Fraser's Highlanders.

Scottish historian Tom Devine writes that "the bond between a Highlander and his officer does seem to have been much closer than the relationship between English soldiers and their superiors."[27] English historian Stephen Brumwell explains that Highlanders "shared a common culture and heritage, and very often the same name. Highland officers were expected to provide an unswerving example of honourable conduct to their men."[28] In fact, English soldiers shared a common culture and heritage, and their officers were supposed to act in an honourable manner, too. Neither historian explains *why* there was a close bond in Highland regiments.

No direct evidence from the time indicates that the close bonds in the 78th were created by the chief-clansmen relationship. The officer-soldier bonding may explain the absence of the use of the lash but, as stated, the exact reason for this bond is difficult to explain. Approximately eleven officers in the 78th were either clan chiefs or sons of clan chiefs.[29] The large Highland clan aristocracy was supposedly close to its social inferiors if only because so many claimed relationship to the chief. Social relations within the regiment likely reflected the structure of Highland society, which was not, in fact, an egalitarian one. On balance, the evidence of the 78th suggests that the officer-man gap was an elastic one in that social distance varied according to circumstances.

Although some officers were chiefs or the eldest sons of clan chiefs, they were also experienced soldiers, partly because "warrior societies thrived in most of the Highlands."[30] In brief, the 78th was a fine regiment, perhaps because officers had clan links to the men, but certainly because they were highly experienced soldiers who could relate better to their men.

The officers were ambitious career soldiers and flowed in and out of the regiment from other parts of the military machine. For example, Captain Simon Fraser of Balnain became a major in the 24th Foot in 1761 for his part in decoying the sentries at Quebec. Nairne's *Orderly Book* records that six officers from other regiments were promoted or bought their way into the 78th. Military writers often portray Highland regiments as "families," though temporary ones at that.

That the 78th Fraser's was a retinue of clansmen rather than of professional soldiers is a common misinterpretation, partly "because it contained fifteen Frasers amongst its officers."[31] According to the Scottish historian D.H. Henderson, the 78th "has become the focus of over-sentimentalized and unsustainable arguments that view Highland units as simply state-sponsored clan levies — a perception that has consistently clung to all kilted regiments."[32]

Another common misconception is that officers in the Fraser's Highlanders paid to obtain their posts. The initial posts were given out free to encourage recruitment, which meant the original officers of the 78th obtained a financial advantage. Each officer "owned" his post. They could sell their posts, but although it was a dangerous job, it was also a valuable one to hold. At the end of a war and the disbandment of a regiment, the officers received a pension of half-pay, and in return were liable to be re-enlisted to fight. Most of the 78th's half-pay officers returned to the Highlands, where they contributed to what author and historian Andrew MacKillop labels the re-militarization of the tacksman officer class.[33]

Several officers, such as John Nairne, Malcolm and John Fraser in Quebec, Sir Henry Seton, and Hugh Fraser in upstate New York, drew their half-pay on the frontiers of the former New France. Lieutenant Allan Stewart migrated to North Carolina with a substantial following in the inter-war years of 1763–76.[34] The sheer numbers and high status of half-pay Highland officers is such that in Scotland they "remained an important element in emigration … until the early 1800s."[35] On the Canadian frontier, half-pay Highland officers, such as the husbands of authors Catharine Parr Traill (*The Backwoods of Canada*) and Susanna Moodie (*Roughing It in the Bush*), became familiar and important figures.

Major Clephane of the 78th sold his post as major because of ill health to Captain John MacPherson.[36] However, Major MacPherson then had to "sell out" himself in October 1760 after being wounded. He was to be paid £1,500 — £800 from a Lieutenant Baillie, who was wealthy, £400 from a Captain Campbell, and £300 from an ensign. The captain was to become the new major and the other two men were to move up into the rank above them. Lieutenant Baillie's youth and short service counted against him, however, and General Amherst refused to allow him to take the captain's post, so the elaborate plan fell apart. In this case, at least, it took more than just wealth and influence to buy a commission in the 78th.

Later, in March 1761, Lieutenant John Nairne, who wrote the *Orderly Book* after he became a captain, was recommended as purchaser of Captain Campbell's post. This led to a bitter, complicated dispute about how Nairne was to pay Captain Campbell for his captaincy. Nairne offered to pay in cash, but Campbell did not want to keep that amount of money in the camp. Campbell preferred that Nairne purchase an expensive bank draft that could be transferred safely to Scotland. The dispute eventually went to an arbitration board, where Captain Archibald Campbell acted for Alexander Campbell and General Murray acted for Nairne. Not surprisingly, the result favoured Nairne and confirmed the huge market value of the post. The arbitrators "inquired into the usual price paid for companies in the 78th regiment, which we find by the concurrent testimony of Captains Archibald and Alexander Campbell of the said regiment, to have never at any time exceeded one thousand pounds sterling."[37]

Commissions were scarcer and more expensive in the reduced army.[38] The cost of a major's commission in the British Army was two thousand pounds in 1766 after peace was declared. As for the new Captain Nairne, he was promoted during the American Revolution to become a major, then sold his commission in the 84th Regiment for three thousand pounds after the American Revolutionary War ended. He did well. However, the point is, selling out could cause a chain reaction and some major problems for other posts purchasing at the lower levels of command.

Warfare in the New World

There were two kinds of warfare in the New World — campaign battles and irregular warfare. Manoeuvring as a regiment, let alone an army, was difficult in the uneven and heavily forested terrain, making large campaign battles uncommon. Fighting in this topography underlined the need for tactical caution.[39] The enemies the British faced, such as the Aboriginals and the French Canadians, tended to favour irregular warfare where they fought in small groups, using the cover the landscape offered. This meant that soldiers had to aim at a specific target, or "mark" in eighteenth-century language, rather than firing volleys in the direction of the enemy ranks. Jeffrey Amherst (1717–97), commander of the British forces, wrote that "Firing at marks is so essential for forming a soldier for this country."[40]

The fight on the Plains of Abraham at Quebec was unusual because it was a campaign battle between two armies. The mere act of transporting a substantial military force to a particular destination was extremely difficult. Much of General Wolfe's success on the Plains of Abraham can be attributed to the British navy, which provided mobility for what was an unusually large body of troops in North American warfare.

The irregular type of warfare, or *petit guerre*, consisted of raids, ambushes, and patrols fought by small groups.[41] General Edward Braddock's two inexperienced regiments, the 44th and 48th Foot, were badly routed in 1755 at the Monongahela River in the Ohio Valley. A British eyewitness account describes the French tactics: "Scarce an officer or soldier Can say that they ever saw at one time six of the Enemy and the greatest part never saw a Single man of the Enemy." Indeed, the enemy's shooting from the cover of the woods was sufficient to "soon put the Grenadiers in some disorder."[42]

During the Seven Years' War the British adopted a variety of new tactics and forms of military organization. General Braddock attributed his defeat in battle to the inefficient baggage train that could not negotiate the rough terrain quickly.[43] As a result Captain Gabriel Christie established a now famous Wagon Corps that proved to be more effective in moving supplies.[44]

To deal with attacks in broken terrain, light companies were formed in the 78th. The British also created the famed Rangers — versatile groups capable of long-distance scouting that could "beat the woods"[45] and successfully engage the Aboriginal fighters on the flanks. Amherst introduced another innovation to deal with irregulars by reducing the regimental line from three to two ranks. This soon proved effective, and the irregulars were unable to withstand this form of attack because the new line did not present such a compact target. Wolfe may have adopted and intentionally employed this tactic on the Plains of Abraham — the first major battle in British military history to do so. However, there is strong evidence that the line may have been three men deep. Wolfe's thin line, if indeed it was thin, probably reduced British deaths in that battle. The two-ranks-deep formation was the "thin red line" made famous nearly a century later by Colin Campbell at the Battle of Balaclava.

Equipment

Fraser's Highlanders were armed with the fusil (*fuzee*) version of the Long Land musket, and they carried broadswords. The musket itself weighed about 5.5 kilograms and the barrel was a little over a metre long. The muskets used were fitted with steel ramrods and the ammunition came in paper cartridges containing both the powder and the musket ball. An experienced soldier could fire on average three balls a minute, four if pushed, and the weapon was accurate to about eighty metres.[46] Pistols were issued by the government to the 78th, but officers and some men bought the famous Doune pistols, worn on a gun belt that reached from the right shoulder to the left waist belt. These were metal pistols manufactured in Doune, Scotland, elaborately decorated and very reliable. They were sturdy enough to be used as a club after firing. Additional weapons used were dirks (daggers), carried on the right side of the belt. Sergeants carried halberds (combination spear and battleaxe) and officers carried espontoons (a type of spear a little over two metres in length). Other equipment issued included powder horns and cartouche boxes which contained cartridges made up of explosive charges and musket balls.

The Fraser's were avid swordsmen. Sergeant James Thompson (1732–1830) spoke in his journal about a contest in which sharpened sticks replaced swords. Large sums of money were bet on this contest to determine who the best regimental swordsman was. According to Thompson, the judges of the duel had been fixed and they failed to count some of the hits. However, the victimized swordsman, Corporal MacPherson, compensated by cutting the face of his adversary, Lieutenant John Fraser, so the judges could not overlook his hits, and he won the tournament. Sergeant Thompson was given money for helping to organize the contest and was probably betting on it, too, so he may have been biased against Lieutenant Fraser.[47] Sergeant Donald MacLeod of the 78th, a champion swordsman in his days before joining up, had cut the arm off an Irish champion in a famous duel. Much of the success of the Fraser's sword charge on the Plains of Abraham can be attributed to their training under the direction of Sergeant MacLeod.

The Fraser's wore full Highland dress. Except for the drummers, the troops wore black bonnets (hats) without cap badges.[48] The soldiers wore white linen shirts with white collars, red waistcoats, and red jackets. A waist belt divided their tartan plaid into the kilt and the spare part which was worn on the left shoulder. A long undershirt tied between the legs acted as underwear, which answers the age-old question about what was worn underneath the kilt. They also had a kilt, or filibeg, that was worn without the plaid.[49] For footwear, black leather regulation-type shoes were worn, and each soldier carried spare shoe brushes, leather soles and heels in case repairs were necessary.

Unfortunately, there are no direct references from the time that describe the 78th's tartan. Nairne's *Orderly Book* states: "As there is plenty of Tartan in town and the men are in great want of hose, Commanding Officers of Companys are Desired immediately to provide their men in three pares [*sic*] of Good hose."[50] However, it is unclear whether this was the government tartan, known as the Black Watch tartan, or whether it was something specific to the 78th. Authors Harper and McCulloch believe the regiment's tartan to have been the flaming red pattern now associated with the Hunting Fraser tartan of today, which is worn by Colonel Fraser in Benjamin West's famous painting *The Death of General Wolfe*.

To distinguish rank, an officer wore a crimson silk sash over the left shoulder and gold shoulder cords around the right shoulder.[51] The Fraser's possibly had fifteen pipers,[52] which was somewhat unusual because bagpipes had been banned in the Highlands as instruments of war after the Jacobite Rebellion.(1745–46).[53] However, an exception was made in the Seven Years' War (1756–63) for Highland regiments employed by the King's forces. On the battlefield, the 78th's pipers probably played the regimental pipe tunes: "Lord Lovat's Lament," "The Frasers' Salute," and "Lord Simon."

Life in the 78th's America, 1760–63

During the winter, most of the 78th Regiment lived in Quebec City. In summer, tents were set up outside the city. Some members of the regiment patrolled the St. Lawrence River on naval ships while others lived in various parts of New France — for the inhabitants, this made it quite obvious that this territory was now British. The 78th had its own tailors, carpenters, and masons, and soldiers received extra money by working for the army on activities outside their normal duties. General James Murray sent troops downriver outside Quebec City, "to cut there ... the men to be paid five shillings for each cord [of wood] put on board; each man to receive a gill of rum; and the officers who were to survey the work to have three shillings a-day while employed."[54]Sick soldiers who were unable to work and needed hospital care had to pay two shillings per week while incapacitated and had two pence per week cut from their pay.[55] Since each soldier received only sixpence per day, or three shillings and sixpence per week, the substantial fee for admittance to hospital probably acted as a deterrent for malingerers. Medical treatment was not free for officers, but officers had a sort of medicare system and could pay their Captain, Alex Campbell, a regular fee for medical coverage, rather than pay a large sum up front when wounded. Dr. MacLean used the *Orderly Book* to let it be known that "The Capt's. [Campbell] Receipt will be sufficient voucher to those officers that Chuse to pay it."[56] Wives of soldiers who worked in the hospital as nurses received sixpence per day plus a ration [worth two pence a day]. Women were also paid for doing the washing, the rates of which were subject to dispute.

There are many references to essential winter clothing in Nairne's *Orderly Book*. A soldier by the name of Major Abercrombie ordered a Sergeant Campbell to "inspect ... and be answerable that the watch-coats be properly made ... and to report Daily in writing the work they will do ... and if they are found Negligent they will be severely Punished."[57] Keeping written records, attributing individual responsibility, and punishing those guilty for bad work seem more like the actions of a modern CEO rather than that of an eighteenth-century major.

Regimental life was marked by money problems and capitalist activities. Both were recurring themes in the peacetime accounts of the 78th. For instance, some officers complained that the British officers in Montreal were receiving an allowance of double rations because of high costs. General Murray investigated, then made everyone equal by reducing the allowance in Montreal.[58]

In Quebec City, there was an acute labour shortage in the 1760s because the British had to rebuild the extensive fortifications that had been damaged during the siege of that city. Sergeants and corporals of the regiment who "understood carpentry or Masonry" were instructed to give their names to the officer in charge if they wanted to be employed. This was hard labour, though: "Working party for the Engineers ... to parade at 5 o'clock in the morning and work till 10 [unclear in original] parade again in the Afternoon at 4 o'clock and work till 7."[59]

In addition, the city's residents needed help to repair private homes and businesses destroyed during the war, and so soldiers could also earn money working for private citizens. However, soldiers had to keep the lines of communication open to other parts of North America and could be away for weeks on journeys by canoe or snowshoes. A major problem, recorded in Nairne's *Orderly Book,* was that Highlanders would fail to inform their officers that they had returned from their journeys and would surreptitiously work for private citizens. Consequently, 78th soldiers were then paid by private employers as well as by the army. The entrepreneurial spirit obviously flourished in the 78th, and there is a record of "a court of Inquiry to sit at the Orderly Room at 12 o'clock on Donald McIntyre, soldier of Capt Alex Campbells Company, Confined for selling wood."[60] It is unclear what wood was being sold to whom and what the findings were, but Mr. McIntyre could perhaps claim that he was working for himself and not for someone else. There were several other instances of crime involving money and one John MacArthur was: "Confin'd for stealing a shirt for John Douglas, merchant." Curiously, the *Orderly Book* reads stealing *for* a merchant not stealing *from* a merchant. The book appears to have been carefully written, so perhaps Douglas was dealing in stolen shirts.

The *Orderly Book* often records that soldiers were abusing the system and would no longer be allowed to work for private citizens. Perhaps as a consequence of prohibiting outside work, a new financial problem appeared. It is possible that soldiers were relying on future earnings from private citizens to pay for goods.: "Some of the none-Commissioned officers and men of the Detachment had Imposed on some Merchants and others in town and taken up God given Credit, which they are not able to pay...."[61] The soldiers who defaulted on their credit could "Depend upon being most severely punished, and if are Non Commissioned officers they will not only be Reduced to the Ranks but shall Also receive such Corporal punishment and a Court Martial shall Judge to their Crime."[62]

Selling alcohol illegally to soldiers was another feature of regimental life. General Murray recorded in a diary entry on November 14, 1759: "I recalled all licenses, and ordered for the future every man who was found drunk to receive twenty lashes every morning till he acknowledged where he got it, and forfeit his allowance of rum for six weeks."[63] The problem of selling alcohol persisted, however, and Nairne's *Orderly Book* for the summer of 1762 states, in wonderful if brutal language, that guilty women "shall be flogg'd and Drumm'd out of the Regiment" and men shall be "punished by the hands of the hangman." Liquor stills were a conspicuous feature of the Lovat estates; therefore, it is quite likely that by 1762 some private soldiers and their wives were also distilling whisky and selling it.

General James Murray, who had become the governor of Quebec in 1763 after The Treaty of Paris ceded New France to Britain, encouraged the establishment of the first official whisky still constructed in Quebec City. We know that Captain Donald MacDonald, one of the Highlanders who fooled the French sentries, was distilling alcohol in Quebec City in the winter of 1759–60. Sergeant James Thompson, who disliked MacDonald for many reasons, describes him in his diary as "a surely cross dog," and writes that he "sent for me to taste some liqueur that he had made and asked my opinion of it."[64] This is the earliest reference to stills I have been able to find and Captain MacDonald deserves recognition as Canada's first whisky distiller. However, I suspect that the poor quality of the whisky, made using the limited materials available during a siege, explains why MacDonald was surly.

The British Army took great care not to antagonize the local French Canadian population and not to appear to be a harsh army of occupation; the comments and directives in the *Orderly Book* reflect this policy. It mentions that "the French people are to have a procession this day and that the men if they Chuse [sic] to see it are to behave Decently & take off their bonnets as if papis (t) es [papists?] & if they don't chuse this they are to stay in their Barracks." On the day of the British king's birthday, it directed: "none of the soldiers do presume to break any windows on account of their not being illuminated, as his Excellency [General Murray] has exempted the French people from putting lights in their windows."[65]

The regiment also had to deal with the thorny problem of soldiers who had taken up with local married women, most of whom were, of

The Jealous Husband, Cornelius Krieghoff (1845). The nineteenth-century public understood the humour in this scene of a 71st Highlander and a habitant's wife. Krieghoff created several versions of this hugely popular painting. (Galerie Alan Klinkhoff, Montreal.)

course, French Canadians. Wives in the eighteenth century were considered the "property" of their husbands. However, the officers apparently dealt very carefully with a John McDonnel, who was hiding the wife of François Aubic. When McDonnel refused to return the wife, they had him confined to barracks and threatened him with a court martial if his friends continued to hide the woman.[66] Presumably, the wife was eventually returned, because no more is mentioned about the affair in the *Orderly Book*. However, a decade later in the Thirteen Colonies, the American revolutionaries used this type of army-civilian problem as propaganda that converted the British Army in the American colonial mind into an undesirable foreign army of occupation.

The relationship between the officers and the men was not always top-down; that is, rules were sometimes imposed by the men on the officers. For example, a Captain Bayard, who was not in the 78th, disobeyed orders by not carrying a lantern and not knowing the password as he walked around Quebec City during the night. Bayard was arrested by the soldiers of the 78th who were acting as sentries in the town and in retaliation, Bayard later arrested the sentries. The officers in the Fraser's resented this action by an officer in another regiment and appealed to General Murray, who sided completely with the 78th sentries. In wonderful language, General Murray directed that "the Sentry is to know no man in the Night but by the Countersign …"[67]

Perhaps the soldiers of the 78th were being officious, and took the opportunity to arrest an officer who did not follow procedure. However, regimental cohesion in the face of outsiders, and pride in a regiment that followed orders regardless of the consequences, are recurring themes throughout Nairne's book.

General Life of a Fraser, 1760–63

Besides the *Orderly Book*, there are only a few traces of the other social and economic activities of the 78th during the three-year span between the fall of New France in 1760 and the signing of the Treaty of Paris in 1763. This time is known as the Military Regime because General James Murray ruled as the military governor of the region while the Seven Years' War continued in other parts of the world. General Murray, allowed two soldiers from the 78th to purchase land in New France before the Treaty of Paris ceded the colony officially to Britain. John Nairne and Malcolm Fraser bought seigneuries at what were probably bargain prices. Land was cheap, not only because it was war-ravaged, but because many of the French elite wanted to quickly sell their lands and return to France. Merchants, farmers, seigneurs, and officials in New France were ruined because of the worthless paper money that the French government had used to finance the Seven Years' War, the same government that then refused to honour the currency at the end of the war. Money was a big reason why many French Canadians rapidly abandoned the concept of a New France and transferred their allegiance to the British colony of Quebec after 1763. In many ways, France imposed far more hardship on the people of New France than did the British. As happened later in post–Second World War Germany, when the deutschmark was useless, British soldiers with hard currency could do well. Nevertheless, buying land in New France before 1763 was a risky endeavour because there was always the possibility that Britain would exchange the territory for some other, such as Guadeloupe.

Perhaps Nairne and Fraser would have sold their land had New France reverted back to a French colony. It is possible that they were prepared to live on the banks of the St. Lawrence River regardless of whether it was New France or Quebec. There were other Scots living in New France besides the Jacobite soldiers, of course, and marriages took place within these families. A Quebec notary record of 1752, seven years before the British conquest of New France, mentioned the marriage of David Somers and Marie Thompson, both originally from the town of Dundee. Records also show that several children were born to soldiers' wives during that 1760 to 1763 period. For example, records for the parish of Saint-François-de-la-Rivière-du-Sud show children of Andrew Ross, Hector Ross, and John MacNeil of the 78th. All three soldiers were married to Scottish women, not to French Canadians.

During the Military Regime, the 78th was stationed downriver from Quebec City as well as in the city, probably for defensive purposes. After New France officially became part of the British Empire, French Canadians became the "new subjects," to use the official term. Many of the 78th then married local women and settled downriver in places such as Fraserville (renamed Rivière-du-Loup). Indeed, perhaps a reason so many Fraser's Highlanders stayed on in North America after the peace was because both officers and private soldiers got married. Yet, while there were marriages to Scottish women in the 1760 to 1763 period, I was unable to trace any official marriages to French-Canadian brides during this time because British soldiers were not allowed to marry foreign nationals while serving in enemy countries. Quebec notary records reveal that sums of money did change hands: for example, a woman by the name of Catherine Voyer received a payment from Major John Campbell of the 78th on September 23, 1762. And another woman, Angelique Fraser, was involved in a land sale detailed in a notary record dated July 16, 1762. Both of these transactions may have involved illegitimate children because Highlanders who wished to take financial responsibility for children born out of wedlock would have to resort to such methods.

Several business transactions involving the Fraser's Highlanders were recorded in Quebec notary records between 1760 and 1763, but, as with marriages, a spate of business dealings begins after 1763 and the signing of the Treaty of Paris. Sergeant James Thompson recounted in his diary what life was like during the Military Regime. From his accounts, it was clear that the sergeants sometimes cheated the men out of wages, but that the men could and did complain about the unfair treatment. Thompson's stories also demonstrate that the pacifist Quakers were anxious to express their patriotism in peaceful ways during the Seven Years' War by sending cloth to the Highlanders to help them through the cold winter. The anecdote also shows how far Highlanders had been rehabilitated in English public opinion since 1745 and reveals the cordial relations they enjoyed with French Canadians; Thompson apparently gave his cloth to a French Canadian, and the only French Canadian that he wrote about not liking was a local parish priest.

A significant comment made by Thompson about the men in the 78th concerns payment of wages. The French Army, he said, paid the habitants (French farmers) by writing worthless paper — "playing card money," as he described it. Thompson made it clear that ordinary French Canadians did not know the value of gold coins until the British Army arrived. The British practice of paying the habitants fairly for produce not only rejuvenated and created a commercial economy, but it played a major role in transferring the habitants' loyalty from New France to Canada.

It has been claimed that the 78th Fraser's Highlanders established a military Masonic Lodge on October 2, 1760, and that both officers and men such as Sergeant James Thompson and Colonel Simon Fraser were members. Although its very existence is in question, a series of murals relating to the organization were painted long after, in the Masonic Temple of Montreal. If it did exist, it tells us that, for an eighteenth-century regiment, the 78th officer-man links were unusually strong. What also indicates a strong officer-man bond is the settlement of North America by so many officers with their men. Officers John Nairne and Malcolm and Alexander Fraser were joined in their Quebec seigneuries by some Highland soldiers after the Treaty of Paris in 1763 ended the war. Hugh Fraser returned to Scotland at this time with the 78th, where they were disbanded, and he married the daughter of a fellow officer, Lieutenant John McTavish. In 1764, Hugh returned to New York State with a group of 78th and other Highland soldiers with his new wife, and her young brother, Simon McTavish (c. 1750–1804). Young Simon, who would become a famous fur trader, and whom I mentioned in an earlier chapter, had McTavish Street in downtown Montreal (adjacent to McGill University), named after him. This pattern of re-migration back to the New World after discharged soldiers returned to Scotland is important and is explored in more detail in chapters 7 and 8. However, the point is that it was neither Highland chiefs nor the battle of Culloden that initiated the massive Highland migration that took place from 1763–76, it was Highland soldiers in regiments such as the Fraser's Highlanders that sparked migration after their victory on the Plains of Abraham.

Overall, the officers of the 78th do seem to have been highly effective leaders. Arguably, the competence shown by these men came not only from their clan backgrounds, but from their professional military experience. It is difficult for me to join the many historians who make statements about clan chiefs or the sons of chiefs in this regiment. Although there are a great many letters, books, journals, and diaries written by 78th soldiers, there are few direct references to the chiefs and their sons. The one exception was Colonel Fraser, who wanted to impress London with his ability as a Highland chief to raise men.[68] "Fraser was arguing that 'clan chiefs,' through their command of military population, were entitled to preferential state patronage."[69] I will later discuss some of the present-day misconceptions that arose because of the comments made by Colonel Fraser about Highland chiefs.

By today's standards, life was grim within the British military machine of the eighteenth century. But life in general was brutal in those days, so, more to the point many Highlanders thought that life in the 78th was better than in the Highlands of the time. Pay was low, work was hard, and violence within the army was also rife. The Fraser's Highlanders had to watch, for example, as two men, Elias Wolfe and Henry Adrien, from the 2nd Battalion Royal Americans, were tried for robbery and sentenced to "suffer death for same."[70] But public hangings for what we regard as trivial offences against property were common in the eighteenth century, so army life probably reflected the level of violence typical of the time in society in general. Records show that few of the Fraser's Highlanders were actually lashed, none were hanged, and all were given free land in North America if they wanted it at the end of their service.

Loyalty and cohesion characterized the relationships between men of all ranks in the 78th. The men fought well, and by and large obeyed their officers because they wanted to. Yet this was an eighteenth-century relationship, and the very real possibility of the lash or the noose was still held over the heads of these Highland soldiers by their Highland officers. The regiment was perceived as a great success at the time and succeeded as a fighting unit, of course, but it also succeeded economically. The free commissions appealed to officers, and the private soldiers also did well financially. General Murray was most surprised by the large amount of funds lent to him by private soldiers of the 78th after asking for money to tide his administration over until the ships arrived from Britain. While the 78th made up only one-eighth of the troops under General Murray's command, their savings constituted one-quarter of the money raised. According to Murray: "The non-commissioned officers and private men of that single regiment [78th] contributed ... 2,000 pounds."[71] At a time when most English soldiers lived from week to week on their wages, these Scots had saved, on average, more than two pounds each — approximately three months' wages per man. Perhaps the 78th were stationed in areas where jobs paid more than where the English regiments were deployed. It may also be that the Scots were more economical with their money than the English soldiers — a common belief then and now.

For the men of the 78th, the British military machine was a success. The regiment did not just "break into" New France from a military point of view. These soldiers also broke into the economic and demographic life of the former French colony, especially those areas that are now part of upstate New York, Vermont, Quebec, New Brunswick, and Nova Scotia. Many private soldiers decided to settle in North America after having worked there with the 78th, an experience that taught them the best ways to make a living in these rugged frontier lands. Militarism turned rebel clansmen into loyal frontiersmen. General Murray became Governor Murray of Quebec (Canada); John Nairne, Malcolm Fraser, Alexander Fraser, James Murray, and Sergeant Lachlan Smith, all 78th Fraser's Highlanders, became seigneurs in Quebec, while Hugh Fraser and Sir Henry Seton became major landowners in upstate New York.

Highlanders used the British military machine as a bridge into the wider society and economy on the other side of the Atlantic. This was a pattern Scottish soldier-settlers had been following for approximately five hundred years.

4

Raising the 78th Fraser's Highlanders

Got by the Effect of money, Linen cloath and Tartan.
— Major James Clephane, 78th Regiment of Foot
(Rose of Kilravock Papers)

The raising of the 78th Highland Regiment of Foot throws light on many different aspects of mid-eighteenth-century life.

Although universal conscription theoretically did not exist in Britain in the eighteenth century, able-bodied men not required for harvest work were often "pressed" into army service. Most Highlanders had to be recruited by persuasion — and money was very persuasive.

Colonel Simon Fraser (1726–82) "owned" the 78th Regiment, and the state paid him three pounds for each soldier he raised. However, the government did not look too closely at who was enlisted or what methods were used to bring these men into the regiment.

British regiments at the time were still built around "great men" who lent their names to the units they commanded or raised. The Black Watch was usually referred to as "Murray's Regiment," named after its colonel, James Murray (who is not to be confused with the General James Murray who became governor of Quebec). Numbers were allocated to regiments in the order that they were raised for British service. Hence, the Royal

Scots was the 1st regiment; the Black Watch the 42nd; Montgomerie's Highlanders the 77th; and the Fraser's became the 78th.

The Politics of Recruitment

On January 1, 1757, the 78th Regiment was officially created, and on January 13 a notice to "beat out" (raise) men was issued. Major James Clephane, formerly of the Scots Brigade in Holland, was ordered to "raise One Hundred able bodied Men." He was told to choose men "of any size who are fit for Service and of any age from Eighteen to Forty.... For each Man sent and approved of at head Quarters you shall receive Three Pounds sterling with Pay from the date of his Attestation."[1] Clephane was paid his three pounds per head through Coutts Bank in Edinburgh.

It was up to the Duke of Argyll to vet all of the officers: "Stewart is not practicable," he said of one potential recruit, "because he is a lowlander and cannot speak the Highland language, which is a rule laid down in these levies." Another, a man by the name of James Murray, who was already in the Prussian army, would require "an application to the King of Prussia"[2] that would allow him to join the Fraser's.

Argyll believed that "if any can be found who have served in Holland, so much the better." Because the Scots Brigade in the Netherlands was Protestant, the men were presumably politically loyal to the Hanoverians, as well as being an experienced fighting force from which recruits could be drawn. The Duke of Argyll also instructed that "the commissions must all be given gratis. The other two Highland Regiments will likewise have the same addition made to them."[3] This meant that, unlike other regiments where individuals had to buy a commission to become an officer, Highland officers received their commissions free. This provision caused some envy amongst the English regiments, but was a way of integrating the Highland and mercenary gentry into the Hanoverian fiscal military state.

Britain's secretary of war, William Barrington, wrote that "the Scotch Dutch officers at present recruiting in Scotland are a great hindrance ... as they can afford to give as much money as he [Colonel Fraser] can ..."[4] In another instance, the Duke of Cumberland complained that men thinking they had been recruited for the Scots Brigade in Holland were, in fact, shipped off to the French army. As an indicator of the eighteenth-century mind, the Duke was not so much complaining about French recruitment in Scotland, just fraudulent recruitment.[5] Indeed, Major Clephane of the 78th Highlanders may well have been one of the Dutch officers deceiving recruits in Scotland. In the early 1750s, Clephane wrote that he was leaving for "Frogland" with eight recruits.[6] Clephane was likely referring to the Netherlands, but it is possible he may have been referring to France.

Captain Donald MacDonald of the 78th, the man who spoke French to the sentries on the clifftop in Quebec, had definitely been recruiting for the French Royal Scots. After Culloden he had been released and was sent back to his regiment in France, the French Royal Scots. In 1753 a British soldier wrote of him, "Donald MacDonald Brother to MacDonald of clan Ranald with another MacDonald, a Cameron and a MacKenzie all officers of the French King's service, are lately arrived in the Highlands from Abroad with the Intention it is said to recruit men for that service."[7] Even in the 1750s the British Army had no monopoly on Highland recruitment.

In 1756, after the amnesty for Jacobites took effect, Donald MacDonald became a captain in the 78th Fraser's Highlanders and proceeded to recruit his quota of men. Major General James Wolfe thought very highly of MacDonald, who enthusiastically fought the French during the campaign in North America. Captain John MacDonald of the 78th could be the "other" MacDonald mentioned in the recruitment for the French Royal Scots in 1753. The tangled loyalties of Highland Scots at this time arose just as much from the professional soldier tradition as from the Jacobite loyalties of these men. There were Irishmen who fought for the French and French Huguenots (Protestants) who fought for the British during the Seven Years' War. Among the Scots, however, there were soldiers like Donald MacDonald and John MacDonald who had recruited and fought for *both* sides.

It is difficult to know how soldiers such as the two MacDonalds mentioned saw themselves and whether they identified with Britain. Nevertheless, both Captain Donald MacDonald and Captain Simon Fraser, his mercenary companion in Wolfe's lead boat, eventually died as soldiers in the service of Britain.

MAP 2: RECRUITMENT OF THE 78TH IN SCOTLAND

These areas and families were also the source of much of the Scottish emigration, 1763 – 1776. For example, the HECTOR, the "first" Scots emigrant ship to Canada, assembled at Beauly, home to Col. Simon Fraser of the 78th. The PEARL, which took many ex-soldiers to upstate N.Y. and Vermont, assembled at Fort William. Skye alone lost about 10% of its population.

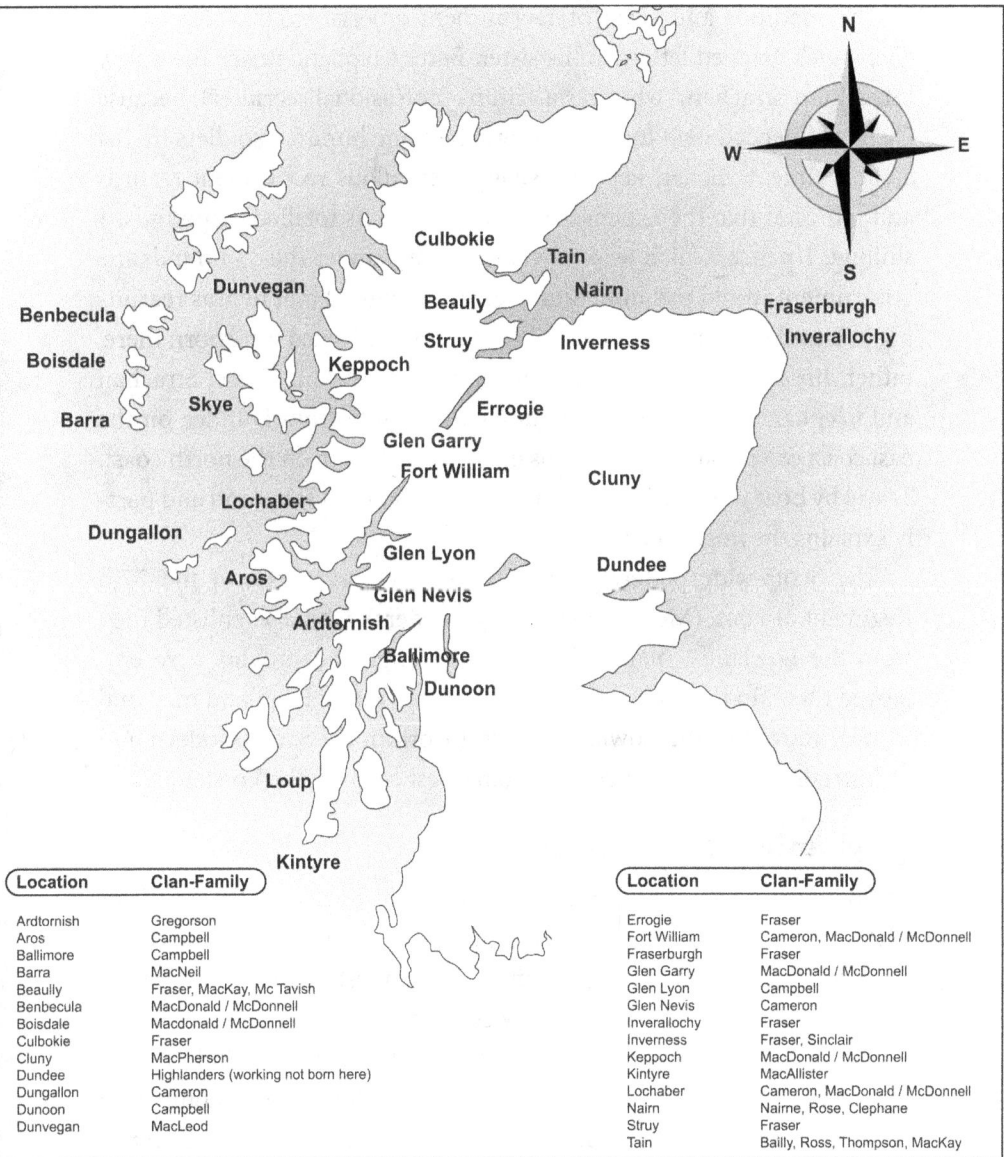

Location	Clan-Family
Ardtornish	Gregorson
Aros	Campbell
Ballimore	Campbell
Barra	MacNeil
Beauly	Fraser, MacKay, Mc Tavish
Benbecula	MacDonald / McDonnell
Boisdale	Macdonald / McDonnell
Culbokie	Fraser
Cluny	MacPherson
Dundee	Highlanders (working not born here)
Dungallon	Cameron
Dunoon	Campbell
Dunvegan	MacLeod

Location	Clan-Family
Errogie	Fraser
Fort William	Cameron, MacDonald / McDonnell
Fraserburgh	Fraser
Glen Garry	MacDonald / McDonnell
Glen Lyon	Campbell
Glen Nevis	Cameron
Inverallochy	Fraser
Inverness	Fraser, Sinclair
Keppoch	MacDonald / McDonnell
Kintyre	MacAllister
Lochaber	Cameron, MacDonald / McDonnell
Nairn	Nairne, Rose, Clephane
Struy	Fraser
Tain	Bailly, Ross, Thompson, MacKay

Colonel Simon Fraser, who lived at the Fraser Clan seat in the town of Beauly (Inverness-shire), selected officers who lived in various geographical regions in order to enlist Highlanders, often their own clansmen from a wide area. The map and its information are based on where the officers lived.

The methods and scale of recruitment emerge from Major James Clephane's detailed letters to his sister, Betty Clephane Rose. The major hired John Strachan,[8] who was a crimp (professional recruiter), because Clephane needed help to recruit more than one hundred soldiers in just a short time. Strachan kept unusually meticulous recruitment records and indicates that the expenses for eleven recruits totalled 32 pounds, 1 shilling, 1 pence, which was conveniently just under the 33 pounds the government would pay him. Strachan also recorded that he was recruiting in Dundee, though none of the Highlanders enlisted were born there; rather, his records indicate they were merely working there. Strachan and Clephane seem to have recruited all the way from Dundee on the east coast of Scotland to the towns of Nairn and Elgin on the north coast. Travel by boat was much faster and cheaper than travel by land and partly explains the huge recruiting area.

The Scots-wide pattern of recruitment was also true of the 77th Regiment of Foot, (Montgomerie's Highlanders), who also enlisted men from the Lowlands, many of them likely Highlanders who were employed there. In the eighteenth century, many young Highland men and women moved to the Lowlands to find work in the more modern and industrializing towns and cities or to harvest crops in the Lowlands.

Mechanics of Recruitment

The officers of the 78th used their political ties to raise men. As Major Clephane wrote: "My most sincere thanks to the Magistrates and Town Council of your good town of Nairn … for … assisting me in the recruiting of my company … accept of my small mite here enclosed to you as Treasurer toward assessing to repair the street at the West End of town …"[9] Clephane became provost (mayor) of Nairn after he came home from the Seven Years' War. Clephane's "mite" (money) allowed him to recruit in Nairn, and a letter from his sister suggested that both the Black Watch and Montgomerie's Highlanders would be unable to recruit there. It seems Clephane had purchased a monopoly on the town's potential soldiers.

There is evidence that women were also involved in the raising of the 78th. Major Clephane's sister was married to the chief of the Clan Rose who fought for the Hanoverians in the Jacobite Rebellion. Betty Clephane Rose wrote about the recruits she gathered and fed at Kilravock Castle for her brother: "There are about a dozen of them, that I call the pigs and these are near the doors; that their bellies may be well filled, and if they be they will cast a dash, for they are really handsome Boys."[10]

There was great competition for recruits among the Fraser's Highlanders, the Black Watch, and Montgomerie's Highlanders. Colonel Fraser claimed that his recruits volunteered because of loyalty to their clan chief and King. However, Mrs. Rose, in her letters, indicates it was money that induced Fraser's Highlanders to volunteer: "Mr. Rose goes mad at not having them cheap, but that they are not, nor indeed in our way couldn't be; others take them out of thar beds by dozens...."[11] She revealed her empathy for the poor widows who enlisted their sons for money: "[M]any a poor woman has since this work began brought me her son and told me that I should have him at my own price, but he was all the help that she had in the world for bread, such a one ... is not a cheap one."[12]

"The King's Shilling," a term that referred to the payment given to recruits joining the British Army during the eighteenth and nineteenth centuries, was a means for families to escape bitter poverty. Sending their sons to the army for as much as three pounds was an economic godsend to many poor Highland widows. Mrs. Rose's comments about mothers bringing their sons to enlist, however, conflict with the conventional views in some history books and in much historical fiction. Most accounts state that Highland mothers did not want their sons to join the British Army. For instance, Sir Walter Scott's famous short story "The Highland Widow" tells of a destitute mother who is mortified to find that her Jacobite son had become a redcoat in a regiment going to America. This fictional mother detains the recruit so long that he is hanged for not reporting for duty. Historian Eric Hobsbawm calls such misconceptions by Scott "invented traditions," which I deal with in detail in chapter 11. Reality is often stranger than the fiction surrounding Highland Scots in America.

Recruitment of Highlanders by aristocratic women was important. Mrs. Rose writes about a recruiter for another Highland regiment: "Lady Munro has named a Sergeant at Nairn to act there for some of her friends ..."[13] In much the same way as women in the First World War would persuade young men to join the army, one young woman wrote about the Fraser's: "I am happy to say I have made out my man."[14] Captain James Grant of Montgomerie's Highlanders wrote: "Mrs. Brodie has got me about thirty men ..."[15] I do not wish to overstate the role played by women in raising Highland regiments; little, in fact, is known about the practice. However, both rich and poor women played a part in the recruitment story of the Fraser's Highlanders.

Colonel Fraser claimed that most of the regiment was raised around the Lovat and neighbouring estates. In actuality, his clan area provided only a minority of the 78th, partly because other regiments were also recruiting there. Mrs. Rose writes about Colonel Fraser's difficulties:

> I think [Fraser] has got the most difficult part to act, for Montgomery's people is just planted round them, for except Mr. Baillie in Rosshire, and Mr. Rose in Moray. I see no other help that poor Fraser has got ... Colonel Fraser is in want of some proper people about him; I was this day up very early giveing him a motherly breakfast and setting him off about his business.[16]

Mrs. Rose recorded that, with the exception of her husband, the Laird of Kilravock, Simon Fraser did not receive much help from his neighbours. The Lovat estate employed 140 soldiers who had returned from the Seven Years' War, so it is likely that Colonel Fraser had raised about two hundred soldiers from Lovat lands and the areas immediately surrounding it, rather than the eight hundred or so that have often been attributed to him. The Frasers were *not*, by and large, recruited locally from the Fraser clan, no matter what historians such as John Prebble may write. Competition for recruits led to Simon Fraser unintentionally taking men who were promised to Colonel Montgomerie. Fraser wrote two apologetic letters to the Duke of Atholl's agent who was sponsoring Montgomerie's recruits. Fraser said he took them to be impressed (conscripted) men[17] who were thus available to join his regiment. This contradicts Mrs. Rose and Fraser's own statements made later about the 78th, namely that people were not pressed into service.

Why Soldiers Joined

Perhaps the best summary of the motives that moved Highlanders to enlist the Fraser's Highlanders was made by Major James Clephane, whose opinion was that men were convinced to join the regiment with promises of "money, Linnen cloath and Tartan."[18] Sergeant Thompson's memoirs, dictated to his son, confirmed the appeal of new clothes to the poor Highlanders: "After I had got myself rigg'd out in the uniform of the Company ... We staid some days at Inverness walking about the streets to show ourselves, for we were very proud of our looks."[19] It seemed that for many young men of the time, life in the 78th Fraser's Highlanders was much more appealing than life as a Fraser in the Highlands.

Clephane wrote, in April 1757:

> I have at last sent of [off] for Glasgow 124 recruits ... not one of them was ever confined, and not one deserted.... I was obliged to put a stop to my friends recruiting more for me in Angus and Perthshire, otherwise my number of men would have run too great, and the expense too high, which God knows are too high already for my poor purse ... I rather choose to have men than money.[20]

By April 1757, the regiment had 41 officers, 40 sergeants, 20 pipers and drummers, and 987 other ranks, for a total of 1,088. There were 130 supernumeraries, some of whom were soldiers' wives, who, as said earlier, were useful for washing, cooking, and nursing.[21] A second group

Present-day squad of the 78th in Montreal. (B. Bolton, photographer.)

was raised and sent out to Germany in May 1758, giving them a total of 1,542 officers and men[22] and approximately 60 women.

The Fraser's and Montgomerie's Highlanders had different recruitment policies. While Montgomerie turned away Jacobites who wanted to join the army rather than remain prisoners,[23] Fraser actively recruited those same Jacobites. Montgomerie's men had to wait until they reached Glasgow to receive their uniforms, whereas Fraser issued the men their uniforms as soon as he could. One of Montgomerie's officers wrote of his men that they all wanted to go home. None of the officers or men in the Fraser's recorded such sentiments, which probably reflects the fact that Fraser had highly experienced officers to plan and carry out his efficient and effective recruiting methods.

Assembling

Recruiting for Simon Fraser's regiment took place in three phases: the first, during the spring of 1757; the second, in the summer of that same year; and the third, starting in the autumn of 1758. In the first phase, each captain's company of approximately one hundred men was assembled at Inverness, marched to Glasgow, then shipped to Ireland where they joined the rest of the British Army to sail in convoy to North America.

Some wives accompanied the first phase of recruits, and there were children born to Scottish soldiers in Ireland. There were more wives wishing to accompany their husbands to North America than places for them. At Cork, a lottery was held to determine which women would sail with the soldiers. The merchants of Cork sponsored a subscription to help those wives who were not chosen to return to their own country. It is not known how many, if any, of the wives with the 78th had to return to Scotland. The second phase took place later in the summer and seems to have followed the same pattern as the first phase.

Recruits of the 78th from the third phase did not reach the regiment until 1759, but the fact that a regiment could be raised and transported from Scotland to North America within months speaks well of the British military machine of the Seven Years' War. British policy was to dispatch regiments quickly, and the speed with which the 78th were sent from Scotland reflects the distrust the government felt about arming Jacobite Highlanders close to home. Major Clephane and Sergeant Thompson recorded that none of the men raised in the Fraser's had deserted during the march from Inverness to Cork. The conspicuous absence of desertion indicates the cohesion of the regiment, even in those first weeks and months. However, Colonel Fraser's letters reveal that, for reasons unknown, about seven men did attempt to desert from the regiment later in North America.[24]

Highland men and women in the late eighteenth century were a mobile, clustered workforce who travelled to temporary jobs in the rural and urban Lowlands, to Europe as mercenaries, and to North America as frontier soldiers. While it is one of those things that are difficult to prove, it is probable that young Highland men and women, accustomed to short-term migration to the Lowlands, would also prove good recruits for permanent migration to America. The Highland people were poor, the population was increasing, and they were used to relocating, either temporarily or permanently, to new locations to find work or better land conditions. The ranks for the 78th filled rapidly because enlistment was not a radical departure from the Highland experience. Highland soldiers in America were similar to Highland harvest workers in the Lowlands: they would stay if the living conditions suited them.

Colonel Fraser cast a Scotland-wide net for his recruits. The raising of the 78th Fraser's Highlanders was an efficient, professional, and national activity, not a local activity around the Lovat Estate in Inverness. It was a remarkable organizational feat, especially considering the size of the recruitment area. In several weeks the men were equipped and then shipped to North America, where the first wave of soldiers arrived by the summer of 1757. However, Lieutenant-Colonel Simon Fraser's later account of the recruitment of this regiment emphasized the importance of his local clan chiefs in the process: "Such a number of men as I raised in the year 1757 in four weeks could not have been procured so speedily by any sum of money, without the concurrence and aid of friends, gentlemen of the country with proper connections."[25] Fraser's words were repeated by historians on both sides of the Atlantic into the late twentieth century. Most of Fraser's contemporaries in the regiment such as Major Clephane, however, believed that money from the British fiscal military state, rather than clan loyalty to their chiefs, played an important role in Simon Fraser's successful recruitment program.

A desperate need for fighting men explains the free commissions, high bounty money, and generous land grants offered by the British to soldiers in the Seven Years' War. In the wake of the 1745 Rebellion, Highland identification with the British state was weak. The present idea of a Highland citizen-soldier fighting for Britain only grew because of Highland military successes in the Seven Years' War, the American Revolutionary War, and the French wars of 1789–1815. By the Battle of Waterloo in 1815, Highlanders saw themselves as the elite forces of the British Army. Therefore, professional Highland soldiers in the 1750s who did not identify with the British and changed allegiances should not be judged by today's beliefs about national loyalty. Mercenary service in the 1750s was not yet considered desertion or treachery, and the officers had to observe procedures by formally resigning and enlisting. Money, then free land after the Seven Years' War, not patriotism, drew recruits.

Samuel Johnson (1709–84), the great English writer, reveals the eighteenth-century mindset about mercenary Highland soldiers. He toured the Highlands in 1773, long after the Jacobite Rebellion, and was sympathetic to the Highland Scots. His Scottish biographer, James Boswell (1740–95) said that England benefited from the Union of Parliaments with Scotland (1707) because the Scots had fought in the Seven Years' War on behalf of the Union. To this, Johnson replied, "We should have had you for the same price, though there had been no union, as we might have had Swiss, or other troops."[26] In other words, Johnson is saying that, Union or no Union, the Scots would have fought for England because the money was good, but he didn't realize the full implication of Scottish successes on the battlefields. Had the Scots fought only as mercenaries in the Seven Years' War, they would not have had the same impact politically. I show in later chapters that the Highland soldier-settlers helped to transform an English empire into the British Empire. Consequently, the thirteen *English* colonies that existed at the start of the Seven Years' War became part of *British* North America after the war, thanks to the new Scottish influence felt on both sides of the Atlantic. In the following chapters I will demonstrate how the economic and socially progressive characteristics of the Scots in the Americas of 1763–76 proved to be disastrous for the short-lived British Empire in the thirteen formerly English colonies.

5

The Fighting Fraser's

Whash went the broadsword.
— Sergeant Thompson, 78th Highlanders
(Ralph Harper, *The Fraser Highlanders*)

The 78th Fraser's played a major role in surprising and defeating the French on the Plains of Abraham — an important turning point in the Seven Years' War. In recent times many historians have argued that the Fraser's Highlanders on the Plains were foolish, impetuous, and "lucky," but I suggest that they were remarkably effective and capable soldiers. Besides telling the fighting story of the regiment in North America, this chapter explains how this first global war, which transferred New France to Britain and Spain, changed the course of history in both the Old and New Worlds. I also outline why Britain won and France lost their long duel for global supremacy.

The Seven Years' War

British prime minister William Pitt believed that during the Seven Years' War, America was won because the Prussians, subsidized by Britain, had forced France into also fighting a land war in Europe. The Seven Years' War was fought more for West Indies sugar and rum than for North

America's fish, furs, and forests. Neither Britain nor France at the time valued North America as much as they valued the West Indies. France, for instance, spent vast sums building forts such as Louisburg to maintain their land claims throughout North America, but profits derived from fur and fish did not remotely compensate for the money spent. Consequently, Canada had "cost much but ... brought in very little," according to Voltaire, the great French intellectual of the time.[1]

Table 3: France and Britain: The Seven Years' War [2]				
	Population (millions)	Army	Warships	Naval Expenditure
France	21.5	330,000	70	30m livres per annum
Britain	10.5	200,000	105–120	150m livres per annum

France was the greatest power in Europe, far larger and richer than Britain. But starting in 1717, John Law (1671-1729) a Scottish economist and banker living in France, created the Banque Générale Privée, which was, in effect, France's central bank, and controlled the paper money used by his Mississippi Company, later renamed the Occident Company. Law spread the belief that fabulous wealth in Louisiana backed the paper money. Share prices in his companies soared, but in 1720 the claims of wealth were shown to be false, and thousands of speculators were ruined when the Occident Company and the bank collapsed. Consequently, distrust in paper money and banking meant that in the Seven Years' War, (1756–63), France had neither a central bank nor a sound financial structure with which to fund that war. Fighting a war in Europe and four other continents was imperial overstretch for France.[3] However, in many ways, Voltaire's quip that the French were "spending more on this fine war than all Canada is worth," applied equally to Britain. It took Britain approximately fifty thousand regular and colonial troops, hundreds of ships, and a crippling national debt to finance the capture of New France.[4]

The St. Lawrence River is the major water route to and from the Atlantic for much of northeastern America.[5] The French controlled not only that strategic waterway, but the Great Lakes and their huge surrounding territories as well. As said, they spent a great deal of money before the war building approximately two hundred forts to guard strategic points along the vast inland waterways,[6] and by controlling these routes through the dense forests, France could claim far more of North America than did the British.

France's waterways empire was dependent upon French Canadians to transport their soldiers and supplies over lakes and rivers in both winter and summer. The Ministry of Marine, who administered the colony as well as the navy, treated the *Canadiens* more as the crew of a warship than as settlers. As a result, all males between the ages of fifteen and sixty were subject to an often harsh conscription. During the building of Fort Duquesne, located at the confluence of the Allegheny and Monongahela Rivers (now in Pittsburgh), "nearly 400 men perished, either from the scurvy or from the excessive strain of carrying these goods on their backs."[7] Militarism hampered the already poor agricultural system by taking farm labourers away from their duties, often for months at a time.

New France was essentially a military outpost, with some fish and furs as the major economic by-products of this colony. Agriculture languished under a system where the habitant rented farms from a seigneur. Few settlers were attracted to New France, partly because of this inability to own land. For example, John Nairne of the 78th had difficulty persuading Highlanders to settle on his seigneury after the conquest. Eighteenth-century people preferred to own rather than rent their lands when given the choice. Furthermore, immigrants to New France had to be Roman Catholic, and this policy kept out the thousands of French Huguenots, many of whom went to settle in New England instead.[8] As a result of these French policies, New France covered a huge area but had a very small population to develop and defend it.

France was unable to send large forces to defend its North American colony, partly because the colony itself was unable to sustain the needs of so many soldiers. This, of course, meant that France's North American army was expensively supplied with goods from France. Famine haunted the colony, hindered the war effort, and was likely one of the causes of their defeat at the hands of the British on the Plains of Abraham. Montcalm had assembled a huge force to defend Quebec City, but was unable to maintain such a large force throughout the siege because he was unable to feed them. The ultimate British victory at Quebec reflected the fact that Britain could project almost as large a colonial force onto the Plains of Abraham as could France.

MAP 3: BATTLE FOR THE OHIO TERRITORY

New France's claim went from north to south via waterways.

British Colonies claimed land westwards from the coast.

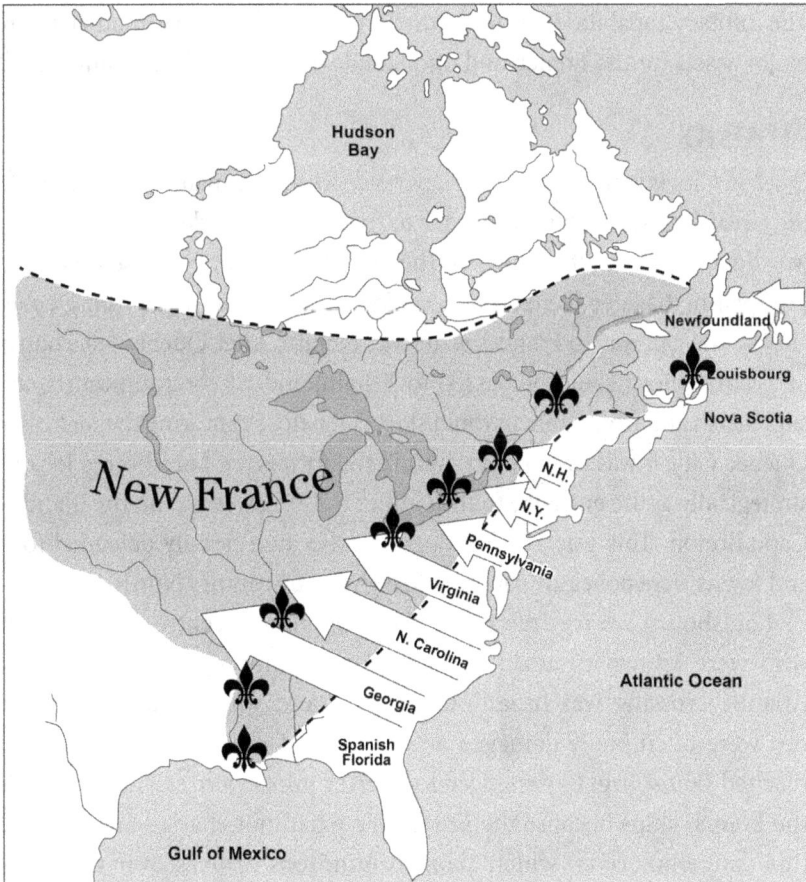

At the start of the war in 1756 there were approximately 1.5 million people living in the British-controlled Thirteen Colonies.[9] Their rapidly growing agricultural population needed military muscle to press inland into the Ohio Territory claimed by both France and the Aboriginal peoples who lived there. The French wanted the Ohio territory for prestige and to expand the fur trade; the British wanted it for farmland.

In the "French and Indian War," as it is known in the United States, British North America was divided, independent, and difficult to coordinate. New France was united, centralized, and militarized to a degree that New England was not. Through the fur trade, New France had at its disposal thousands of experienced bush fighters, while New Englanders were mainly farm boys unaccustomed to fighting and canoeing in the forests. The military capabilities and maritime mobility of French Canadians were major assets for the French and often made up for their lack of numbers.[10]

Strategy

Quebec City is located on the St. Lawrence River, the main water route into the Great Lakes, which in turn leads to rivers that meander their way all the way down to the Gulf of Mexico. The new British prime minister, William Pitt, planned Major General James Wolfe's expedition to capture Quebec City — the gateway to France's waterway empire. After Quebec fell, control of a vast region would be passed to Britain, and all communication and supplies to and from France would stop. But before capturing the fortress at Quebec City, it was essential to capture the fortress of Louisbourg, located strategically at the entrance to the Gulf of the St Lawrence, on the island of Cape Breton. This was a major operation because heavily defended forts and towns were not easily captured in eighteenth-century North America.[11]

Louisbourg, an ice-free port, was at the time a centre for privateers who were known to attack New England's shipping. Just making the Atlantic crossing was hazardous enough, and ships making the journey were often badly damaged and in need of repairs by the time they reached Louisburg. Experienced local river pilots were essential to guide the French ships because the French navy had not charted and mapped this dangerous river, which claimed hundreds of lives over the years.

Consequently, the inhabitants of Quebec City thought they were more or less safe from an invading British naval force.

The Attack on Louisbourg

Although thousands of British troops had assembled in Halifax, Nova Scotia, by the autumn of 1757, the attack on Louisbourg was called off for that year. Nova Scotia, as well as parts of upstate New York and New England, were garrisoned by Fraser's Highlanders. Colonel Fraser wrote of his company: "We ... go to Cantonments in Connecticut ... among a set of Cromwellians imported about the year 1640."[12] Colonel Fraser, an ex-Jacobite, was expressing his dislike of the New England Yankees who sided with Cromwell and the Roundheads against King Charles Stuart and the Cavaliers in the English Civil War of the 1640s. The regiment continued training throughout that winter, albeit in different parts of New England, New York, and Nova Scotia.

In the spring of 1758, Fraser's Highlanders and the rest of the British Army assembled in Boston and sailed again for Halifax on April 22. While in Halifax, the regiment practised climbing, musketry, marching, and embarking-disembarking from boats. In June, the British Army arrived at Gabarus Bay off Cape Breton Island, but had to wait several days before attempting a landing on the defended coastline near Louisbourg because of bad weather. The attackers had great trouble finding a landing spot because of huge waves. In addition, Sergeant Thompson of the 78th records the horror of sitting in a crowded boat under constant fire:

> [M]usket balls fired from 24-pounders came whistling about our ears.... One 24-pound shot ... passed under my hams [the back of the thighs] and killed Sergeant McKenzie, who was sitting as close to my left as he could squeeze, and ... passed through Lieutenant Cuthbert, who was on MacKenzie's left, tore his body into shivers, and cut off both legs of one of the two fellows that held the tiller of the boat, who lost an astonishing quantity of blood, and died with the tiller grasped tight in his hand![13]

Thompson continued, "[W]hat affected me most was the loss of my captain, Captain Charles Baillie.... He was struck mortally, and expired without the least struggle. Poor fellow! He was my best friend, and it was to be with him that I had volunteered to come away from Scotland."[14]

Colonel Fraser lamented the deaths of his officers because they were his friends, and he had too few of those to spare.[15] It was Sergeant Donald MacLeod of the 78th who found a way up the cliffs, according to the account in his memoir.[16] General Wolfe, the second in command of the expedition, landed soon after, and a foothold was established.

Thompson reveals that the Fraser's were not yet used to operating as a unit, and when they landed, prematurely attacked the French, but subsequent events showed that the Fraser's became disciplined soldiers. Since many of the Fraser's had been Jacobite rebels and this was their very first engagement in British service, some of the army thought them unwilling to fight for Britain: "You see most of them had servd in the Rebellion of 45 and they were thought not to be Game."[17] Thompson recounted the exceptional sense of duty displayed by a 78th soldier who remained at his post despite derision from other soldiers:

> [T]he sentries, when they were planted [posted] it was some-what low water, but the tide soon began to rise, and as it did so, the other Sentry moved away, but devil a peg did Duncan budge from the spot where the relief had posted him ... at last it comes to the ears of General Wolfe ... and he thought very highly of him."[18]

Duncan MacFee, an ex-cattle thief, had refused to budge from his post as the water rose to his chest. MacFee then became a special bodyguard to General Wolfe, and the general, guarded by MacFee, would wander around Louisbourg trying to find weaknesses in its defences.

The British Army captured Louisbourg after a siege of two months, which was long enough to delay the attack on Quebec City until the following year.

However, the French press had frightened the French women by saying that the Highlanders were savages. One woman came into their camp and Thompson writes, "afaith it wasn't long before we had a great deal too many of the Canadian women amongst us begging for victuals, as they were in a starving state. And so it turnd out that the Highlanders, instead of being eaters of human flesh, lived the same as other civilized people."[19]

Besieging Quebec City

After the capture of Louisbourg, the 78th Regiment sailed for New York City, from which they proceeded to winter quarters throughout New England, including upstate New York.[20] The fall of 1758 and spring of 1759 found the Fraser's guarding the frontier from Indian and French attacks. There was comparatively little fighting during that time, and Major Clephane's letters home are filled with everyday business matters, the purchase of food, and the payment of soldiers. During this time, the men, and possibly their wives, worked for the locals in the district, where they learned about frontier life.

In the spring of 1759, the Fraser's marched down to New York City and set sail for Louisbourg, which was now being used as a British staging post for the attack on Quebec City. When Major Clephane and some of the other men fell ill, many with scurvy contracted by poor diet in the winter, they were left behind. Clephane ended up selling his commission and returned to Scotland where he entered local politics, became provost (mayor) of Nairn, and lived with his sister at Kilravock, where he died in 1768 at the age of fifty.

The British fleet carried the Fraser's back to Louisbourg, but discovering there was still too much ice on the St. Lawrence, they were redirected, and the troops landed at Halifax in May. Additional troops soon arrived from Britain, and a huge fleet of 49 Royal Navy warships and 119 merchant navy transports set off from Halifax on June 6, 1759, to attack Quebec City.[21] A smaller group of stragglers followed later. There were approximately 13,500 Royal Navy sailors and at least 4,500 merchant navy men (estimates vary) in approximately 200 ships (including the small fleet of large collapsible flat-bottomed troop-landing crafts). Approximately 8,500 soldiers formed the landing party of the British navy, arguably the first modern amphibious operation in history. To put this in perspective, the British attack force numbered approximately 25 percent of the entire civilian population of New France.

Thanks to navigational care and expert seamanship of sailors such as James Cook (the future explorer), the navy brought the attack force upriver swiftly and without loss.[22] Not to say the twenty-day voyage up the uncharted St. Lawrence River was easy, as they had to contend with dangerously high tides, rocks, a winding shoreline and powerful currents. The voyage finally ended on June 26, 1759, and the twelve-week siege of the city began.

As I said earlier, the French imagined it would be too difficult for large British warships to navigate up to Quebec City. In fact, one French soldier even wrote that the British navy "found none of those imaginary difficulties upon which the Canadian seamen were so relying."[23] Many French ships, including supply ships that the commander of the French forces, General Montcalm, was counting on, had been wrecked on the St. Lawrence en route to Quebec that spring. The defenders had such a large area under siege and such a small population to defend it, that they were unable to fortify and guard the cliffs and rivers around the city, let alone places downstream from Quebec.

Quebec, the Algonquin word for "where the river narrows," is located on a treed sixty-metre clifftop above the junction of the St. Charles and St. Lawrence Rivers about 1,200 kilometres from the Atlantic. However, the St. Lawrence is still tidal at this point, creating beaches at low tide and a very fast current in an ebbing tide, natural features that played a role in the capture of the city. The upper town was walled; indeed Quebec was an impressive fortress on the north side of the St. Lawrence.

As can be seen in the accompanying map, the French built defensive trenches guarding the St. Lawrence shoreline east and downriver from Quebec City to the Montmorency River.[24] The series of maps about the battle in this chapter are a good guide to understanding how, what, when, and why events unfolded as they did.

The opposite side of the river was within range of the fortress's floating batteries, which protected the Lower Town's harbour from attack. Dense forests surrounded the entire region, but a swath of trees had been cleared

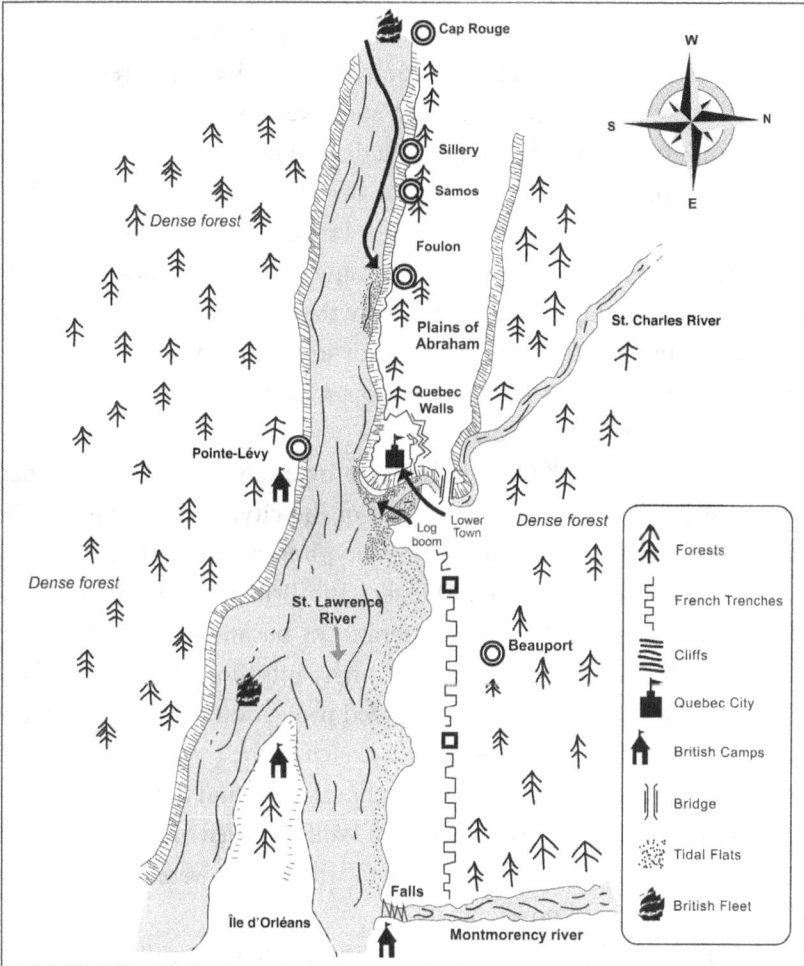

MAP 4: SIEGE OF QUEBEC: JUNE – SEPTEMBER 1759
British attack from East to West: June – August

for farmland about a hundred metres up the banks. The low population in the area meant that few roads had been built through the woods — travel at the time being mainly by river. Montcalm had assembled about fifteen thousand men from the surrounding areas to defend the city, a remarkable proportion — 23 percent — of New France's population, which numbered only sixty-five thousand. However, the disadvantage of amassing such numbers was that it meant there were a large number of mouths to feed, and supplies were scarce, with or without control of the river.

The French had relied on ships that set sail from France, crossed the Atlantic, and travelled up the St. Lawrence for the majority of their supplies. But now that the British controlled the river, the French stores of food, weapons, ammunition, and such were not being replenished. Another issue that put the French at a disadvantage was that Montcalm held one of three separate commands over the French forces guarding the city. Vaudreuil, the governor of New France, controlled some troops, as did Jean-Baptiste Nicolas Roch de Ramezay, the governor of the city guard. While Montcalm was supposedly the supreme commander, this divided command structure had a major impact because the other two commanders refused to allow their troops to join Montcalm's in the final Battle on the Plains of Abraham.

General James Wolfe began the siege by establishing three fortified camps: at Île d'Orléans, an island east of the city; at the mouth of the Montmorency River also east of the city; and at Pointe-Lévy, directly across the St. Lawrence from Quebec. The British were free to attack Quebec City without fear of counterattacks because of the protection the river afforded them. Though the high cliffs along the shore of the wide, swift flowing tidal waters provided protection for the French, the British were highly mobile along that stretch of the river and the French were not. The highly professional naval personnel and the flat-bottomed landing craft made available to General Wolfe allowed him to ferry guns, men, and supplies safely and quickly to where they were needed, often without the enemy's knowledge.

On July 12, 1759,[25] the British let loose a volley of artillery fire from Pointe-Lévy that eventually reduced much of Quebec to rubble.[26] The ability of British guns to range across the St. Lawrence to the Upper Town was a contingency the French had not planned for. The city was constantly under bombardment for weeks on end, and the sweeping fires resulting from the bombardment compounded the inhabitants' misery.

Wolfe's first major attack took place at Beauport, east of Quebec, about 6:00 on the evening of July 31. General Wolfe, accompanied by some of the Fraser's, landed by boat, and other Fraser's had come over a ford in the Montmorency River with Brigadier-General George Townshend. But the attacks proved to be a fiasco, [27] with Colonel Fraser being wounded, and Wolfe losing several hundred men and then having to retreat back across the ford because the boats had become stranded on rocks uncovered by the ebbing tide. An incident then followed that some historians, such as the Canadian C.P. Stacey, have used to criticize the 78th Fraser's Highlanders.

Brigadier-General Townshend had complained that the Highland companies that day "would not retire with him until they knew the regiment had re-embarked."[28] The Fraser's (apparently) had waited at the ford to cover the withdrawal of their comrades who could not re-embark on the unusable boats and until the wounded had been saved from the Native forces. In writing about the incident, C.P. Stacey, in his book *Quebec, 1759*, gave an opinion that has seeped into conventional historical views: "The 78th were really less a British regiment than a war party of Clan Fraser."[29] In reality, the 78th behaved as a highly cohesive professional regiment. In his journal, Ensign Malcolm Fraser makes it clear that Wolfe had, in fact, given the 78th "the honor of covering the retreat of the entire army,"[30] and that Wolfe himself marched back with the Highlanders. Wolfe was demanding and highly critical of everyone, including himself, that day, yet he had only praise for the 78th. Wolfe later wrote: "Amherst and the Highland regiments alone, by the soldier like and cool manner they were formed in, would have beat back the whole Canadian army if they had ventured to attack them."[31]

I believe that Townshend's comments about the battle were made out of malice. He had fought at Culloden with Wolfe, whom he disliked intensely and denigrated constantly both in public in private in words and in cartoons that he drew. Townshend would succeed Wolfe in command after his death.

Stalemate

The failed July attack on the Beauport trench lines was followed by weeks of indecision on Wolfe's part. The prevailing winds made it difficult to sail ships west of the city, yet the navy managed to slip more than twenty ships upriver from Quebec. When Montcalm discovered this, he ordered two French sentries hanged for failing to sound the alarm.

The 78th, in conjunction with other British regiments, began to attack the French at locations above and west of Quebec City in order to destroy the enemy's food supplies and disrupt communications. Montcalm and his army remained in the city. Both Montcalm and Wolfe used their resources cautiously throughout the siege. Montcalm was hoping to hold out until winter forced Wolfe away, while Wolfe was saving his forces for a huge thrust that would capture the walled city.

The Fraser's played an active role in the skirmishes that took place in the surrounding villages that they were ordered to destroy west of Quebec. This destruction was conducted reluctantly by the Fraser's, but enthusiastically by the American Rangers who fought alongside them. The Highland Scots saw themselves as professional soldiers with a code of conduct towards the enemy, whereas the American Rangers saw themselves as avenging Protestants.[32] Ensign (later Lieutenant) Malcolm Fraser wrote in his journal concerning several incidences of scalping that took place: "This barbarous action proceeded from the cowardice and barbarity which seemed so natural to a native of America whether of Indian or European extraction."[33]

There was a very famous incident involving Wolfe's reaction to the killing of French Canadian prisoners that illustrates one of the differences between the British and the British Americans — a difference that would later surface during the American Revolution. Ensign Malcolm Fraser recorded in his journal that a Captain Montgomery,[34] as the head of a company of [American] Rangers, had "a few prisoners taken, all of whom the barbarous Captain Montgomery, who commanded us, ordered to be butchered ... two, who I sent prisoners by a sergeant, after giving them quarter ... were one shot and the other knocked down by a Tomahawk ... and both scalped in my absence."[35] Ensign Fraser's report of the killings prompted General Wolfe to issue his famous order prohibiting scalping "except when the enemy are Indians or Canadians dressed like Indians."[36] Ensign Fraser's concerns for captured soldiers apparently became well known on the French side and partly explain the good feelings expressed by the French Canadians toward Highland Scots after the war.

Another incident tells us about wily tactics used by soldiers in the regiment. The 78th had obtained an agreement from the French defenders of Quebec City not to fire on a boat that was taking captured French prisoners back to the British camp.[37] The 78th used this agreement to load several other boats with cattle and sheep to feed their men and sailed them with the prisoners' boat together under the guns. The French did not fire.[38]

Changing the Attack

Knowing that he had at his disposal a large naval force lying west (upriver) from Quebec, General Wolfe was able to shift some soldiers to that area. At the end of August, Wolfe's three brigadiers suggested landing a strong permanent force fifty kilometres west of Quebec, which would cut Montcalm's supply lines overland. Quebec City was already deprived of supplies from farms downriver by virtue of the British presence. While war prices were in effect for goods in the British camp, famine prices for food prevailed in the French.

Wolfe's thinking began to change when he started to weigh the possibilities of attacking the Upper Town of Quebec from the west rather than the Lower Town from the east. Consequently, well above Cap Rouge, about twenty-two kilometres west of Quebec City, boatloads of red-coated soldiers were rowed up and down the river or drifted with the tide on warships. In reaction, Montcalm detached a force of about three thousand men under the command of Louis Antoine de Bougainville, who wrote that the British "had designs on our communications, a thing essential to us, but difficult to guard, [we] being obliged to follow on foot with much inferior forces the movement and rapid advances of their vessels and barges."[39] Such intense marching rapidly exhausted Bougainville's men, who were subsequently dispersed to guard the St. Lawrence riverbank above Cap Rouge. Consequently, it took time to reassemble the three thousand men back into one unit, a factor that helped them miss the decisive battle.

Two wooded ravines edged the promontory where Quebec City's Upper Town was located — one side bordered by the mighty St. Lawrence and the other by the St. Charles River. This geography created a problem for Wolfe: if he landed his troops at Cap Rouge, they would have had to march twenty-two kilomtres under fire from the French Canadians who used the woods as cover. Eventually, Wolfe decided to land his force as close to the Upper Town as possible.

How Wolfe determined they were to land at Foulon, about 1.6 kilometres from the Upper Town, is a great mystery, because for security reasons he kept this vital information from even his second-in-command. It would have been obvious to him that the men, after travelling downriver and disembarking from their vessels, would have to find some practical way from the shore up the steep promontory. The most likely source of information about the existence and location of a path up from the Foulon was Robert Stobo, a Glasgow man who had been held hostage in Quebec City for several years, but who had escaped, joined Wolfe, and passed on several pieces of intelligence.[40] J.R. Harper claimed that Captain Simon Fraser made a lone reconnaissance in a canoe to explore the area, but gives no source.[41]

Wolfe went to observe the path at Foulon using a telescope. It is speculation, but he probably observed that there were no sentries at the foot of the cliff, and that sentries at the trailhead could not see down because of the trees. Wolfe, unknown to Montcalm, massed his men in secret on the British ships west of Quebec City.

Planning the Attack

Much farther west from Cap Rouge, the British navy had been trying to intercept French supply boats from Montreal and informed Wolfe that supply barges were being prepared by the enemy. Based on the tidal flows, it was estimated that the night of September 12–13 would be the optimal time for the French to send the supply barges to Quebec City. French deserters confirmed the timing, and Wolfe knew that the French sentries on the cliffs would have been alerted to expect the barges and not to fire upon them. Wolfe figured that to mislead the French sentries, British boats could pretend to be the expected barges.

To mislead the rest of the French army during the evening of September 12 and through to the dawn of the 13th, Wolfe ordered that the British fleet be conspicuously active *east* of the Lower Town of Quebec City. Sailors laid out coloured marker buoys in the St. Lawrence off the

Beauport trenches as though preparing to guide an attack. A British Army and marine skeleton force that was camped out on Île d'Orléans east of the city was alive with activity from evening to early dawn with fires burning, figures marching, and drums beating. The naval ships were instructed to fire their guns after dark as though attacking the French. The actual British attack force west of the Upper Town of Quebec heard the mock attack, as did the French sentries along the cliffs. In the Beauport trench lines, five kilometres east of the Lower Town, the French army stood to arms through the night of September 12 and into the morning of the 13th, waiting for an attack on Quebec that would never come. Governor Vaudreuil was completely deceived by the feint attack and thought the real attack, when it came, was the fake, refusing to send the approximately two thousand men at his command to fight in the decisive battle outside the Upper Town.[42] Much of the French army remained in their trenches guarding against something that was not happening, leaving Montcalm undermanned to fight what was actually happening. In a small way, Wolfe's deception was similar in results to that practiced by the Allies during the Second World War prior to the Normandy landings.

The sentries posted on the shore at Sillery, along the clifftop at Samos and at the trailhead at Foulon, were vigilant — likely the hanging of two French sentries just a few weeks earlier for not reporting that British warships were running upriver under the city's guns was fresh in their minds. The supply barges expected by the French on the night of September 13, however, had been cancelled at Cap Rouge, but Bougainville had not bothered to inform the sentries along the clifftop.[43] This was, in fact, the only "luck" Wolfe had that night. Communications along the clifftop of the promontory were poor, partly because of the darkness and the absence of roads.

Sailing Down the River

At Cap Rouge, on the night of the 12th and morning of the 13th, the moored flagship *Sutherland* stealthily loaded soldiers into thirty troop landing crafts on the side away from the French observers on the north shore of the St. Lawrence. For swift movement up the cliffs, Wolfe ordered the soldiers to carry only basic equipment. The first of the landing crafts, holding approximately fifty soldiers and rowed by twenty sailors, intentionally went upstream with the tide to fool any French guards and returned with the ebb tide. General Wolfe had such confidence in the abilities of the 78th's officers that he placed two of their fluent French-speakers — Captains Simon Fraser and Donald MacDonald — with eight other Frasers of the "climbing party" in this lead landing craft. Wolfe told Captains Fraser and MacDonald that the French sentries knew about the expected supply boats. At midnight, a lantern was hoisted on the *Sutherland*'s mast to signal a rendezvous for the thirty landing craft that had flat bottoms and ramps enabling troops to disembark quickly on the sandy shores. This was possibly the first example in modern history of an amphibious attack using specially designed craft for the purpose. At 2:00 a.m. on September 13, a second lantern was hauled up the *Sutherland*'s mast to act as a starting guide. The thirty landing craft containing about seventeen hundred soldiers rowed off in a long line for what must have been a tense journey on a turbulent river. A second wave of nineteen hundred men in small sloops followed the rowboats a short time later, and a third wave would be rowed across the St. Lawrence to their landing point at Foulon.

An ebbing tide, the fast-flowing river, and sailors at the oars propelled them downstream at about fifteen kilometres per hour. Lieutenant Chads of the Royal Navy navigated in the moonlit night and deserves much recognition for his accomplishment. Even today it would be a remarkable amphibious achievement to load and ferry approximately 4,500 soldiers secretly through hostile territory on a turbulent river at night and then unload them at an exact location so far away. This feat can be attributed to a superb British navy that allowed Wolfe to use natural features to his advantage: darkness, river current, a noisy ebbing tide creating a sandy beach, a path up a huge cliff, and, to cap it all, the landing area and path hidden by trees from the trailhead sentries.

The line of silent landing craft stretched for about a quarter of a mile. Lieutenant Chads proceeded for most of the journey in the middle of the river. However, he had to navigate only about twenty yards offshore for two or three miles before reaching the exact landing spot at Foulon. Past Sillery, just before Foulon, the shadows of the cliffs blocked the moon-

Wolfe's Cove, Foulon, where the landing crafts disembarked, is shown as it was in the early nineteenth century. The image brings out the steep wooded cliffs and the huge beach that Wolfe encountered in 1759. The extensive timber industry, like the houses, only appeared after the conquest. (Folios Willis v.2 p. 12, McGill University, McGill Rare Books and Special Collections.)

light from hitting the water and giving away their position. As General Townshend wrote, "ye French Centries on ye banks challengd our boats, Captain Frazer who had been in Ye Dutch service and spoke french, answered — *la france* and *vivre le Roy*, on which ye French Centinels ran along ye shore in ye dark crying *laisser les passer ils sont nos Gens avec les provisions* ['Let them pass. These are our people with the provisions']."[44]

Captain Fraser was challenged several times from the rocky shore at Sillery. The French sentries saw the boats, and those in the boats saw at least one sentry come to the water's edge. Yet, the boats were travelling much faster than the sentries could run along a rocky shore at night to question the soldiers in the boats. One sentry shouted "Which regiment?" and Fraser replied "de la Reine" (the Queen's Regiment), which was stationed in Montreal and on Lake Champlain. The reply was obviously thought out beforehand and saying this was a specific French regiment from far away justified the great number of soldiers in the boats to the sentry. The French

had no password to challenge Fraser's assertions. The deception continued long enough that the thirty landing craft started unloading at about
4:00 a.m. unchallenged at Foulon, where the outgoing tide had created a
wide landing area. I found no records about the actual unloading of the
troops but assume they disembarked via the ramp at the front in military
formation and probably waited on the wet beach in those formations until
ordered to climb the path again in formation. It was a tremendous feat of
crowd control to process 4,500 troops quietly and in darkness from boats to
their eventual lines across the Plains. The noise of the choppy river drowns
out sounds from below even today, so the sentries on the clifftop could
neither hear nor see the troops below them. The alert French sentries on
the Sillery shore eventually realized who were in the boats, but they could
not communicate the news quickly enough to warn their comrades at the
Foulon trailhead. By the time the gunners on the Samos clifftop received
word, the first wave of boats had already passed by, but the gunners took
aim and fired at the second wave consisting of naval sloops.

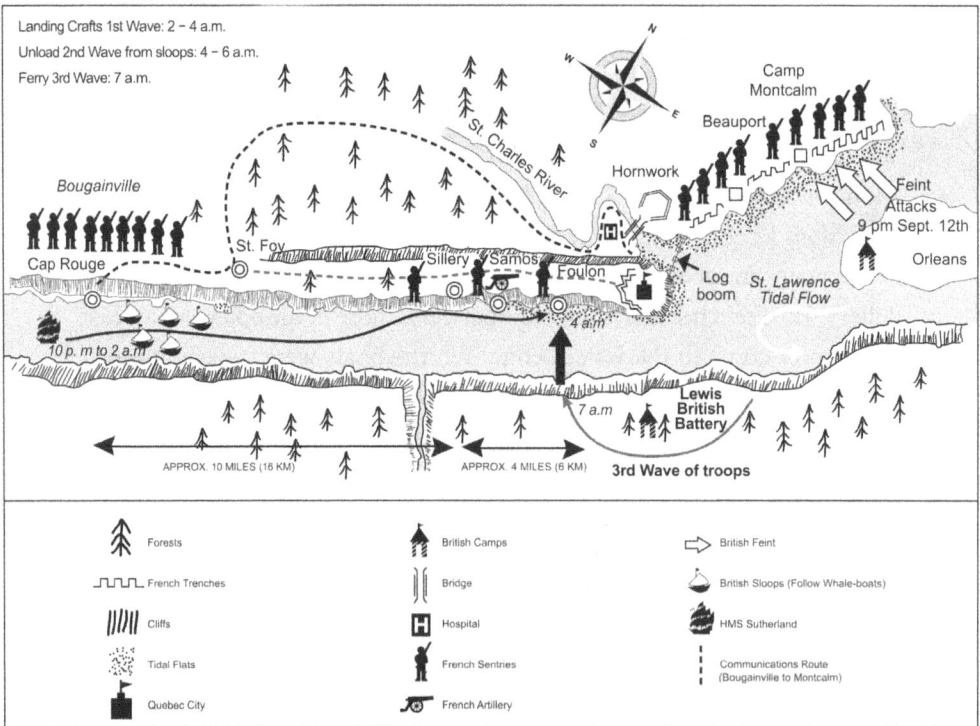

MAP 5: BRITISH ARMY ATTACK: SEPTEMBER 12–13 1759
WOLFE'S MANOEUVRES TO MOVE NORTH

The inability of the groups of sentries to communicate with each other along the clifftop as fast as the boats could travel along the foot of the cliffs handicapped the alert French defenders. The failure by the French to post sentries at the Foulon's tidal beach also contributed greatly to Wolfe's success.

Climbing the Cliffs

The lead boat had come ashore in the dark at the predetermined spot, and Captain MacDonald of the 78th, with eight light infantrymen from the regiment, climbed up the cliff about one hundred metres east of the path itself.[45] MacDonald's party was followed by approximately two hundred light infantrymen from the other landing craft. A Malcolm Fraser family legend says that a Highland poacher reached the clifftop first. However, it is probable that the bilingual MacDonald climbed first to fool any sentries. Climbing guarded and stony vertical cliffs in the dark by clutching slippery, wet bushes must have been an unpleasant and nerve-wracking experience. The sentries were guarding the trailhead, of course, but not the area where the eight Fraser's Highlanders and the other two hundred light infantrymen climbed up. Some writers claim that that Vergor, the commander of the trailhead post, allowed half the guards to go and help with the sorely needed harvest.

Whatever the number of sentries, MacDonald and his men misled them by approaching along the clifftop from the direction of Quebec City, not from up the path itself, as would be expected. When the sentries did address the Highlanders in the darkness, they had no password with which to challenge them, and so Captain MacDonald assured them that his special unit had come to relieve them, and told them to go and tell their sleeping companions to disperse. The sentries would have been severely punished if they fired on their own men. Nevertheless, according to French sources, "a Canadian sentry there … fired his musket at them."[46] It is unclear when the sentry fired or even whether he hit a Highlander, but MacDonald's clever reply confused and delayed the guards long enough for the Highlanders to drive them all off and then secure the clifftop. The attackers gave a loud cheer, thus informing Wolfe and the others below of their success. Sadly, MacDonald was killed the following year, and because the full story of his actions was not recorded, historians have often undervalued his dramatic confrontation on the lip of the cliff. British soldiers at the time thought that MacDonald had saved a great many of their lives because even a small party of defenders could have held off the British Army in the dark on a steep cliff.[47] General Wolfe's army started to come up the path itself, and Wolfe sent the Light Infantry to silence the cannons at Samos, which, as was said, were now firing at the second wave. Just how big the path was in 1759 is difficult to tell because it was greatly enlarged soon after as a link to the lower area's beach, which the British began to use as a timber cove.

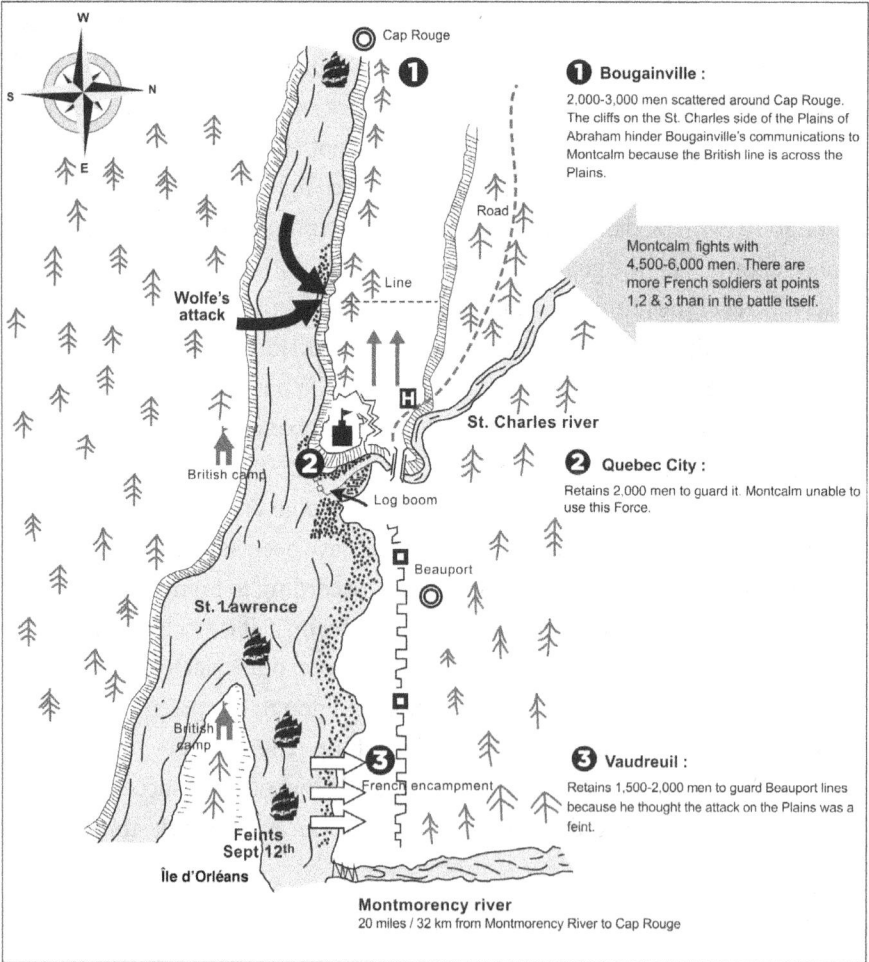

MAP 6: FRENCH FORCES: SEPTEMBER 13, 6:00 – 10:00 A.M.

❶ **Bougainville :**
2,000-3,000 men scattered around Cap Rouge. The cliffs on the St. Charles side of the Plains of Abraham hinder Bougainville's communications to Montcalm because the British line is across the Plains.

Montcalm fights with 4,500-6,000 men. There are more French soldiers at points 1,2 & 3 than in the battle itself.

❷ **Quebec City :**
Retains 2,000 men to guard it. Montcalm unable to use this Force.

❸ **Vaudreuil :**
Retains 1,500-2,000 men to guard Beauport lines because he thought the attack on the Plains was a feint.

Montmorency river
20 miles / 32 km from Montmorency River to Cap Rouge

The second wave was landed at the beach by 6:00 a.m. and was less fortunate than the first wave. General Townsend mentions the landing craft sheltering behind the sloops to load because they were being battered by enemy cannon, and Ensign Malcolm Fraser wrote, "[W]e were fired on in the boats by the enemy, who killed and wounded a few."[48] The thirty landing craft sped across the river to pick up the third wave of men under colonels Burton and Carleton. This latter group had marched in secret through the night from Pointe-Lévy, assembled on the south shore facing the cliffs, and about 7:00 a.m. joined the main body.

On the Clifftop

The "Plains" of Abraham is a bit of a misnomer because the plains are not flat but composed of an endless series of small hollows and wooded ridges. The "Heights of Abraham" refers to one of the narrowest and steepest ridges across the Plains. At about 8:00 a.m., when some 4,500 troops had been assembled on the clifftop, Wolfe lined them up, drums beating, pipes and flutes playing across the Heights of Abraham on to their final dispositions. The 78th stood to the left of centre on the British line about a kilometre and a half from the city walls, hidden from the Upper Town by an even higher ridge. This proved to be a clever tactic. Admiral Holmes wrote that the inequalities of the ground hid much of the army from Montcalm.

Since Montcalm could not see the British Army from his vantage point in the city, he was unsure of their numbers and exact position; consequently, he could not hope to figure out what their next move would be. By about 8:00 a.m., Generals Montcalm and Chevalier Johnstone, the Edinburgh Jacobite who was Montcalm's aide de camp, were on horseback organizing their force. They eventually assembled their available troops into three columns about nine deep containing French Regulars, the regular Colony troops, and the colonial militia, each of whom had different methods of marching and fighting. Some historians dispute that there were columns, and state that there were three sections of the attacking force.

Estimates of the British forces on the Plains range from 4,300 to 4,800; whether the line was two or three men deep, and how far the line stretched, is still subject to dispute. Only about two thousand of the men were positioned on the actual firing line. Many others had been sent to guard the rear in case Bougainville marched his two thousand men from upriver to attack the redcoats. Others patrolled on either side of the British line edged by wooded cliffs and concealing Montcalm's Native forces and colony militia.

General Wolfe's firing line took full advantage of the terrain; the fifty metres of steep downward slopes from their line meant the French had to coordinate their columns uphill and around hollows. The heavy rain in the previous days probably filled the hollows and made the slope slippery for the French troops trying to run up in a coordinated manner. Wolfe, however had months to train his men, ensuring that they fought cohesively in line. The 78th, for instance, were no longer the uncoordinated unit that they were at the start of the attack on Louisbourg. They had loaded their muskets with two musket balls to increase the effectiveness of their first volley. Round musket balls spin and veer in the air; consequently, soldiers in each platoon fired their muskets simultaneously so as to kill or wound more. Two musket balls greatly increased firepower as subsequent shots from unreliable muskets and excited troops were never as effective as the first volley. Some authorities claim that Sergeant Donald MacLeod of the 78th had even placed markers thirty paces ahead of the men to ensure they would not fire too soon.[49]

In contrast to this, many of the men in General Montcalm's force were irregulars, and in addition "were in any case poorly armed since they had simple hunting muskets without bayonets [and] were a hindrance to the operation."[50] Unlike the British, the French had not practised charging in the columns they employed in this battle. Indeed, the regular French army apparently had never drilled alongside the colony troops, let alone charged with them in columns.

Estimates of the French forces that fought on the Plains of Abraham are even more varied than the British numbers. Many French officers, including the top three, who may have known how many soldiers they had, were killed that day. The Aboriginal fighters and members of the colony militia who fought from the wooded cliffs were not properly counted and are often left out of the calculations. Consequently, Montcalm's numbers on the field could have been as low as 4,500 or as high as 6,000. Ensign Malcolm Fraser of the 78th, who stayed on in Quebec after the war, wrote:

> The Enemy's numbers I have never been able to get an exact account of. We imagined them seven or eight thousand, [but] this has since been disputed since. However, I am certain that they were greatly superior to us in numbers, as their line was equal to ours in length, tho they were in some places nine deep, whereas ours was no more than three deep. Add to this, their advanced status and those in the bushes, on all hands, I think they must exceed five thousand.[51]

It should be noted that Ensign Fraser states that the British line was no more than three men deep, the standard practice up until this battle. Perhaps the 78th, Wolfe's largest regiment, in order to fit their section of the line had three, while the other smaller regiments had two men in line.

The combined forces of the three French commanders — Montcalm, De Ramezay, Vaudreuil — had been reduced from sixteen thousand at the start of the siege to about ten thousand, probably because "we had to contend with more than one enemy: famine, at all times inseparable from war, threatened to reduce us to the last extremity."[52] Although, some of the men had simply deserted and returned to their farms.

De Ramezay, who commanded the approximately two thousand guards of Quebec City, was ill, and his second-in-command refused to let his troops join Montcalm's proposed attack. Vaudreuil, who, as mentioned earlier, thought the clifftop attack was just a ruse, kept his command in the trenches east of the city. Wolfe's line across the Plains divided Bougainville from Montcalm. Communications sent to Bougainville at Cap-Rouge had to be sent along a circuitous route that followed the St. Charles River Valley, then cut up and across the table-top to avoid the British line. Consequently, Bougainville wrote of the British landing that, "I was not informed of it until nine in the morning,"[53] a situation that also made it difficult for him to inform Montcalm

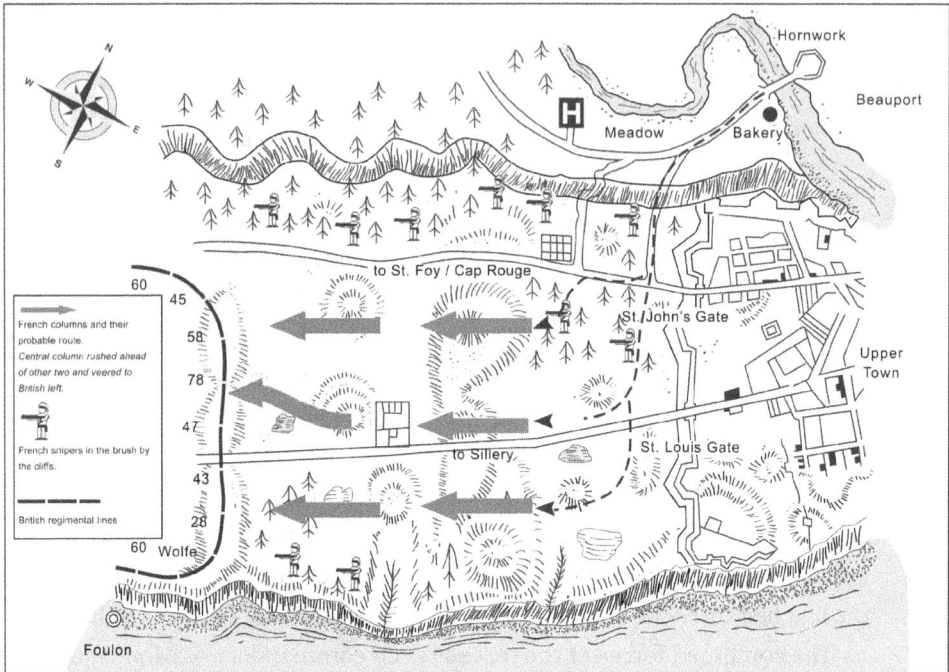

MAP 7: THE THIN RED LINE ACROSS THE HEIGHTS OF ABRAHAM
10 A.M. SEPTEMBER 13, 1759

when he could arrive with his men. Bougainville claimed that he had, "marched at once, but when I came within range of the battle, our army was beaten and in retreat."[54] His command had to march approximately twenty kilometres from Cap-Rouge to the battle. The rain of the previous days created muddy conditions that would have slowed their progress. Montcalm organized a force that most historians seem to think was approximately the same size as Wolfe's, about 4,500. It was a surprised and divided command in the French forces that prevented Montcalm from mustering all ten thousand of the available defenders.

The Attack on the Thin Red Line

Montcalm's strategy was to smash his three columns through the British line, but he has often been criticized for attacking too soon (at approximately 10:00 a.m.). By that time the British had already managed to haul two light cannons up onto the Plains and had many more on the way up.[55] Montcalm perhaps realized that his Canadiens, who were unused to fighting out in the open, could not withstand a barrage of cannon fire. Plus there was always the possibility that Wolfe could have started to build trench works, as Montcalm thought, or bombard the bridge across the St. Charles River, thus cutting Quebec City off from Vaudreuil's men still in the trenches. But in reality, the redcoats decided to lie down and catch up on some sleep around 8:30 a.m., thus avoiding the snipers in the bushes along the cliffs on either side of the battlefield.

Time and the terrain were on Wolfe's side from about 9:00 a.m. onward, not on Montcalm's, something that modern historians often dispute. Montcalm's already tired men had to march many miles from the Beauport Camp outside the Lower Town up to the Plains outside the Upper Town, and it took Montcalm as long to muster 4,500 French soldiers on the Plains outside Quebec City as it took Wolfe to muster an equal number from a much greater distance.

General Wolfe and his army were only 150 metres from their own ships, which could supply them with extra men, ammunition, and food. The cliffs along the rivers protected Wolfe from attack from either the left or right. The longer Wolfe was camped across the Heights, the more options he had — he could dig in and haul guns up to batter the city walls, which had not been designed to withstand a siege of this nature.

In addition to his concerns about dwindling supplies and mustering all the French troops, Montcalm had difficulty maintaining his existing force. British and French diarists record stories of French soldiers sliding off to fight from the bushes and trees on either side of the Plains. The colony militia was unused to set battles, and many of the men were reluctant to march in the open against the lines of enemy soldiers. Chevalier de Johnstone, Montcalm's aide, recorded that even as the columns were starting to march, Montcalm realized it was a mistake to mix the types of soldiers. The fighters in the irregular troops fired much too soon to be effective, then threw themselves on the ground to reload, jumping up to fire again just as the regulars were trying to step over them.

Just about 10:00 a.m., Montcalm ordered his troops to advance. Eighteenth-century military psychology held that both the French and the Highlanders were "hot" peoples, best on the attack. The Lowland Scots and the English were thought to be better in defence. Montcalm worked his men into a state of excitement by riding in front of the columns waving his hat and by having each regiment unfurl its colours as he passed.

The silent red line on the ridge waited for the inevitable attack to come. There was a ripple effect recorded by Sergeant Thompson as the men of the line were hit by long shots and the man behind silently stepped in to take their place. This is when the discipline of the British Army became evident. There were as many British as French wounded in this battle; however, most of the British wounded recovered, so it's likely that the long shots accounted for the lack of mortal wounds.

The white-coated French began their charge from their ridge a little over a half kilometre from the British lines and had to run through thickly sown wheat fields to reach their targets. According to one French soldier by the name of Pouchot, this charge winded the men before they had even reached the British lines.[56] The running soldiers also had problems coordinating as columns. Perhaps because of the distance and terrain, the centre column ran ahead of the other two. There are surprisingly few descriptions of the battlefield terrain by historians, or even by onlookers of the time. However, accounts such as those of Volunteer Henderson, who carried Wolfe back after he was hit, make note of the small hillocks that can still be seen today. As they were charging, the two British cannons tore holes in the French ranks, and by all accounts were far more effective than the French cannons.

Sir John Fortescue's *History of the British Army* states that the first volley on the Plains of Abraham was the most perfect volley ever fired on a battlefield.[57] Wolfe's army did not fire one volley in unison as Fortescue claimed, however, but how they actually did fire is a source of much discussion. After the initial volley, they probably fired one by one, platoon after platoon in each regiment; then each platoon in turn would step forward through the smoke to continue firing. Some commentators estimate that the two armies were only twenty metres apart by the third or fourth volley. For the French, the effect of this was described as follows:

"We never opposed such a shock as we received in the centre of our line. Every ball seemed to take effect with such regularity and discipline we had never before experienced. The English fire was *comme un coup de cannon* [like a cannon shot]."[58]

Commentators speak of the French columns veering away from the British lines, but they do not explain why they would do this. The undulating terrain probably caused the exposed sides of the columns to become a target for British volleys. The columns were at an angle when the British fired into them, which would explain high French casualty rates. However, it would take further research to say definitely that the terrain placed the French attacking columns at a severe disadvantage. Quebec City has been built over and around the actual battle line, so it is difficult to know exactly what the terrain looked like on the day.

The two thousand British soldiers could fire three to four rounds a minute and so they shot approximately thirty to fifty thousand musket balls in all into the French. Since there were approximately one thousand to fifteen hundred French dead, it seems that it took about thirty musket shots to kill each French soldier in this battle. No white-coated soldier reached the red-coated lines on the crest before the French survivors began to retreat. This part of the battle lasted about ten minutes, the time it took for the French to charge up to approximately twenty-five metres from the British line then to run back down again which of course signaled General Wolfe that it was time to follow up on a retreating enemy.

Ensign Fraser writes: "[We] continued firing very hot for about six or (as some say) eight minutes.... Our Regiment was then ordered by Brigadier-General Murray to draw their swords and pursue them, which increased their panic but saved their lives."[59] It is then a myth that the ordinary Highland soldier initiated this charge. Canadian and American historians since Francis Parkman, in *Montcalm and Wolfe* (1884), often claim that the Fraser's charged out of excitement and threw away their fusils. In fact, no diarist or commentator of the time suggested that the Fraser's threw down their muskets. Contemporaries would have been quick to note faults because Highland soldiers had not yet been fully accepted into the British Army.

The Highland Charge

After giving the order to charge at about 10:15 a.m., Wolfe, on the right of the British line, was shot. According to a few sources the bullet was fired by a deserter from the Royal Americans who was himself then wounded. The wounded deserter who shot Wolfe was supposedly in turn shot by British officers who held a drumhead court martial. However, there is no direct evidence from the time that I traced, so it is probably one of the many historical myths added over the 250 years since the battle. Sergeant Donald MacLeod of the 78th claims to have carried Wolfe's body wrapped in his 78th plaid down to the British ships, and this is widely believed and related in Scottish history books.[60] As the 78th Fraser's Highlanders were nowhere near Wolfe during the battle, I suspect that this was added to MacLeod's book to increase sales.[61] As often happens, time has added many myths to this battle, and the Literary and Historical Society of Quebec objected to "the false theatrical versions of some truly dramatic stories like Wolfe and Gray's Elegy ... the famous volleys (absurdly misrepresented as having been fired by the whole line together...); the dashing down of Highland muskets and the charge with Highland claymores."[62] Causes and effects of historical myths about Highlanders and this battle are explored in greater depth in a later chapter.

It is interesting that Ensign Malcolm Fraser in the above excerpt believed that using swords rather than more musket shots saved French lives. This contradicts most observers who testified to the effectiveness of the Frasers' sword charge. A French soldier wrote that he would "never forget Fraser's Highlanders flying wildly after them, with streaming plaids, bonnets and large swords, like so many infuriated demons."[63] According to Thompson: "If the French gave themselves up quietly, they had no harm done to them, but Faith! If they tried to outrun a Heillandmon, they stood but a bad chance for *Whash!* went the broadsword."[64] The Frasers' charge was made with directed violence, not uncontrolled fury. The officers were highly professional and aware of their men's military strengths. The Highland charge was one of those strengths, as was their firepower — they were equipped with muskets and Doune pistols. Charles Clephane, a relative of Major James Clephane of the 78th

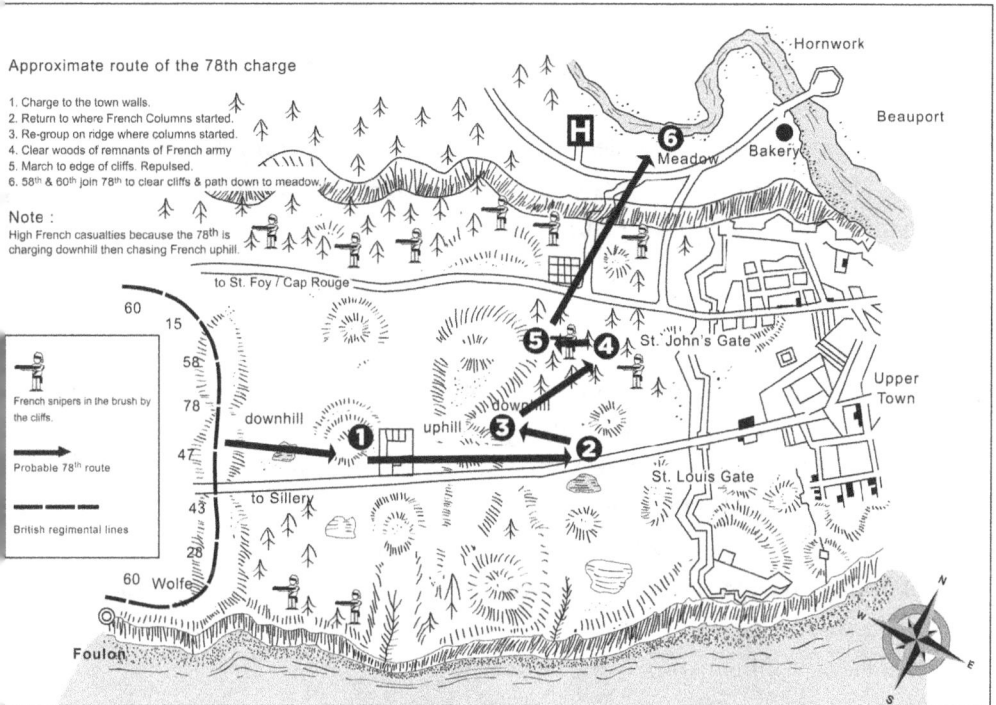

MAP 8: THE FRASER'S CHARGE
SEPTEMBER 13, 1759

Approximate route of the 78th charge

1. Charge to the town walls.
2. Return to where French Columns started.
3. Re-group on ridge where columns started.
4. Clear woods of remnants of French army.
5. March to edge of cliffs. Repulsed.
6. 58th & 60th join 78th to clear cliffs & path down to meadow.

Note :
High French casualties because the 78th is
charging downhill then chasing French uphill.

French snipers in the brush by the cliffs.

Probable 78th route

British regimental lines

and first mate on the *Prince of Orange*, one of the naval ships present at the siege, wrote, in what to us is rather strange language, that it was a common saying throughout the fleet that the Highlanders had behaved like "angels" in the battle — perhaps he meant angels of death, or that they were fleet footed.[65] In the same way that the volleys were "the most perfect" ever delivered by British regiments on a battlefield, the charge was also one of the most effective ever made. The success of this sword charge can be explained by the fact that the French army was trapped by cliffs and could not flee to the left or right. Highlanders were charging downhill into the side of a column exhausted by having run nearly a kilometre down from a ridge over muddy ground, then up a ridge to the British line. The fresh Highlanders could easily outrun the tired and often wounded French retreating back up the muddy ridge they had come from. Slashing and stabbing with swords is much more lethal than just stabbing with a bayonet in those circumstances, and Sergeant Thompson writes: "The casualties lay on the field as thick as a flock of sheep ... and [the French] had no opportunity of carrying away their dead and wounded. We killed 72 officers alone."[66] Captain Knox, states that after the battle the British "victors were opening the turf"[67] for the many French dead on the Plains.

After the Charge

According to Malcolm Fraser, after their charge, the 78th were the first regiment to rally around General Murray who "ordered them to face to the left and march thro the bushy woods, towards the General Hospital ... but we had a few men killed and Officers wounded by some skulking fellows with small arms, from the bushes."[68] The two narrow paths down the cliffs to the St. Charles River had acted like a funnel for the thousands of fleeing French soldiers and consequently stranded many of the militia in the woods and ravine. Malcolm Fraser destroys the myth that the 78th had discarded their rifles when he writes:

> We soon dispossessed them from the bushes and from thence kept firing for about quarter of an hour on those under the cover of the bank [cliff bank down to the river], but as they greatly exceeded us in number, they killed and wounded a great many of our men, and killed two officers,[69] which obliged us to retire a little and form again, when the 58th Regiment with the second Battalion of Royal Americans having come up to our assistance ... and drove them first to the Great Meadow between the Hospital and Town, afterward over the River St. Charles.[70]

Chevalier James Johnstone, the Edinburgh Jacobite and Montcalm's aide-de-camp, wrote a book in the form of a dialogue between Montcalm and Wolfe. Johnstone's book has been translated, re-translated, and reprinted somewhat freely over the years. Time and re-translations have probably altered what Johnstone himself wrote. In a version printed by the Quebec Literary and Historical Society, Montcalm "says" to Wolfe that the Canadian militia in the ravine "disputed the ground inch by inch from the top to the bottom of the height, pursued by your troops down to the [St. Charles River] valley at the bakehouse, opposite to the hornwork. These unfortunate heroes — who were most of them cut to pieces...."[71]

Nuns at the hospital in the valley described the fight in the woods: "We witnessed the carnage from our windows. We were in the midst of the dead and dying, who were brought to us by hundreds, many of them close connections."[72] This description points to more of a massacre of the militia by the 78th, rather than a victory by the militia that is sometimes claimed by modern historians. The original accounts indicate clearly that the Fraser's destroyed the Canadian militia both in the woods and in the ravine. The same cliffs that had stopped the British from climbing up to the Plains now stopped the French from climbing down from the Plains.

In this battle, the Fraser's suffered a total of eighteen killed and 148 wounded, the highest of any British regiment.[73] They killed approximately two hundred men in the bushes leading down to the hospital, though British sources often quote the numbers as much higher. The exact figures will never be known, as the French field army was shattered and the Indians and colonial militia scattered. In total, the British had about fifty-eight dead and six hundred wounded.[74] French deaths far exceeded British deaths by at least ten to one and maybe by as much as twenty to one. Many French dead were buried by the British, so it is possible that British estimates of fifteen hundred French dead were accurate. The British soldiers of the time stated that the "thin nature of their red line" explained "why we lost so few men in this Battle and the Enemy such a vast number."[75] The proportion of the French army in the battle who were killed could be as low as a fifth or as high as a quarter. It is no wonder that the contemporary press linked the Highland charge to British national prestige: "When they took to their broadswords, my God! What a havoc they made! They drove everything before them and walls could not resist their fury. Those breechless brave fellows are an honour to their country."[76] In sharp contrast, modern Canadians usually believe that both sides suffered equally in the fifteen-minute battle and so the *Historical Atlas of Canada, Vol. I,* edited by R. Cole Harris, estimates that 658 British troops and 644 French troops were killed or wounded.[77]

De Ramezay, the Franco-Scots governor of Quebec City, surrendered the town five days after the battle, on September 18, 1759. The Fraser's played a role in mopping up the battlefield during this time, and militiamen trapped in the woods for days were apparently surprised to become prisoners rather than being killed by American Rangers.

Occupying Quebec After the Battle

After the surrender, the impending winter freeze-up of the St. Lawrence meant that the British fleet was forced to withdraw to Louisbourg in the fall, leaving only a garrison to hold Quebec City. While the French army had been decimated, it had not been destroyed, and they still had about ten thousand men (compared with only six thousand in the British force).

General Murray succeeded Wolfe as commander of the British Army in Quebec. Later he would become the colony's first British governor after the Treaty of Paris was signed in 1763. Murray did well to hold the largely destroyed town through the winter freeze, surviving French attacks, malnutrition, and scurvy, which killed more than six hundred of his soldiers. It is rumoured that during this time the nuns of Quebec knitted leggings for the Fraser's who were wearing kilts in the harsh Canadian winters.

Captain MacDonald, who deceived the sentries on the clifftop and defended Quebec City on snowshoes, was greatly admired by both Wolfe and Murray. In the battle of Sainte-Foy in April 1760, he played an important role commanding the far left flank of the British Army and was killed after his position was overrun. Sergeant Thompson wrote about his Captain's death: "He himself was found cut and hack'd to pieces in the most shocking manner. There was an end of him."[78]

The Battle of Sainte-Foy was the last major fight in the struggle for North America. The French had marched from Montreal in the spring in an effort to dislodge General Murray and his men from Quebec. In response, Murray ordered his troops to march out and line up in approximately the same place the French had lined up the year before. Once again the Fraser's behaved in a spectacular fashion and fought the elite French Grenadiers for possession of a flourmill. The mill changed hands three times, and a piper from the 78th stood outside as both Fraser's and Grenadiers jumped in and out of windows fighting for the building.[79] General Murray retreated into the city, leaving Captain MacDonald and Lieutenant Cosmo Gordon dead and a great many Fraser's, including Colonel Simon Fraser, wounded. Captain Charles Stewart, who had been badly wounded at Culloden under the Jacobite Lord George Murray, found himself yet again wounded, this time at Sainte-Foy and under the Hanoverian Lord James Murray. In hospital after the battle, Stewart made the famous quip, "From April battles and Murray generals, good Lord deliver me!"[80] Murray heard about the comment and, to his credit, laughed and went to the invalid to wish him better luck next time.

The 78th lost more men under Murray in the second Battle of Quebec than they had under Wolfe in the first.

Table 4: Fraser Losses in the Battles for Quebec		
	Wolfe (1759)	Murray (1760)
Dead	18	59
Wounded	156	148

After the battle there was great anxiety within the town about the arrival of a relief fleet. The besieged thought wrongly that a French fleet could arrive first. Historians believed their fears and often suggest that the recapture of Quebec would have been possible if the French fleet had arrived first. However, the French fleet had been destroyed at Quiberon Bay after the fall of Quebec, and the British navy was guarding the St. Lawrence and blockading France itself. The French sent only a few supply boats, which did not, in fact, slip past the British navy. Sergeant James Thompson writes, "In about three days after the arrival of the Lowestoff [fishing trawler], the remainder of the fleet came up to Quebec."[81]

By July 1760, General Murray was ready to advance on Montreal. Lieutenant-Colonel Simon Fraser was promoted to command a brigade. En route from Quebec to Montreal, Thompson wrote: "The habitants were very friendly disposed, and we made it a rule not to molest them in any way.[82] General Murray ... accordingly gave orders to the men to club their firelocks; that is to carry the Butts upwards, in token of friendship."[83]

Three British armies converged on Montreal at the same time — one of the great military feats of the Seven Years' War. On September 8, 1760, the governor of New France signed the capitulation, and New France passed into the hands of the British Army. A great parade including Fraser's Highlanders and the Black Watch marched, triumphant, into Montreal.

The 78th's last action in North America involved some of their companies in Halifax, Nova Scotia, re-taking a position held by the French. In 1762, the French captured St. John's in Newfoundland, and four Fraser's, including Captain Charles MacDonnell of Glengarry, were killed at the Battle of Signal Hill after their remarkably brave surprise attack on the fortified French positions there.

Naval supremacy was the reason that the only two expeditions ever to capture Quebec City were those of General Wolfe and the Kirke brothers, the Franco-Scots privateers of the 1630s. British naval supremacy is the reason for military success at Louisbourg, and the capture and the retention of Quebec City. While Wolfe's dramatic capture of Quebec was a spectacular triumph, it also established a naval beachhead in a New France isolated from its homeland by a naval blockade. Wolfe did not destroy the French army in America, he did what was asked and captured that beachhead. The British lost the Battle of Sainte-Foy, but it did not matter: General Murray held the landing place for the navy at the only entrance to New France. America was won on the Atlantic, not only on the Plains of Abraham, and in this British versus French contest of wooden walls versus stone walls, ships defeated forts. With the capture of Quebec, the French no longer had a land base from which they could maintain a fleet off the North American continent. The rise of Britain, which replaced France as the world's leading power, was a work in progress before the Seven Years' War and was not completed until Waterloo, which ended the Napoleonic Wars, in 1815. However, the Seven Years' War transformed North America into a largely English-speaking area — that alone was to have a global impact in the following centuries.

Victory on the Plains of Abraham can also be attributed to the fact that British used tactics that had been drilled into them: superior firepower, the sword charge, and strategic use of terrain account for the high French death rate, yet natural features are often omitted from the story. Military intelligence, speed, and naval coordination allowed Wolfe to deceive, divide, and defeat. Within eight and a half hours, the victors boarded their ships, travelled, and disembarked in silence, then scaled a guarded cliff, before obtaining the high ground from which to fight.

The Highland charge was at first romanticized, then criticized, in literature over the years. The notion that the 78th threw away their muskets, like the idea that Wolfe read poetry aloud to the troops on the boats, is a theatrical gesture that historians and novelists have written into the story of this battle as embellishment. This was the last time swords were used by a British regiment in a major battle, since they were replaced by bayonets, and their use as a major feature of British tactics came to an end. Such was the effectiveness of the Highland charge that it entered into nineteenth-century military lore.

This charge also changed the eighteenth-century public image of Highlanders: from savage rebellious malcontents on the fringes of Britain, to passionate and loyal defenders of the Empire who played a central role in British society. The United Kingdom of Scotland and England had defeated the Auld Alliance of Scotland and France in a battle for the New World. The Murrays, Frasers, and MacDonalds in British service defeated the de Ramezays, Johnstones, and Douglases in French service. Scots Highlanders would never again participate in ventures such as the Jacobite Rebellion of 1745, nor flock to French, Swedish, Spanish, Dutch, Austrian, and Russian military service. According to Yale University historian, Linda Colley, Highland soldiers after this time became the very arsenal of the British Empire.[84] I will show in later chapters that Highlanders were also on their way to becoming spearheads of migration into that new and growing Empire.

6

Veterans Home from America

[T]hough I have been so long behind you in Scotland,
my heart is in America.
— William Russell, from Bernard Bailyn, *Voyagers to the West*

The Fraser's Highlanders were disbanded when the Treaty of Paris ended the Seven Years' War in 1763. According to the official lists, approximately eight hundred Fraser's Highlanders took their "sword-money" (discharge) in Glasgow, Scotland. Approximately 170 soldiers were discharged in Quebec, and many were drafted into North American regiments, such as the 60th Royal Americans. Major John Campbell held command of the Fraser's because Colonel Simon Fraser left in March 1761 to take up his seat as the elected Member of Parliament for Inverness. Thousands of veteran Highlanders returned from the Seven Years' War and had a major impact on postwar Scotland. This chapter describes how extensive Scottish military activity in the New World of 1756–63 led to extensive migration from the Old World.

Perceptions

The 78th was greeted upon their return to Scotland with lavish praise in books, magazines, and newspapers. Samuel Johnson, essayist and literary historian, wrote in the 1770s that "England has for several years been filled with the achievements of seventy thousand highlanders employed in America … their behaviour deserved a very high degree of military praise, but their numbers have been much exaggerated."[1] Historian Hugh Trevor-Roper states that Colonel Fraser elbowed his way into the British Parliament because "the attitude of Englishmen and Lowland Scotchmen towards the Highlanders rapidly changed…. Their loyalty to their chiefs, which had hitherto been regarded as contemptible servility, now became admirable and touching constancy."[2]

The Impact of Returning Veterans on Scotland

Migratory attitudes also changed during the years after the Highlanders returned home. Before the Seven Years' War, very few Scots went to America.[3] On the Island of Barra, in the Outer Hebrides, the chief of Clan MacNeil wrote, "From the time Roderick the Resolute went to Canada with the Fraser Highlanders to the departure of his son Roderick XL for the American Revolutionary War, about 1776, the imagination of the Clansmen was aroused by the reports of the most wonderful conditions in America."[4]

Returning veterans made Scots more favourable towards emigration. The author J.D.V. Loder, in his book *Colonsay and Oronsay in the Isles of Argyll*, writes: "Emigration first stimulated by soldiers returned from Canada at the conclusion of the Seven Years' War in 1763, soon assumed large proportions."[5] Argyll, like so many other areas in the Highlands with high enlistment in the 78th, had high emigration rates after the War. Highlanders began to imagine they could all "obtain land for themselves and their flocks of cattle at a trifling rent or of conquering from the Indians with the sword the most desirable holding of any for a Highlander."[6] The Highland-wide recruitment of the 78th ensured that "Discontent … even reached the small islands, and two families have migrated to America,"[7] said T. Pennant, a Welsh travel writer in the Highlands of the 1770s.

A woman by the name of Janet Schaw, in her diary about a trip she took to America in the early 1770s, recorded the presence of veterans among the migrants on her ship: "Should levys be again necessary, the recruiting drum may long be at a loss to procure such soldiers as are now aboard this Vessel, lost to their country forever, brave fellows, who tho' now flying from their friends, would never have fled from their foes."[8]

Samuel Johnson and his Scots biographer, James Boswell, wrote the finest contemporary account of Highland emigration after the Seven Years' War: *A Journey into the Western Isles of Scotland*. Johnson met with the famous Flora MacDonald, who had smuggled Bonnie Prince Charlie over the sea to Skye. She subsequently immigrated to North Carolina. Johnson emphasized the group nature of Scottish migration, and wrote of the soldiers already in America: "Those who have obtained grants of American lands, have … invited settlers … the accounts sent by the earliest adventurers … including many to follow them; and whole neighbourhoods formed partners for removal."[9] In other words, localities would join together to hire ships, and citizens would emigrate en masse to join those soldiers who had remained in North America. I shall tell the story of those Frasers who stayed in America in the following chapter.

Perhaps the best indicator of the impact of emigration on the Highlanders of this time was Johnson's description of a contemporary folk dance, "A Dance Called America." He wrote: "Each of the couples successively whirls around a circle until all are in motion; and the dance seems intended to show how emigration catches, until a whole neighbourhood is set afloat."[10]

Emigration was made easier after 1763 by the rapid increase in the Glasgow tobacco and sugar trades. By the 1770s, Glasgow was easily the world's largest tobacco port, importing from Virginia and exporting to Europe. Consequently, there were Scots ships in large numbers returning to North America to provide a cheap passage to America. The rise of tobacco and other trade with North America created a new European economic pattern that shifted Scotland to a central geographic place in the Old World. In turn, the Scots population began shifting away from the East and the Highlands to settle in the West and the Lowlands.

Scots military service overseas helped to eventually depopulate the Highlands, but did not do so immediately. The Fraser's Highlanders who had stayed in America established communities in North America that

Fraser House, Fraserville (renamed Rivière-du-Loup) was occupied by four generations of Frasers, the seigneurs (landowners with tenants) of the area. Alexander Fraser of the 78th had his seigneury on the St. Lawrence River downstream from Quebec City. (Photograph by Sam Allison.)

acted as bridgeheads on the eastern seaboard, attracting thousands of Scots from across the Atlantic. It's quite telling what the attitudes toward eighteenth-century migrants were by simply looking at the titles of some of the books on the subject that have been written, including *Willing Exiles* and *People's Clearance*.

Regular census records did not start in Scotland until 1801, so there is debate about the numbers involved in this mass migration.[11] Harvard historian Bernard Bailyn's figure of forty thousand people emigrating between 1760 and 1775 is perhaps the closest to the truth because he analyzed arrivals in North America as well as the less-documented departures from Scotland.

University of Glasgow historian W.R. Brock wrote, "It is a persistent myth that the Highland migration was caused by the failure of the Jacobite risings in 1715 and 1745."[12] He points out that 936 people were sentenced to "transportation" after the 1745 Jacobite Rebellion and that only 610 arrived in the American colonies. Yet, according to popular Scots culture and many distinguished academics,[13] emigration began after 1745, not in the 1760s as brought out by Bailyn's figures. For instance, Flora MacDonald immigrated to North America in 1774, almost thirty years after Culloden. In fact, about 3 percent of the entire Scottish population migrated between 1760 and 1775,[14] which led to Samuel Johnson's memorable description of the situation as an "epidemical fury of emigration."

During the last half of the eighteenth century, Scotland was experiencing a population explosion, and this continued well into the nineteenth. In the words of the Duke of Argyll, the head of the powerful Clan Campbell and one of the most important political figures in Scotland, the Highlands were "overstocked with people ... the emigration began ... and, in spite of it ... in 1790, the inhabitants were then so crowded that some relief of this sort [emigration] seemed absolutely necessary."[15] The Scottish population increased from 1,265,360 in 1755 to 1,608,420 in 1801 and again to 2,888,742 in 1851.[16]

A consequence of the population explosion in the Highlands was that there were many young men available for the army. The dozens of Highland regiments that fought in British wars, from the Battle of Quebec (1759) through the American Revolution and Napoleonic Wars to Waterloo (1815), were partly a consequence of Highland overpopulation. Contrary to popular belief, there was no population decrease in the Highlands after 1745, nor were the thousands of Highlanders in the eighteenth-century British Army decimated by war. There were only 103 Fraser's, 110 Montgomerie's, and 381 Black Watch soldiers — a total of 594 — killed in the Seven Years' War.[17] These numbers do not include the many Highlanders serving in other British regiments who were also killed, nor do they include those who died of disease. While historians sometimes include disease-related deaths with those killed in battle, it is difficult to know whether more eighteenth-century people died of disease in the army or in everyday life outside the army.

More than half of the 78th soldiers who enlisted returned home to Scotland. However, many of these re-migrated back to America before the American Revolution. Many others joined the 71st Fraser's Highlanders to fight in the Revolution and then were given land afterwards. Such emigration to North America had little impact on the Highlands because of the ongoing population explosion resulting from better nutrition, peace, and vaccination against smallpox.[18]

In places such as the Isle of Skye, 10 percent of the population left in the twelve years between 1763 and 1775. According to Rosalind Mitchison, a Scottish historian, this emigration rate was comparable to the seventeenth-century Scots emigration to Ireland and east to Poland, Sweden, and the Netherlands.[19] However, after 1763, Scots were instead picking up and moving west to an empire where Highland migrants could retain their cultural identity. It was indeed a New World for the Scots.

The Migration of a Military People, 1763–1812

Historian Bernard Bailyn analyzed the migratory patterns of the late eighteenth and early nineteenth century and found that the Scots displayed very different demographic characteristics to immigrants from other countries. Although most Highland migrants during this period were not soldiers in the Seven Years' War, the American War of Independence, or the War of 1812, those emigrant soldiers skewed Scots demographic patterns by acting as "important initial facilitators of emigration to a wide range of destinations, not just to areas of military settlement. Half-pay officers were thus conspicuous in organizing emigration."[20] In other words, those soldiers who had returned from the New World convinced others in Scotland — friends, relatives, neighbours — to immigrate to North America.

Most Scottish historians see this "exodus from Gaeldom" that took place between 1760 and 1815 as involuntary and, as T.M. Devine states in his book *Scotland's Empire, 1600–1815*, "a reaction to the radical changes in land settlement, rentals and tenure which were destroying the old way of life."[21] Devine points out that it "puzzled many observers at the time that the Gaels [Highlanders] were prepared to leave Scotland en masse for an uncertain existence in a far-off wilderness."[22] In reality, the North American wilderness *was* familiar to many who had served there.

Scottish immigration patterns were also impacted by the fact that an unusually large number of veterans were *re*-migrating back to America, but were counted among other migrants. Bailyn's research showed that almost half of the Scots emigrants arrived in nuclear family groups — a husband, wife, and children — while only one-fifth of English emigrants were in such groups.[23] Scots did *not* emigrate as clan groups, but more usually as family groups.[24] To illustrate this point, fully two-thirds of English migrants were young single men, whereas only one-third of Scottish migrants were.[25]

Although the total number of English migrants was greater than the Scots, there were two-and-a-half times more children and one third more women among the Scots.[26] The higher number of Scottish women and children can be explained because these migrants accompanied re-migrating veterans. Family, rather than individual migration, helps explain the impact that the Scots had on North America. Family groups tended to retain their Scots identities rather than feeling the need to enter into the "melting pot" immediately, as was more likely to happen with young, single men.

So, strictly speaking, the Clan Fraser did not emigrate; the 78th's soldiers with their families did. The subtle distinction gives credence to Bailyn's findings that extended families as a migratory unit scarcely existed at that time.[27] His research showed that Highland migration was a movement of the rural proletariat leaving the land. The Highlanders had the highest percentage of labourers (56.8 percent) of any British group, and many classified themselves as "servants" — meaning farm servants as opposed to farmers or landowners. "But," as Bailyn states in *Voyagers to the West*, "precisely who these labourers were, and precisely what their social position was, remains to be seen."[28] In reality, those ex-soldiers *were* Bailyn's labourers, as private soldiers were drawn from the labouring class in the Highlands. This fact would explain the high percentage of labourers amongst the emigrants, although Highland aristocrats such as Sir Henry Seton of the 78th were also departing their homeland at that time. In short, although the percentage of labourers was high, the entire social range of Highland Scots was emigrating in the eighteenth century.

As emphasized, many of the Scots emigrants were, in fact, ex-soldiers re-migrating back to North America, where they had already served for six or seven years. This explains why the average age of the Scottish men who arrived was higher than that of the English men. Other evidence indicates the regimented, organized, cohesive group nature of Scots emigration at this time — two-thirds of Scots emigrants came as groups that travelled in large vessels bearing 150 or more passengers, whereas only one-fifteenth of English emigrants came in such large vessels. The Scots sailed as a network of people travelling aboard vessels hired for the purpose; English emigrants came in smaller groups of isolated individuals who took a chance at finding passage on commercial ships leaving from commercial ports. Scots chartered ships that came to pre-arranged transit points all over the Highlands; English migrants went to the ships, whereas the ships went to the Scottish migrants.

Even the Scottish destination patterns differed from those of the English. The Scots clustered in New York State, Vermont, and North Carolina, whereas the English scattered. Few Scots appeared to go to Quebec, Nova Scotia, or Prince Edward Island before the Revolutionary War shifted migration patterns. However, official British statistics are contradictory, and some surveys about the Fraser's in Prince Edward Island, for instance, suggest that more emigrants landed before the Revolution than official figures indicate. Some Scots appear to have simply squatted rather than legally claimed land.

The migrating Scots of this time were not, then, the starving masses. The sheer cost of emigration excluded the very poor, and Bailyn wrote: "They appear to have been ambitiously enterprising people attempting to exploit opportunities they knew about and which they thought they could plan for."[29] Highlanders were pulled to a land they knew and pushed from a land that was unable to support their increasing numbers.

Bailyn destroys the myth that the Scots were indentured emigrants in the eighteenth century. Despite Scotland's poverty and the comparatively low socioeconomic status of Scottish migrants, only 18 percent of the Scots were indentured.[30] He points out that 68 percent of the English migrants were indentured (had their fare paid in return for many years of labour) in North America. Regardless of occupational category, the Scots were far less likely to be indentured than the English. Part of the explanation for the Highland Scots' ability to pay emigration fares lay in the fact that they sold their livestock and agricultural equipment. Re-migrating soldiers used capital saved from military service to finance their families' emigration. In addition, because the Scots migrated in larger groups, it was cheaper per head to travel. The indentured service entered into by many English arrivals meant that eight to twelve years of earnings were lost to them, resulting in a much shorter working life than those who arrived free and clear of any debt. The comparative absence of indentures helps explain the greater success of the Highland masses in the New World.

Veterans' Re-Migration

Bailyn records that a commentator at the time remarked: "It was not poverty or necessity which compelled [emigration], but ambition."[31]

The Duke of Argyll summed up what he believed had happened among the Highlanders at the time:

> [T]hey had seen the New World ... new scenes ... new visions ... opened up before them. Within a few years of the close of the War in 1763, a steady stream of emigration to the colonies poured out from many parts of Scotland, but especially from the Highlands. It began ... with the most intelligent and educated classes — Those who had occupied the position of Tacksman — the officers and non-commissioned officers of the military Clans.[32]

The perceptive comments made by the Duke of Argyll stressed the importance of military clans such as the Stewarts of Appin, the MacDonnells of Glengarry, and the Frasers of Lovat in triggering migration. All of these clans were well-represented in the 78th. Militarism and migration went in tandem.

I referred earlier to Lieutenant McTavish of the 78th, whose son founded the NWC, Montreal's huge fur trading organization. The elder McTavish began to make plans for re-migrating to New York because

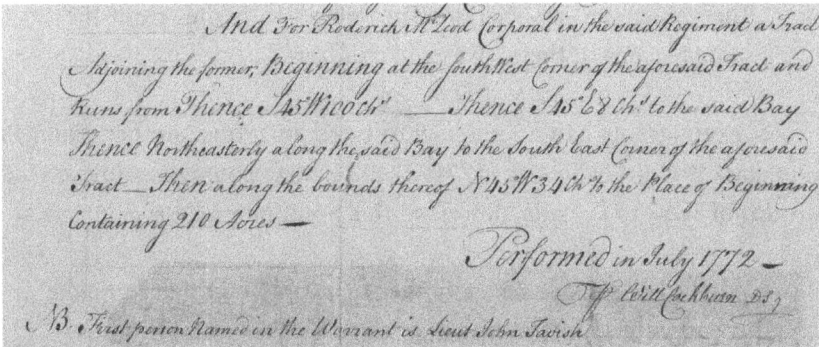

Pictured here is the official land warrant issued by the Scots surveyor William Cockburn. Although Lieutenant John McTavish of the 78th was not in upstate New York in 1772 to legally claim the land, his name is on the warrant (Tavish). He never did get the land. His famous son, Simon, was there in 1772 and perhaps could have claimed the land had the Revolution not broken out in 1776. (New York State Archives A0273-78-780.)

he was being taxed heavily to pay for improvements on the Fraser estates. In the end, he did not return to America, but sent his son Simon McTavish with a petition for his military land. Although the land was apparently set aside, it was not granted to Simon, and he obviously struck out on his own, succeeded, and eventually made a fortune. Years later he brought out his nephew, William McGillivray, a grandson to Lieutenant McTavish. McGillivray also made a fortune and brought out relatives.

As with the aforementioned McTavishes, the chain of emigration often began with soldiers from the 78th, but had an intergenerational demographic impact that continued long after 1763. The Highland Scots made up a network of military-migratory people who flowed back and forth across the Atlantic from 1758 to 1812.

An official report in 1774 explains:

> This spirit of emigration to America, which first began in the Highlands, begins to spread itself to the Low Country.... Various associations have been formed for purchasing lands in the Colonies upon a joint-stock, to be afterwards divided amongst the contributions upon their arrival in America....

They enter into associations, and go off in bodies from the same place with their wives and children.[33]

Scots emigrants had a tendency to bond with one another. Thomas Douglas, 5th Earl of Selkirk (1771–1820), who encouraged and even led groups of Scots to Canada, described this bonding process:

> When any considerable number of people had determined to emigrate, some leading man circulated a subscription paper, and a regular contract was entered into between the subscribers, and some one of their own number who acted as agent and contractors for the rest — perhaps they themselves had a strangely surviving feeling of military desertion.[34]

The high emigration rates, combined with socio-economic change, began to alter the nature of Highland society. Historian Duane Meyer writes that "without clan ties, the Highland population became far more mobile. The chiefs who earlier had been concerned with 'man-rent' [i.e., warrior service] now began to exploit their lands for the largest possible return of money rent."[35] The prevalence of manrent declined sharply as more families bonded together to migrate.

In North America, there were already some large immigrant groups being led and helped by former Scots soldiers. For example, according to the Johnson papers, passengers of the *Pearl* were aided by Hugh Fraser, the 78th lieutenant who had emigrated in the 1760s. John MacDonell of the 77th Montgomerie's Highlanders led several hundred of these Highland emigrants from Fort William in the Highlands to upstate New York, also on the *Pearl*.[36]

Bailyn described these newly arrived immigrants as "Genteel People of Considerable Property," and it is thought that the group was carrying about six thousand pounds with them.[37] Many ex-soldiers also arrived at that time on the *Pearl*, including John MacDonell's brother Allen, who had been a mercenary in French service; another brother, Alexander, who was principal tacksman on the Glengarry estates; and a cousin,

John MacDonell (a.k.a. Spanish John, 1728–1810), an active Jacobite who had been a mercenary in the Spanish army fighting the Austrians in the Italy of the 1740s. Donald MacKay of the 78th Fraser's was among the private soldiers on board. However, Simon Fraser, whose son Simon (1776–1862) was to become the great explorer after whom the Canadian river in British Columbia is named, was perhaps the most famous passenger aboard the ship. Many Highlanders had served in upstate New York, which is the most likely reason why many migrated there. As we have seen, after 1763, Highland emigrants were linked through military service in Highland regiments and through clan family ties.

The most famous Scots-Canadian emigrant ship was the *Hector*, which arrived in Pictou, Nova Scotia, in 1773. The *Hector* carried at least two ex-78th men and the brothers of several 78th veterans.[38] Beauly, Inverness-shire[39] — the home of Colonel Simon Fraser of the 78th —, was the gathering place for most of the *Hector*'s passengers, who then walked from there to board the ship, which picked up more passengers in Skye before sailing to Nova Scotia.

Simon Fraser (1776–1862), who explored the river in British Columbia that bears his name, was born in the New York/Vermont area and joined the North West Company. Fraser was arrested in 1817 as an accessory to the murder of the governor of the Red River Colony, Robert Semple. These events occurred during the massacre of Lord Selkirk's Highland settlers at Seven Oaks, Manitoba. (McGill University, McGill Rare Books and Special Collections.)

The best-documented immigrant group at this time was the Scots American Company of Farmers (SCAF). In the 1770s, a Bond of Association was drawn up and signed by 138 men and women who were members of the SCAF in Scotland.[40] The cost of membership was two pounds, ten shillings, a considerable sum in those days, and each member, including the women, had one vote. The group sent out a scouting party of two and they travelled more than 4,500 kilometres across the Thirteen Colonies from North Carolina to New Hampshire in 1773 before deciding to buy land in Ryegate, Vermont (Caledonia County). Although SCAF's recruiting links to Scotland were hampered by the American Revolution (1776–83), it continued successfully until 1820. Members came out from Scotland gradually, and membership ensured that migrants had "friends in America," which made the process a bit easier. The SCAF sold lots to settlers, sponsored members, lent money to settlers who needed help, and sent goods from Scotland for sale in America.[41] These were not rich people, but their co-operative activities led to their success.

In nearby Barnet, Vermont, the United Company of Farmers for the Shires of Perth and Stirling proved a less successful example of bonding for emigration purposes during this period, the Revolutionary War having seriously hindered this group by making passage to America dangerous and arousing anti-Scots feelings in the Thirteen Colonies.

According to Bernard Bailyn, pre-industrial rural Scots migration was very different to pre-industrial Irish migration in the nineteenth century. Scots migrants recruited in an organized, cohesive fashion, targeted specific American regions, and settled in rural as well as urban areas. Bailyn viewed Highland Scots emigration as a transfer of farming families to North America. I interpret the Highland migration as a military network on the move to where they served or had relatives.

Soldiers returning to Scotland with their half-pay were able to pay more for farm rentals, and half-pay officers became a major source of income for Highland landowners.[42] The period between 1763 and 1775 was, as stated in an earlier chapter, characterized by "a distinct re-militarization of the Highland tacksman officer class."[43] As a consequence of serving under British colours rather than European colours, more retired officers settled in Scotland rather than in Europe. However, qualifying that view, the Duke of Argyll wrote that as a consequence of the military-migration that took place between 1763 and 1775, the kind of people who enlisted in Highland regiments was changing. Rather than recruiting from clan areas, "it was chiefly among those Highlanders who had already left their own country [locality] that enlistment continued to be successful."[44]

Military-Migratory Land Relationships

Many of the 78th officers, such as Hugh Fraser in New York, John Nairne in Quebec, and Allan Stewart in New Brunswick (after the American Revolution), acted as North American landlords, and encouraged Highland emigration to build up their lands. However, some veterans seem to have transferred their experiences in recruiting soldiers to recruiting emigrants.

Major Simon Fraser was one of the most successful emigration agents during the 1790s and into the 1800s, and "made a trade of the business."[45] He was the son of Captain John Fraser of the 82nd Regiment, who had fought in the American Revolution and was given land in Pictou, Nova Scotia. Both father and son appear to have conducted an emigrant trade, and the son continued working at this endeavour into the nineteenth century.

None of this is to suggest that all Highland officers encouraged emigration. Many, in fact, were opposed to the practice because it decreased the number of soldiers available for military service at home. Captain John Ross of Balnagown near Tain, Ross-shire, where so many of the 78th originated, wrote in 1772, in reference to the local minister, "I hope by his good advice to his people he may put a stop to this emigration."[46] Some others were neutral in the debate. The father of Captain Charles Baillie of the 78th received a letter stating, "I see numbers of people are going from all our Northern parts to America. For my part tho' I'm sorry for the loss of people as it is a natural loss yet I see great advantages to arise from it in time."[47]

After 1763, British trade followed the flag to the former New France, and Highland emigrants weren't far behind. The reasons for the Scots leaving their homeland for a new start across the sea differed, however, from other migrants: "The motives of these emigrants were fundamentally unlike those of New England Puritans, Delaware Quakers and even Virginia Cavaliers. Among the North Britons there was no talk of holy experiments or cities on a hill. These new emigrants came mainly in search of material betterment."[48]

Both the Highland Scots and the Ulster Scots — Irish Protestants of Scottish descent — had materialistic motives for immigrating to North America. They migrated not for religious or political reasons, but for economic betterment. However, a majority of the Highland Scots also had a military background, and so it was that the 78th Fraser's Highlanders laid down the foundation for a pattern of relationships that were built around the migration of thousands during a period that was to last until the War of 1812.

Lieutenant Allan Stewart's story encompasses many of the aspects of Scottish emigration patterns I have discussed in this chapter. Despite the myth that Jacobites emigrated in large numbers, Stewart appears to be the only active Jacobite from the 78th who recruited emigration parties for North America. Allan Stewart's clan position in the Stewarts of Appin helped him to recruit clansmen and become an officer in the clan regiment in the Jacobite Rebellion of 1745. In 1756, he recruited again among his clan and joined the Fraser's Highlanders to fight for the Hanoverians. After serving for six years in North America, Lieutenant Stewart returned home in 1763 to the annexed estate of Appin,[49] located in a remote coastal area in the West Scottish Highlands, and was granted a ten-year lease on a farm there. However, at the end of the ten years, a Jacobite relative who had made a fortune in the East India Company was able to pay more, obtained the lease, and Stewart had to vacate the property.[50] His military position in the 78th allowed him to claim free land in North Carolina, and he led a group of eighty-five emigrants from Appin on the ship *Jupiter* of Larne, according to *The Records of Emigrants from England and Scotland to North Carolina 1774–75*. Also aboard the *Jupiter* was another group of fifty-one emigrants from nearby Glenorchy, led by a man by the name of John Stewart. There was yet another Stewart — Kenneth, a ship's master — who was travelling with Allan Stewart's group. The records show that both Allan and Kenneth had personal servants travelling with them, but, as Bailyn's study of the Scots indicated, this group of migrants was unusual because not one of them was travelling to become an indentured servant once they reached America.

In 1775, at the start of the Revolutionary War, Lieutenant Allan Stewart became an officer once again and enlisted a group of Scots immigrants, including a Kenneth Stewart who became an ensign, for the Loyalist North Carolina Highlanders Regiment. Later in the war, Allan became colonel of the Black Pioneers Regiment, with Kenneth a lieutenant in the same regiment. This Black Pioneer Regiment was composed of escaped African-American slaves who were promised their freedom if they fought for the British. I write more about this in the chapter about the Revolutionary War. At the end of the war, Allan led another group to Nova Scotia and New Brunswick — the African Americans to obtain their freedom and the various Scots to obtain the promised Loyalist land. Allan was encouraged to recruit followers to North Carolina, and then Canada, because it was in his interest to develop his new land.

Although Allan Stewart probably did not recruit exactly the same people for his different military-migratory ventures,[51] he did recruit from the same pool of Appin families, who emigrated and enlisted with him. The names Carmichael, MacIntire, McCole (MacCall), and Stewart formed the numbers for the Appin regiment at Culloden, for the 78th, for the North Carolina Highlanders, and for the Nova Scotia/New Brunswick land grants at St. Andrews in what is now New Brunswick but which was part of New France before the Seven Years' War. Stewart did not claim one giant estate, but instead claimed a variety of places with valuable attributes such as land on the ocean, by a town, and at a waterfall where a timber mill could be erected. Allan Stewart died in the 1790s in Scotland, apparently while trying to recruit settlers from Appin and the surrounding areas to make the move to his new lands in Canada. His will was disputed, and several years after he died, his land appears to have been absorbed by an influential group that dominated life in the new colony.[52]

After the Seven Years' War, the new military-migratory relationship westward put such a strain on the mercenary migration eastward to the

Continent that employers hoped that "the recruiting of the Scotch regiments in Holland from Scotland will be discouraged from the future ... the want of hands is more sensibly felt than ever, when such numbers are daily giving over to the new settlement in America."[53]

Veterans of the Seven Years' War often returned home with new ideas. For instance, Robert MacPherson, Chaplain to the 78th, "having naturally a taste for farming and improvements ... remained nine months in England, in order to observe the method of farming in that country."[54] In 1770, MacPherson started to implement his "improvements" and had eighty people evicted from Aberarder near Tulloch and Loch Laggan, Inverness-shire, to implement those improvements. However, MacPherson failed as a farmer and seemed to have no real knowledge of successful farming techniques, though he claimed to be able to "introduce a better method of farming."[55] His experiment took place before the successful introduction of sheep into the Highlands, and it is not known exactly what MacPherson attempted to do. Returning veterans had an environmental and demographic impact in that some introduced farming methods that reduced the need for labour, which subsequently forced out many of the inhabitants. Migration was also prompted by the population explosion and the vision of America as told by returning "professional soldiers" — the "wild geese," as mercenaries were often called. Samuel Johnson brilliantly characterized the re-migrating 78th Fraser's as "those who are fluttering on the Wing ... collecting a flock that they may take their flight."[56]

7

Choosing America

Where One Scot Comes, Others Soon Follow
— Craig Maskill, Master's Thesis, Mount Allison University

Why Stay?

After disbandment in 1763, the 78th Fraser's Highlanders received sword-money (discharge) of three pence each and a Royal Bounty of fourteen days' pay. In addition, any soldier who chose to take his sword-money in North America, as opposed to returning to Scotland, received fifty acres of land.[1] Non-commissioned officers (NCOs), such as sergeants and corporals, received two hundred acres, while captains received three thousand. Officially, it was stated that "grants are to be made only to such officers as have served in North America during the late war, and to such private soldiers as have been or shall be disbanded in America, and are actively residing there."[2]

However, the part of the 78th who disbanded in Glasgow also received free land when they re-migrated back to North America. Approximately ten officers took up different pieces of land in New York/Vermont, three claimed land in Quebec, two in Prince Edward Island,[3] one in North

MAP 9: BRITISH NORTH AMERICA, 1763

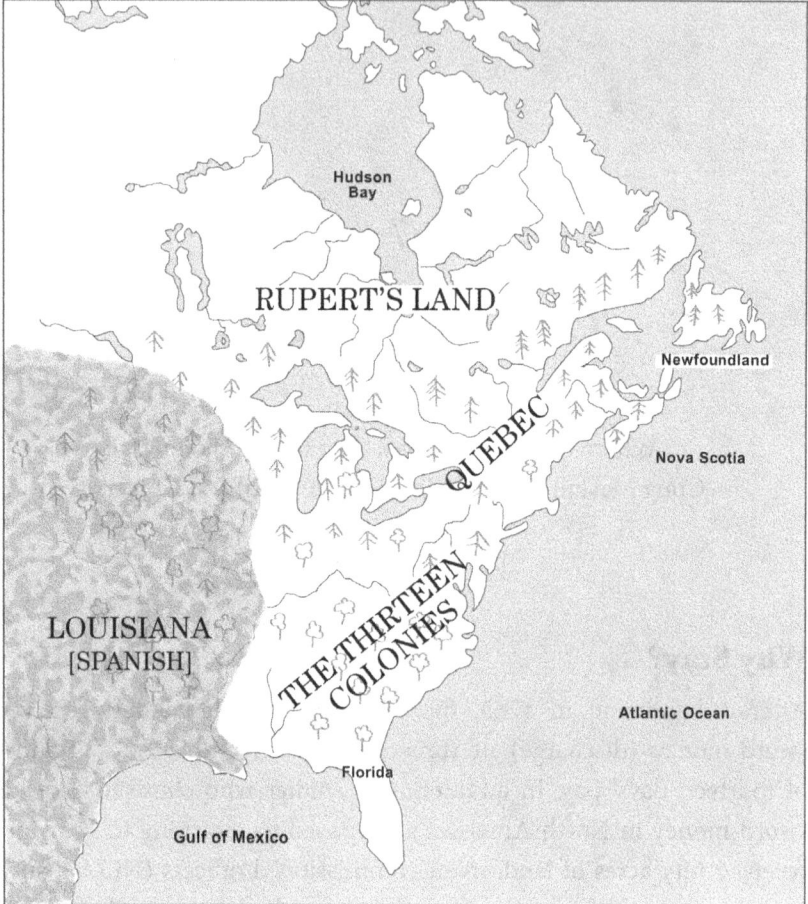

Hudson Bay

RUPERT'S LAND

Newfoundland

QUEBEC

Nova Scotia

LOUISIANA
[SPANISH]

THE THIRTEEN COLONIES

Atlantic Ocean

Florida

Gulf of Mexico

Carolina, and one (and possibly others) in East Florida.[4] At least two — Lieutenant Hugh Fraser in New York and Captain John Nairne in Quebec — planned to bring out settlers to North America even before the Treaty of Paris (1763) was signed.[5]

One hundred and seventy private soldiers and NCOs took their discharge in North America. In addition, approximately one hundred private soldiers and NCOs returned with the regiment to Scotland in

1763, then re-migrated back very quickly. The *Indorsed Land Papers 1643–1803* of New York indicate that 78th veterans discharged in Quebec took land alongside 78th veterans who had been discharged in Scotland. Individual 78th soldiers often appear with groups from other Scottish regiments to claim New York land. Networks of Scots from various regiments who had served in America coordinated the migration of women and children from Scotland.

Clusters of Highland soldiers and their relatives migrated to North America during this time. They did not emigrate individually, en masse, or at the bidding of the government. As I stated in the previous chapter, the Scots migrated in large groups from pre-arranged parts of the Highlands.[6] Some officers invited their men in North America to re-migrate with them after they had returned to Scotland. Some officers in Scotland posted notices to this effect and collected 78th veterans there. Those wishing to accompany them would "enlist" by signing an agreement and paying perhaps half the fare. The cost was about three pounds, ten shillings per adult — an immense sum at the time, and one that kept out the destitute.[7] The officer or NCO in charge would coordinate with one or two other networks to hire a boat. Some 78th veterans joined with their own officers and some joined officers from other Scottish regiments. Large groups hired boats, then, once landed, dispersed among veterans already on the frontier.[8]

Thousands of British soldiers and sailors had served in North America during the Seven Years' War. However, the Highland Scots, more than any others in the British forces, chose to stay for the free land. Among the three Highland regiments that served in North America, far more of the 78th took their discharge in the New World. The assertion is often made that Highland soldiers stayed because Highlanders were poorer than Lowland, English, and even Irish soldiers. Poverty fails to explain the differential in discharge patterns among the three Highland regiments themselves, however.

A major reason that the members of the 78th decided to stay in such great numbers lies with their frontier experience. Both the Black Watch and Montgomerie's Highlanders moved to fight in the West Indies, though they later returned to North America. However, the 78th Fraser's

Highlanders spent the entire Seven Years' War on both sides of the vast New France–New England frontier.

The 78th Fraser's were dispersed first among New England settlers (1757–59), then among French-Canadian settlers (1760–63). Sergeant James Thompson records working for a rope maker and learning that trade in Saratoga, located in upstate New York. Corporal William Ross worked for French Canadians on the St. Lawrence River, learned to be a ship's pilot, and, after his discharge in 1763, settled on the Lower St. Lawrence piloting British ships. Highland soldiers on the North American frontier were like magpies, taking after their mercenary ancestors, who acquired skills from the local people they met.

The *Orderly Book* of the 42nd Regiment, the Black Watch, mentions some of the Scots soldiers who were involved in frontier forestry activities:[9]

> The following carpenters ... James Frazer, George McDougall, [another] James Frazer, John McColme, John Robinson, James Cumming and James MacDonald ... to be at the sawmills. The following sawyers are to attend Lieut. Col. Eyre tomorrow at 5 o'clock Robert Kennedy, John McFarling and Robert Bain. The following masons are likewise to attend ... Dougal McKeafter and John Stewart.[10]

Highland soldiers at Crown Point on Lake Champlain helped the British Army to build a fort: "Field Officer for the work Major Reid. The men of the Royal Highland Regiment (the Black Watch) who have been employed in making baskets will be paid for the same."

Then, at Fort Edward, "The Royal Highlanders and Montgomery's [sic] Regiments to send as many men this afternoon at 4 o'clock as are necessary to clean [clear] the ground where the Light Infantry is to encamp. They will receive axes on applying to the store-keeper in the fort."[11]

These facts will perhaps change the mental picture many people have of Highland redcoats in eighteenth-century America. It is surely no historical accident that John Reid, the Highland officer mentioned as helping to build Crown Point, claimed land on behalf of himself and "eleven sergeants, ten corporals, and thirty-four privates who served during the war." As in the 78th, NCOs were numerous.[12] Reid, who set the words of "Garb of Old Gaul" to music, and established a professorship of music at Edinburgh University, married an American lady and owned about thirty-five thousand acres around Crown Point, though he left after the Revolution.[13]

Even Highland soldiers in the 42nd, the 77th Montgomerie's Highlanders, and the 55th, acquired forestry skills. These clansmen became woodsmen. I would like to emphasize that we are talking about the average Highland soldier in North America. A few soldiers, such as Robert Kirkwood of the 77th, were captured by the members of the First Nations and lived with them long enough to become expert frontiersmen.[14] Indeed, under Lord Howe, the 55th Regiment adapted so well to the methods made famous by Rogers' Rangers — partisan warfare, marksmanship, tracking, scouting, surviving in the forest, canoeing — that they became the model for the British Army in matters of frontier warfare.[15]

The 78th's apprenticeship in the rugged territories of North America transformed these Highland Scots into frontiersmen. The 78th was a cohesive military unit, but by 1763 the regiment was being dissolved. Consequently, many of the soldiers chose to make their break into civilian life together and decided to remain in the New World. Then, throughout the 1760s and 1770s, the veterans not only encouraged and financed new Scots immigrants; they helped season those immigrants into their new life. The success of Highland Scots in the rugged lands of the United States and Canada has been attributed to just about everything except this wilderness apprenticeship.

In *Memoirs of an American Lady*,[16] Anne Grant (1755–1838) of Laggan, Scotland, wrote about her childhood with her father, Duncan MacVicar, a Highland officer of the 55th Regiment in New York and Vermont. Duncan MacVicar received help from the Aboriginal peoples when he chose his lands. Grant writes, "For by the aid of ... the old inhabitants, and friendly Indians ... he could expect to get advantageously some lands ... which it required much local knowledge of the country to discover ... he could get information of those secluded spots here and there that were truly valuable. Accordingly, he became a consequential landholder."[17]

Anne MacVicar Grant (1755–1838) was the daughter of a Highland officer in the 55th regiment serving in North America. The family returned to Scotland just before the American Revolution and lost their lands. Anne married the Reverend Grant in Scotland, but became a widow with eight children when he died in 1800. Writing became a highly successful means of support for her family. Sir Walter Scott promoted her work partly because she wrote romantic literature about the Highlands and pre-Revolutionary America.

Highland officers seldom claimed huge tracts of land as a giant "estate" but rather selected the valuable terrain in an area. The story of Duncan McVicar indicates that Scots used their position as soldiers to enrich their life as frontier settlers in eighteenth-century America. The ability of Highland officers to obtain the best units of land for their profit did not endear them to incoming New England settlers, who resented that much of the best land was already taken. Mrs. Grant was highly critical of the New England squatters who displaced her family from their lands and forced them to return to Scotland.

Lieutenant Allan Stewart of the 78th was Anne Grant's uncle, one of the members of the 78th who can be traced through the unusual number of letters, books, diaries, memoirs, that provide stories about their lives; but the only comments on the subject of emigration refer to Lieutenant Allan Stewart. One report states: "He goes with an Intention of settling in the Lands granted him by the Government at the End of the last War [Seven Years' War]. But should the Troubles continue in America he is Determined to make the Best of his way to Boston and Offer his Services to General Gage."[18] As told in the previous chapter, Stewart took up land in North Carolina, which was unusual because the 78th did not serve there.

This author searched the *Statistical Account of Scotland*, a parish-by-parish survey of the 1790s. Not one stated that the Jacobite Rebellion prompted Highland migration. Despite this, as mentioned in the previous chapter, most historians, especially those from North America, explain Highland migration in much the following way: "Many Scots hated England.... After the Highland rebellion of 1746, tens of thousands lost their land as well."[19]

Very few of the migrants I traced appear to have been active Jacobites. Lieutenant Allan Stewart appears to be the only 78th Jacobite to have emigrated during that period. Even his Highland brother-in-law MacVicar, father of the writer Mrs. Grant, was a Hanoverian.

The 1745 Rebellion was a civil war. Even General James Murray, first British governor of Quebec, had Jacobite brothers lurking in the family cupboard, as did the James Murray who commanded the Black Watch during the Seven Years' War.[20] John Nairne of the 78th is claimed by the *Dictionary of Canadian Biography* to have had Jacobite sympathies, but having Jacobite relatives such as Lady Nairne, author of many Jacobite songs, does not necessarily mean that John Nairne was a Jacobite. During the 1745 Rebellion, Nairne was stationed with the Scots Brigade in Holland.

So, despite the views of many other historians over the years, the evidence I have uncovered suggests that most of the 78th veterans chose North America because of the economic "pull" of free land and paid passage rather than a "push" from Scotland to North America because of Jacobite sympathies.

Where Did They Take Land?

Following their victory in the Seven Years' War, the British wanted military settlements set up in Quebec's Lower St. Lawrence area to guard against any future French attacks, and also to link up their newly acquired colony of Quebec with their colony of New York. The Fraser's Highlanders had been stationed in these areas and knew how to make a living there. Circumstances — "fortune" in eighteenth-century language — placed these men in the right place at the right time.

Most Fraser's Highlanders settled on the New York-Vermont border in the former colony of New France (Vermont was a part of New

The First Settlement. Life in the woods of eastern North America was hard toil for the whole family. Sunlight streams down through the dark woods onto the cabin indicating hope for an enlightened future. (Folios Willis v.2 p. 99, McGill University, McGill Rare Books and Special Collections.)

France and became a state only after the Revolution). Scots veterans played a major role transforming this geopolitical frontier of major battles, forts, and military activity into what is now upstate New York and Vermont.

Even the New England states contested this area bitterly among themselves. New York and New Hampshire granted the same land to different people, causing mass confusion between 1763 and approximately 1790. The whole question of who controlled land from the former New France was divisive, even after the Revolution when Vermont almost joined British North America rather than the new United States. In some ways this area was the "Poland of North America"; claimed and divided but settled by forgotten Scots soldiers.

Before the Revolution, (1763 to 1775), a smaller group of 78th veterans inhabited the former New France along the St. Lawrence up to Montreal. To link up the settlements in Montreal to those in New York/ Vermont, the British encouraged the Fraser's to farm the Lake Champlain area down to Albany, a north-south axis. However, after the Revolution,

Skenes Mill in Skenesborough was founded by Major Philip Skene, whose father had taken part in the First Jacobite Rebellion in 1715. Wounded by the French at Ticonderoga, he commanded the fort at Crown Point then claimed land nearby on Lake Champlain. Skene built roads, ships, and timber mills, all of which he lost during the American Revolution. His town was renamed Whitehall, and this part of New France is now Vermont. (NY Public Library Image 1102483.)

many of the veterans migrated up Lake Champlain and the Richelieu River and along the St. Lawrence to what is now Glengarry County. This divided Quebec into Lower and Upper Canada, settlement patterns along an east-west axis. Highland Scots military settlements were then a geopolitical weather vane indicating the flow of the general population at the time. Settlement in British North America (Canada) continued on an east-west direction for over a century.

The map on page 156 indicates where the 78th veterans claimed land and is intended only as an approximate guide to 78th settlement. There were more Fraser's veterans in this area than were listed in the New York-Vermont land records for 1763–76. These areas were not entirely dominated by 78th veterans, nor were the areas entirely settled by Scots. There were, however, approximately ten to fifteen thousand Scots who moved into the New York-Vermont frontier area.

It is extremely difficult to write about the land grants that were parcelled out between 1763 and 1775 because most Scots left the region

MAP 10: 78th FRASER'S SETTLEMENT PATTERNS: 1763–1775; 1783–1812

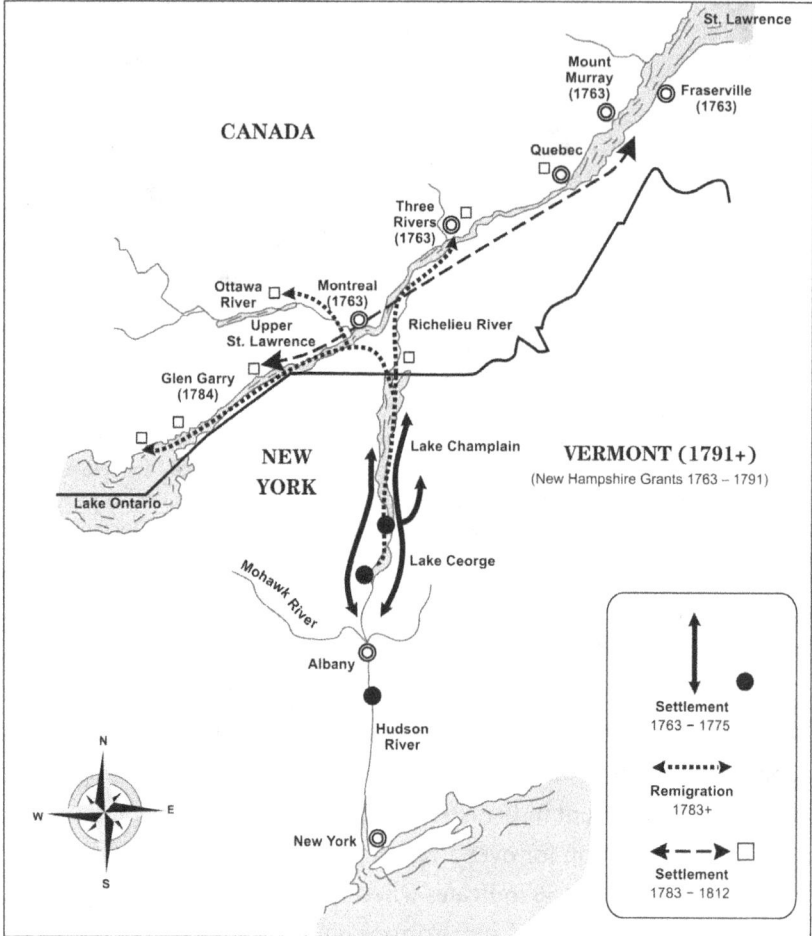

during or after the American Revolution, and records of their presence were destroyed. However, what was apparent when I examined the *Indorsed Land Papers 1643–1803* of New York and Vermont, was that a great number of Scots soldiers moved on to farms. Even though some officers received up to three thousand acres and privates only received fifty, this was a land transfer of great importance to the common soldier.

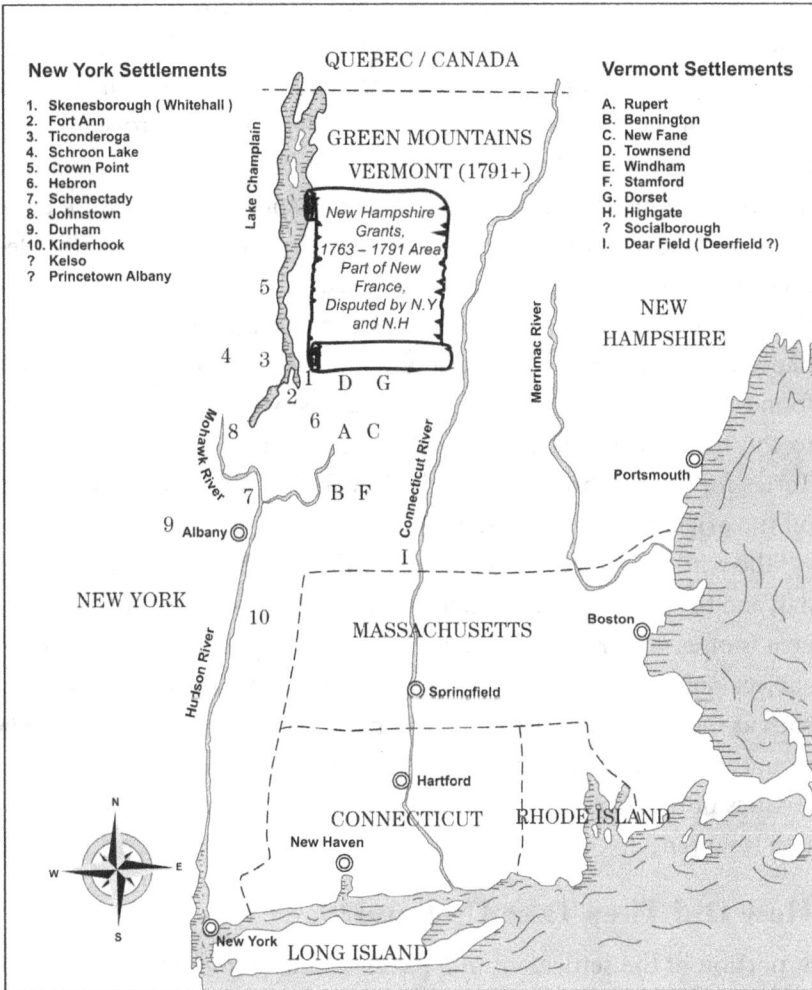

MAP 11: 78th SETTLEMENTS 1763–76

New York Settlements

1. Skenesborough (Whitehall)
2. Fort Ann
3. Ticonderoga
4. Schroon Lake
5. Crown Point
6. Hebron
7. Schenectady
8. Johnstown
9. Durham
10. Kinderhook
? Kelso
? Princetown Albany

QUEBEC / CANADA

GREEN MOUNTAINS

VERMONT (1791+)

New Hampshire
Grants,
1763 – 1791 Area
Part of New
France,
Disputed by N.Y
and N.H

Lake Champlain

Mohawk River

Merrimac River

Connecticut River

Vermont Settlements

A. Rupert
B. Bennington
C. New Fane
D. Townsend
E. Windham
F. Stamford
G. Dorset
H. Highgate
? Socialborough
I. Dear Field (Deerfield ?)

NEW
HAMPSHIRE

Portsmouth

NEW YORK

Hudson River

Albany

MASSACHUSETTS

Boston

Springfield

Hartford

CONNECTICUT   RHODE ISLAND

New Haven

New York   LONG ISLAND

Former Highland farm servants (labourers) became landowners over-
night by virtue of a redcoat and a kilt.[21]

Geographically, Highland Scots settlement in the New York-Vermont
area was more extensive and dispersed than is often stated. For instance, a
great deal of attention has been focused on the *Pearl* and the three hundred

Highlanders who settled west of Albany with William Johnson, the Scots-Irish Iroquois leader.[22] In reality, the majority of Scots Highland settlers owned land north and east of Albany during the years between 1763 and 1774. Only after the destruction of the Iroquois Confederacy (1776–83) did the immigration stream pour west of Albany rather than north.

Many of the Scots settlements in New York were destroyed during the American Revolution, and the ideological baggage that accompanies revolutions changed the evidence of Scots presence in the area. For example, Skenesborough, New York, the oldest European settlement on Lake Champlain, was renamed Whitehall, Vermont, after the war and the Scots soldier-settlers driven out.[23] Many of the 78th had settled around Rupert, Vermont, but the only oblique reference I found about them in libraries and local history associations referred to the fact that the town "was in the possession of the British and Tories for two or three years in the Revolution" and that they carried off the original official records.[24]

The anti-Scots rhetoric generated by the Revolution echoes even today, and the extent of Scots soldier-settlement in the New York-Vermont area is often underestimated. Even Bernard Bailyn's classic study of the subject only analyzes the non-military Scots settlements of Vermont, such as the Scotch-American Company's colony of Barnet, in Caledonia County.[25] However, Bailyn does acknowledge the quasi-military characteristics of the Scots-American Company, such as its bonds of association (manrent).

How Did They Take Up Land?

A portion of the settlement in New York and Vermont was led by approximately ten ex-78th officers. These officers operated a bewildering, often overlapping series of consortiums claiming land. Men of the lower ranks, and thousands of other Scots, joined with them and claimed land near the officers. For instance, Lieutenant Hugh Fraser was with several consortiums: a high-ranking group containing such soldiers as Captain Sir Henry Seton (an ex-78th officer who became aide-de-camp to General Monckton), and another group consisting of lower ranks, such as Privates John and Donald Fraser. As stated earlier, Lieutenant Fraser also brought out his famous brother-in-law, Simon McTavish, son of Lieutenant McTavish, from Scotland to claim land. In addition to all that, Lieutenant Fraser also helped the *Pearl* passengers from Glengarry to settle in New York State.

Clan ties overlapped with military ties in these Highland land consortiums. Campbells from various regiments claimed the carrying places (where cargo had to be taken by land between Lake Champlain and Lake George) near Fort Ticonderoga. In addition to officers in the three Highland regiments, Highland officers from other regiments, the marines, the navy, and the artillery, co-operated in these land consortiums.

Table 5: Approximate Number of 78th Veterans Claiming New York/Vermont Land			
Year	Veterans	Year	Veterans
1763	3	1770	6
1764	16	1771	21
1765	16	1772	8
1766	8	1773	1
1767	11	1774	1
1768	5	1775	0
1769	1	1776	0

Calendar of NY Colonial Manuscripts: Endorsed Land Papers 1643–1803

Yet there were clusters of soldiers who arrived separate from the officer-led groups. For example, Sergeant Duncan Weir, Private Alexander MacDonald, and Private Duncan McArthur, all of the 78th, petitioned for land on their own near Dear Field on the west side of the Connecticut River in 1767.[26] Sergeant Weir had been discharged in Quebec, and the other two had gone back to Scotland in 1763. These men chose an unusual site near the river rather than near Lake Champlain, where most of the soldiers settled. Perhaps Weir had found unusually good land, or they found work in the area while they built their farms. Corporal Roderick McLeod, Donald Stewart, and sixteen others claimed land on the valuable waterway leading from Lake Champlain to the Hudson River. The land warrant was also granted to Lieutenant McTavish of the 78th, who was not there to claim it. According to the surveyor's map, not only does Corporal McLeod have more land than the sixteen private soldiers, but he owns the falls where a timber mill could be erected.

When Did They Settle the Land?

The 78th Fraser's Highlanders did not move en masse onto frontier land at a time and a place determined by military authorities. The *Indorsed Land Papers 1643–1803* show clusters of Highland soldiers moving gradually onto farms from 1763 to 1775. The evidence suggests that, by and large, the men chose where, when, and with whom they settled. They seemed to have held other jobs to support themselves and squatted before formally claiming their land. Yet the New York and Vermont land records have to be treated with caution. These lists are sometimes inaccurate, contradictory, incomplete, and misspelled. Indeed, the often-bizarre spelling of Scots names in the United States arose at this time as land agents struggled with illiterate Gaelic speakers to record their landholdings. Names such as Calhoun replaced Colquhoun and Mackag, McCullock, McChombick, McKachern, McKann, and McKlennon were first used.[27] Large groups of soldier-settlers are inadequately recorded. Consequently, the chart made from the *Indorsed Land Papers* underestimates the number of veterans who claimed land. Some Fraser's were drafted into the Royal Americans in 1763, after which they then claimed land as members of that regiment.

Who Settled North America?

When I analyzed those Fraser's Highlanders who emigrated between the years 1763 and 1775, I found that approximately 10 to 15 percent of the officers in the Fraser's emigrated, but the proportion of sergeants and corporals was a staggering 85 to 90 percent. Emigration was primarily a phenomenon of the non-commissioned officer group in the Fraser's Highlanders. Thirty-five sergeants, twenty-eight corporals, and Drum Major Kennedy took their sword-money in North America. In total, sixty-four — almost 40 percent of the 170 who stayed in 1763 —were non-commissioned men. In addition, some of those who claimed New York land were NCOs who re-migrated back from Scotland immediately with their families. These men received two hundred acres each, compared to the enlisted men's fifty acres, so economics probably accounts for the large proportion of NCOs.

Military Ranks Among Fraser's Highland Emigrants

Officers, including Sir Henry Seton, were often promoted to other regiments, but continued to co-operate with their former comrades in 78th emigration ventures after the war. Consequently, there are different ways to estimate the proportion of the officers who took up land. However, although the majority of these military migrants to North America were private soldiers, as many as one-third were from strata above, demonstrating that the upper and middle social groups of Highland society were emigrating along with the clansmen. Officers formed less than 10 percent of the 78th Fraser's Regiment at any one time, but it can be argued that Highland migrants in North America were successful at this time, because many of them were educated and ambitious people who wanted land. They valued the Crown because it gave them security and upward mobility because of that land.

There has been very little written about NCOs as immigrants; however, Highland migration to North America was dominated statistically if not socially by this class of Highland society. The information I managed to trace about these men gave the impression of very formidable settlers indeed. It is perhaps significant that a sergeant, James Thompson, left as testament information about the 78th Highlanders recorded by his son — some of the most comprehensive stories available about this regiment.

James was six foot two and had fought heroically during the American Revolution. He is mentioned by many historical figures in their writings, and his massive four-storey stone house still stands today in the Upper

James Thompson's grand four-storey house in Quebec City was an unusually large property for an eighteenth-century sergeant who was comparatively low in military, economic, and social rank. Successful Fraser's soldiers such as Thompson, not failed Fraser clansmen, were the motor of Highland emigration 1763 to 1812. (Photograph by Sam Allison, June 2009.)

Town of Quebec City. It is difficult to know how typical Thompson was among the men of this regiment. However, his life of great upward social mobility was not unusual for Highland soldiers in North America.

Other Fraser's NCOs succeeded in bettering their lives after emigrating. Sergeant Lachlan Smith, for example, is supposed to have contracted five marriages and eventually became the owner of a seigneury in Quebec. Sergeant Sinclair, who had been a drummer boy at Culloden for King George, became an officer and later died a magistrate. After a shot in the head ended his military career, Sergeant John Fraser became the first and most respected teacher of English in Quebec.

And, while he did not emigrate, it is perhaps significant that the best-selling author in the 78th was also a sergeant: Donald MacLeod.

Turning to the officer group, I suggest that, although they were not statistically important, they did contribute greatly to their new homeland. Men such as John Nairne and Malcolm and Alexander Fraser in Quebec, John Fraser in Montreal, Sir Henry Seton and Hugh Fraser in upstate New York, and Allan Stewart in North Carolina made an impact, socially, economically, and politically. Indeed, in contrast to other waves of immigrants, Highland Scots had representation at the very highest social levels right from their first presence in North America. Consequently, Highland success on this continent is demonstrated by ex-officers such as Montreal judge Captain John Fraser (1729–95), who, in a not-too-egalitarian age, quite cheerfully — and often against the evidence — ruled in favour of his countrymen.[28]

Judge Fraser had been educated in France, and at some point fell afoul of the British authorities, losing his position in 1777. He was, however, immensely popular and respected by French Canadians, fifty of whom signed a petition to have Fraser's judgeship restored, citing his knowledge of French law, language, and people.[29]

These men, along with other officers from the 78th, had a significant impact on their adoptive countries, partly because they fought their way into the governing elites in both Quebec and Vermont–New York. In Quebec,[30] for example, they formed the nucleus of the "French Party" — spokesmen for the French Catholics, but a misnomer, because the group was led by the Scot Adam Mabane. While the members benefited themselves, at the same time they helped preserve the laws, language, religion, and rights of French Canadians. They sided with Governor Murray, then with Carleton (Lord Dorchester), against the majority of British-American traders in the colony. Through these efforts, the officers helped bridge the French-English divide in the new Canada.

The high social status of these military veterans mattered in the eighteenth century. The French Party had transformed what was potentially a race conflict into a political conflict by the time Lower Canada's (Quebec) Parliament opened in 1791. The group then helped to transfer the allegiance of French Canadians from New France to Lower Canada.

During this time, some of the men, both privates and officers, from the 78th, married locals and some of their descendants became French rather than English-speaking Canadians. These men lived alongside one another and French Canadians regardless of previous social status. Consequently, the British conquest of Quebec after 1763 never developed into a caste system with a British ruling elite. The Constitutional Act of 1791 had established an advancing democracy in Lower Canada where both French and English settlers were represented. The United States and Britain resumed close ties after the American Revolution, but France and the new Quebec cut themselves off from each other demographically, culturally, intellectually, and politically. In the wars of the French Revolution (1789–1815) many French Canadians even fought for Britain against France.

It is ironic that the 78th Fraser's Highlanders have been remembered, if at all, for toppling New France in 1759. The postwar role that the veterans played in the building of a new Canada has been largely ignored. The loyalty of some French Canadians to the Crown, and the neutrality of most French Canadians in the American Revolution backed by France, had immense consequences for the history of North America. The veterans of the 78th formed the backbone of the military defence of their new colony during the American Revolution. Less obviously, the political failure of the American revolutionaries in "French" Canada can also be partly attributed to these veterans.

How Did They Migrate?

After 1763, as I emphasized earlier, clusters of Highland soldiers coordinated moves with their families to North America. Reverend William Fraser described emigration in the 1790s: "Soldiers … have migrated to North America … and sent home money to their aged parents. By comparing their present with their former condition in this country, they have done much to excite others to follow their example."[31]

Soldier-settlers who arrived alone or stayed on after their service had ended were joined later by family and friends because they wrote to them extolling the virtues of making the move. Members of the educated officer class played an important role in this process. While some scholars challenge the notion of high educational levels among Highland Scots, the 78th officer corps and their NCOs appear to have been much better educated than their contemporaries in English, French, or American regiments. Certainly no regiment, British or French, had anything remotely approaching the bilingualism found among Fraser's officers, several of whom had been better educated in the French language than their French counterparts.[32] Sergeant Thompson was scandalized that one Fraser's NCO was illiterate and thought he should never have been promoted because he was unable to read or write orders. Chevalier Johnstone in Louisbourg and John Nairne in Quebec recorded their annoyance that many of the French officers and seigneurs were unable to read and write.

Arguably, higher levels of literacy help explain how this military group succeeded in different parts of North America over a period of many years. Perhaps high levels of education among some soldiers may simply have reflected the absence of other economic opportunities in the Highlands for educated people. Whatever the reason, the men of the 78th appear to have left behind more letters, books, diaries, and memoirs than their contemporaries in other British, American, or French regiments. The works of Ensign Malcolm Fraser, Captain (later Judge) John Fraser, Captain Nairne, Sergeant Donald MacLeod, and Major James Clephane are still worth reading 250 years later. While Sergeant Thompson's stories, dictated to his son, were recorded long after the war and contain some slight inaccuracies, they are powerful descriptions of regimental life. Many of the American letters of the time are interesting, but most are written at an elementary level, whereas those written by the Fraser's would be graded at a secondary or university level of English. A comparatively high level of literacy and numeracy (arising from the army paying cash to soldiers) characterized both the officer corps and the NCOs of the 78th.

Highland Social Characteristics

The presence of so many educated people meant that these migrants were linked by letter to their far off home country over a long time. In contrast to other ethnic groups, the Highland Scots maintained "their contacts with their home communities, maintained with extraordinary persistence, kept their ethnic identity alive and the recruitment of their fellow countrymen continuous."[33] The migration of the Fraser's Highlanders was part of a process; a flow of veterans who migrated then re-migrated over changing times to changing places from 1759–1812.

Contemporaries in Britain, including Samuel Johnson, attribute the prevalence of Highland migration to America after 1763 to the exchange of letters between those who were already in the New World and those still living back home in Scotland. The authors of these letters were, by and large, Highland soldiers. *The Statistical Account of Scotland,* written in the 1790s about everyday life, asked ministers across the country to describe their parishes. Minister after minister in the Highlands emphasized the importance of "friends (relatives) in America" writing letters to persuade Highlanders to migrate. Letters united relatives and friends even after many years of separation, which led Highlanders to being clustered together in settlements.

Politically, Highland migrants were overwhelmingly opposed to the American Revolution. Many historians (and historical fiction writers) have explained this loyalty to the Crown as a subservient feudal Highland attachment to the monarchy, their "rightful king" as Sir Walter Scott labelled it. In fact, the backbone of Highland immigration was the en masse arrival of sergeants and corporals (NCOs), all of whom had received substantial land grants. The NCOs were living proof that fighting for the British Army brought major rewards. This middle-class upwardly mobile group of NCOs were role models who encouraged lower-class Highland soldiers to support the Crown in opposing the Revolution.

The fact that the 78th officers were receiving half-pay from the Crown obviously helped the royalist cause in that had they opposed the Crown, they would have lost this money. However, the added presence of a large number of NCOs helped those half-pay Highland officers to enlist the formidable pool of soldier-settlers, most of whom had obtained substantial free land from the King. The willingness of these Highland settlers to fight for the officers and the Crown may have come down to the fact that many of these men wanted to secure even more land for themselves and their families.

Ideologically, sergeants and corporals have been the bedrock of the British Army. As a social group, NCOs were incredibly loyal to their regiment, king, and country. Throughout British history, the sergeants and corporals were the ones most likely to fight to the last man and the least likely to surrender to the enemy. In turn, Highland loyalty to the Crown in the 1770s is not so surprising when we look at the presence of so many NCOs among the migrants. Those who emigrated represented the very heart of the 78th Foot and probably the heart of the various other Scottish regiments, too. Asking men such as Colour Sergeant Sinclair to rebel against their king and country would have been futile.

The rhetoric generated by the American Revolution distorted the migratory story of the Scots. After the Thirteen Colonies became the United States, most of the Fraser's soldier-settlers moved to Canada, back to Scotland, [34] or even to Ireland. [35] Many veterans who had returned to Scotland after the Seven Years' War were reactivated in order to fight for the British in the Revolution, then subsequently took up free land in Canada.

The importance of NCO settlement fits the various accounts of Highland emigration of the 1763 to 1775 period. While the tacksmen, or officer class, often organized groups of Highland migrants, the evidence suggests that those ranked slightly below these men in the social scale were also important in explaining high levels of emigration. Many of the sergeants, such as James Sinclair — a "standard bearer" as he proudly claimed — were upwardly mobile because of the army. Other sergeants, such as James Thompson, appear to have been from the "sunken gentry"; that is, his family had been wealthy, but had fallen on hard times. Consequently, the men who had fallen out of the tacksman class, such as Thompson, and the men who aspired to that class, such as Sinclair, played a part in shaping emigration patterns.

Emigration as popularly envisioned — one move to a permanent farm in North America — is a misnomer in describing the adventurous, migratory, military lives led by the Fraser's Highlanders. As soldiers, then later as veterans, these people traversed the North Atlantic to a remarkable degree. [36] It is difficult to enumerate, let alone classify, the migratory patterns that characterized these men. Highland Scots soldiers established a land relationship with North America that lasted well into the nineteenth century.

Ensign Malcolm Fraser of the 78th described the fall of New France thus: "This has been a greater acquisition to the British Empire than all that England has gained by Conquest ..."[37] This pride in their achievements is partly explained if we see Highland actions in the context of other great wars. The veterans of the Battle of Quebec in 1759 were held in just as much regard by their contemporaries as the veterans of Waterloo, Gettysburg, the Charge of the Light Brigade, Vimy Ridge, or the Normandy landings. The survivors of the Black Watch at Ticonderoga were held in just as much regard as the survivors of Dieppe, Dunkirk, or Pearl Harbour. Psychologically, Highland Scots in America at the start of the Revolution were the victors at Quebec, not the vanquished of Culloden. A confident belief in their right to settle after 1759 explains their actions and impact on North America. These Scots were in the New World because they had fought and won on the Plains of Abraham. They had climbed the wet, steep cliffs in the dark to win this land. They had suffered huge casualties at Ticonderoga. To paraphrase George Orwell, Highland settlers had mixed blood and labour for their land. They cleared it of the French as well as of trees. Consequently, when George Washington in the republican cause asserted a right to America, the Highland Scots asserted that they too had a right to this land. Highlanders were not just fighting other people's wars in North America as is often claimed. Highland Scots were fighting for *their* America.

8

Redcoats, Revolution, and Re-Migration

Scotch and Foreign mercenaries invade and destroy us.
— Thomas Jefferson (*American Scripture*, Pauline Maier)

The American Revolution (1776–83) was a revolt against taxation to pay for the British Army and the Seven Years' War. Not surprisingly, Highland soldier-settlers sided with the cause that paid the army. The Revolution, although a conflict of "enlightened" ideals, became a vicious civil war and a European war.[1] In this chapter, I will examine why so many veterans re-enlisted for the King's Shilling then re-migrated from the new United States to Canada. I suggest that Highlanders as soldiers rather than as clansmen were the motor of Scots migration. The Jacobites, Hanoverians, and mercenaries of the 78th Fraser's Highlanders morphed into frontier landholders after the Seven Years' War. In turn, these veteran soldier-settlers became a core culture of Loyalism during the American Revolution because it was to their economic and political benefit to support the status quo.

Re-Enlistment

The officers from the disbanded 78th raised new regiments for British service in the American Revolutionary War of 1776–83. Ten of the

Table 6: Military Careers of Former 78th Officers Recruited in Britain		
Rank in 78th (1756–63)	**Rank in American Revolution (1776–83)**	**Post-American Revolution**
Colonel Simon Fraser	Colonel 71st (Fraser's Highlanders)	Major-General
Captain Archibald Campbell	Lieutenant-Colonel 71st (Fraser's Highlanders) Major-General	Governor
Lieutenant John MacDonnell	Captain 71st	Major-General
Lieutenant Simon Fraser	Major 71st	Colonel 133rd Highland Regiment
Ensign Harry Munro	Captain 71st	
Ensign James MacKenzie	Major 73rd	
Major John Campbell	Colonel 74th (Argyle Highlanders)	
Captain Ranald MacDonell	Major 74th	Colonel
Captain Simon Fraser	Brigadier-General (killed at Saratoga, NY)	
Major James Abercrombie	Colonel 22nd (killed at Bunker Hill, MA)	
Ensign Charles Sinclair	Lieutenant 22nd (Light Dragoons)	Captain 22nd
Captain Hugh Montgomery	Major (Argyle Fencibles) Earl of Eglinton	Colonel Western Lothian Fencibles
Ensign Duncan Cameron	Captain 43rd	Colonel 91st
Captain-Lieutenant Donald McBean	Captain 10th Foot	
Ensign William Robertson	Captain 10th Foot	Lieutenant-Colonel
Ensign Lachlan MacPherson	Captain (Corps of Foot in Africa) died 1760s	
Ensign Archibald Fraser		Major Glengarry Fencibles
Lieutenant Archibald MacAllister	Captain 35th Foot	Lieutenant-Colonel 35th Foot
Lieutenant Alexander Fraser	Major British Marksmen	Lieutenant-Colonel 45th Foot

Table 7: Military Careers of Former 78th Officers Recruited in North America		
Rank in 78th (1756–63)	**Rank In American Revolution (1776–83)**	**Post American Revolution**
Captain John Nairne	Major 84th (Royal Highland Emigrants)	Lieutenant-Colonel
Lieutenant Alexander Fraser	Captain 84th (Royal Highland Emigrants)	
Ensign Malcolm Fraser	Captain 84th (Royal Highland Emigrants)	
Lieutenant Allan Stewart	Colonel (North Carolina Highlanders)	Lieutenant-Colonel
Lieutenant Alexander Fraser	Captain (Br. Marksmen) Major	Lieutenant-Colonel 45th Foot
Sergeant Lachlan MacDonald	Lieutenant Caledonian Volunteers (Tarleton's Regiment)	
Sergeant James Sinclair	Quartermaster Brit. Merchant Regiment, QC	Magistrate Trois-Rivières, QC
Ensign Ken McCulloch	Captain British Legion (Tarleton's Regiment)	

thirteen new British regiments raised were Highland ones and evolved into the Highland Light Infantry, the Seaforth Highlanders, and the Cameron Highlanders, some of the most famous and effective military units in British history. The mass promotions in the two right columns in the following diagrams indicate that the 78th was a regiment of career soldiers, not a clan retinue raised by the chief of the Frasers of Lovat.

The veterans of the 78th who had remained in North America, and whom I managed to trace, enlisted in various regiments. Many had similar names to those in other regiments such as the Black Watch, which made identification difficult, and so the accompanying tables underestimate the numbers of 78th veterans.

Despite the larger Irish and immigrant English populations in North America at the time of the Revolution, only two Irish regiments and no specifically English regiments existed. Unlike the Scots, most of the Irish and English migrants were indentured, so had difficulties leaving their service to enlist for military service on either side of the conflict.

Most 78th soldier-settlers re-enlisted into military service on the side of the British when war broke out, especially the common soldiers I tracked. Indeed, this author was unable to find any ex-78th veterans who fought for the Patriots. Unlike the 1745 Rebellion, the American Revolution did not divide the veterans of the 78th, it united them: "The virtual unanimity of the Scots … found no parallel elsewhere."[2] There were a few Scots, such as the poet Robert Burns, who supported the Revolution, but the Scots, more than the English, overwhelmingly opposed the rebels.

It is beyond the scope of this book to discuss the fighting in detail. The British lost, and the Highland Tory Loyalists suffered "political failure, losing not only their argument, their war, and their place in American society, but even their proper place in history."[3] The United States nationalism that wrote the Highland Scots out of American history will be explored in detail in a later chapter, but suffice to say, the reasons the Scots fought, their success in some battles, their treatment by the Patriots, and their impact on Canada have often been overlooked.

The Revolution brought great hardship to Scottish immigrants whose settlements were attacked. Many Scots fell victim to Patriot mobs, and those who were not arrested, imprisoned, or killed often had to flee their homes. New York Loyalists, unlike North Carolina Loyalists (many of whom were Scots) had the ability to flee to the comparative safety of Canada. Some prisoners, including a Captain Simon Fraser (c.1727–79), who was not in the 78th, died after being imprisoned underground in a copper mine.

The large military defeats suffered by the Highland Scots in North Carolina at Moore's Creek (1776) and King's Mountain (1780) have coloured American history writing about Highland Scotland "with its Celtic impetuosity, its clannishness, its yearning for the heroic to the point of foolhardiness."[4] At Moore's Creek, it is true that Highlanders foolishly charged with claymores against Patriots with rifles. At King's Mountain, it is also true that Colonel Patrick Ferguson (1744–80), attached to the 71st Fraser's Highlanders, died leading an inexperienced militia unit that had been surrounded by a superior force of Patriots. However, in general, throughout the war, Highland soldiers were not clannish or foolishly heroic, but modern and highly professional, especially in Quebec, New York, and in the southern state of Georgia: "They were to become perhaps the finest infantry in the war against America ... the 71st Foot (Fraser's Highlanders) would see more action in America than any other British regiment."[5]

Since many of the 71st Fraser's Highlanders, including their Colonel Archibald Campbell, had served in North America with the 78th Fraser's Highlanders, it is not surprising that they were highly effective in the Revolutionary War. As for Colonel Patrick Ferguson, he created the only great technical breakthrough of this war, the invention of a workable breech-loading rifle. In 1776, Ferguson patented a rifle-barreled gun that could be loaded through its chamber far more quickly than muskets or rifles loaded down through the muzzle. Rifles that propel bullets, rather than musket balls, are far more accurate and powerful than muskets. However, Ferguson's rifle died with him because it cost four times as much as a musket, and in the days before factories, took much longer to make. The idea evolved but was only resurrected for large-scale military use in the American Civil War (1861–65) then the Franco-Prussian War (1870–71).

At least two 78th veterans became successful British generals during this war. Simon Fraser, who spoke French to the sentries from the boats in 1759, helped to drive out the invading Patriots from Quebec City and led the British to victory at Three Rivers in 1776. Fraser's experiences were typical of how clan and military networks intertwined in the story of the Highland Scots in the New World. At Fort Ticonderoga in New York, Fraser met his cousin, Mrs. McNeal, who was with the unfortunate Jane McCrea when the latter was killed and scalped by Natives in the employ of the British.[6] Fraser also received information from James MacIntosh, a veteran soldier-settler of the 78th, that a high mountain overlooked the fort.[7] This led Fraser to place cannon on the mountain, which led to the capture of Ticonderoga in the spring of 1777. As Fraser was reputedly the brains of the British force, his death on October 7, 1777, at the Battle of Saratoga in New York, may have contributed greatly to the eventual British defeat.

Although Colonel Simon Fraser of the 78th raised the 71st Fraser's Highlanders, he did not accompany them to America. The 71st was led by Lieutenant Colonel Archibald Campbell (1739–91), who was captured by the Patriots in 1776 after a battle in Boston Harbor. The British

Army had abandoned Boston but did not inform the navy, so Campbell and much of the 71st were captured when they landed in Boston from Britain.[8] Eventually, the Patriot leader Ethan Allen was exchanged for Campbell, who was then promoted to major-general and went on to capture Savannah and much of Georgia with the 71st Fraser's Highlanders. He also stepped in as interim governor of the state and re-established the legislative assembly, which lasted for two years in Augusta, Georgia's capital. Campbell struck a severe blow to the Patriot cause and claimed he had torn a star and stripe from the Patriot flag.

Not surprisingly then, after the fall of British power, the state of Georgia passed into law in 1782 a measure stating that "no Person a Native of Scotland shall be permitted or allowed to emigrate into this state ... or to carry on Commerce or other trade ... but every such Person being a Native of Scotland shall within three days after his arrival within this state be apprehended and Committed to Gaol."[9] Hence, Campbell's successes earned him everlasting anonymity in the story of the Revolution as told by generations of American historians.

The Royal Highland Emigrants (RHE), composed of many 78th veterans, was another highly successful regiment at a key stage early in the war. The Patriot-Whigs led by Generals Montgomery and Benedict Arnold captured Montreal in the late fall of 1775, and soon after began a siege of Quebec City. In a blinding snowstorm on the last night of the year, the Royal Highland Emigrants killed General Montgomery, wounded Arnold, captured hundreds of enemy troops, and drove the attacking Patriots back. Yet, it is Montgomery and Arnold who are remembered, not the veterans from the 78th.

Sergeant James Thompson of the 78th buried Montgomery and kept his sword as a trophy. John Nairne, with the help of a French Canadian, captured an entire Patriot regiment after killing its colonel. Nairne's letter to his sister on May 14, 1776, illustrates his attitude toward the Revolution: "It is certainly a disagreeable necessity to be obliged to put one another to death, especially those speaking the same language and dressed in the same manner as ourselves. These mad people had a large piece of white linen or paper upon their foreheads with the words 'Liberty or Death' wrote upon it."[10] Nairne thought the Patriots were mad fanatics who had to be defeated for the sake of the realm. He deeply regretted fighting against men who spoke his language and who had been brought up as he had.[11] Nairne was a brave if ruthless professional soldier, but he harboured little ideological or nationalistic hatred of his opponents.

John Richardson, the Highland Scots founder of the Canadian banking system, blamed the two Jacobite rebellions for holding back Scotland, which may explain why so many Scots at that time opposed the American rebellion. The Patriot rebels of 1776 believed that after they had driven the hated British out, they would create a perfect utopia based on Liberty and Equality. But Nairne and other veterans who could be labelled Scots of the Enlightenment were "consummate realists who imagined no … utopias crafted by man…. They believed in common sense: the innate power common to all human beings…. A perfect society was impossible."[12] However, many American historians would probably disagree that Nairne's views reflected those of the average Highlander. For instance, in his Pulitzer Prize–winning book, the great American historian D. Fischer states that Scottish regiments' "writings show that they despised the American rebels and the Revolutionary cause."[13] Fischer does not explain that some Highlanders "despised the American rebels" because some Highlanders abhorred slavery and prejudice against the Aboriginal population. Historians have failed to analyze the range of views held by Highland opponents of the Revolution.

The actions of two other veterans of the 78th indicate some of these "enlightened" perspectives. As stated earlier, Lieutenant Allan Stewart became colonel of an African-American regiment of escaped slaves: the Black Pioneers. Information about this unit is quite sparse, however, and little is known about its actual size, actions, and movements, though it is known to have been active in Pennsylvania, New York, and Nova Scotia.

A second veteran of the 78th, Alexander Fraser, who canoed down the Mississippi from Fort Pitt after the Seven Years' War, also operated with the Revolution's "internal enemies." Fraser, who was attached to the Indian Department, coordinated a formidable ranger unit of French Canadians, Scots frontier Loyalists, and First Nations fighters. He "frequently dressed as they did, and covered his face with war-paint."[14]In brief the Highland military culture, loyalism to the Crown, and their unique collaboration with both the First Nations and African Americans, has been overlooked or severely criticized by many historians over the years.

Why 78th Veterans Took the King's Shilling in the Revolution

On April 3, 1775, Allan MacLean, an ex-Jacobite and ex-mercenary with the Scots Brigade in the Netherlands[15] was authorized by King George III to enlist "our subjects who have at different times emigrated from the North West parts of North Britain [Scotland] and have transported themselves, with their families, to New York." The recruiting poster promised: "Each soldier to have two hundred acres of land in any province in North America he shall think proper. Each married man gets fifty acres for his wife and fifty for each child on the same terms."[16]

Notice the major incentives for married soldiers. "The Promised Land," as it was referred to by Highland soldiers of the time, constituted a huge increase from the fifty acres awarded to private soldiers after the Seven Years' War. The proven ability to grant land was an important military asset held by the Crown. Land ownership was an important economic step up in the eighteenth century and explains the huge enlistment of Scottish soldiers between 1776 and 1783.

Historians have emphasized that, culturally and politically, Highlanders were taking the King's Shilling. However, the story of the 78th clearly shows that Highlanders had been supporting the King and taking his shilling since the Seven Years' War and continued to do so up until the War of 1812. Hence, Highland and Lowland Scots were a core culture of Loyalism during the American Revolution, though primarily for reasons of self-interest. Lowland Scots believed that Virginians were trying to renege on their substantial debts to Scots tobacco factors. (Glasgow at that time was the world's biggest tobacco port, importing

The Arrival of Captain John Nairne at Murray Bay, Quebec, 1761, by C. W. Jefferys. John Nairne of the 78th received extensive land grants for military service in the Seven Years' and American Revolutionary Wars. This twentieth-century print shows Nairne and other Highland soldiers moving on to his seigneury. Nairne started settling in Quebec even before the Treaty of Paris (1763) ceded New France to Britain. (Library and Archives Canada, C 040563K.)

tobacco from Virginia then re-exporting it to the rest of Europe.) Scotland was a poor but economically aware nation, and fought hard to keep its share of America, for both King and shilling.

In the original version of the Declaration of Independence, Thomas Jefferson wrote that King George sent "not only soldiers of our common [English] blood, but Scotch and foreign mercenaries to invade and destroy us." A newspaper of the time lists mercenary soldiers as: "Hessians, Hanoverians, Mechlenburghers, Scotch Hollanders [Scots Brigade in the Netherlands], and Scotch Highlanders" who were being sent to fight the rebels.[17] Implications about the Scots being mercenaries, as suggested by newspaper articles of the time and by Jefferson's statements, have largely been ignored by historians. Blind Highland loyalty to the King is a later construct in history writing.

Highland economic and ideological reasons for supporting the King overlap. As Scottish historian Nial Ferguson points out, the Revolution was not a "straightforward fight between heroic Patriots and wicked Nazi-like redcoats."[18] The Revolution was an intellectual civil war, "one kind of Enlightenment in conflict with another."[19] This was a conflict of good and bad principles distributed between both sides. Adam Smith, author of *The Wealth of Nations* and opponent of slavery and the American Revolution, summed up the Highland ideology during this war when he wrote that a philosopher is not so different to a street porter.[20] By stating that "a man's a man for all that," Smith was saying that African Americans, Aboriginals, French Canadians, Jews, and Scots were not so different. This was just as radical an idea in the eighteenth century as anything Jefferson wrote.

As was pointed out earlier, the Scots Enlightenment urged the "freeing" of clansmen by establishing a cash relationship to chiefs. Not surprisingly, Smith and others advocated the destruction of the plantation system by changing slaves into paid employees who would be more productive. Smith was a radical reformer who opposed the Jacobite and American Rebellions because, he said, they destroyed the wealth of the "nations" — that is, of ordinary people. Smith advocated capitalist relationships to free ordinary people from clan servitude in the Old World and from slavery in the New. The King's Shilling established Highlanders in North America as capitalist farmers rather than as clansmen renting land from their chiefs.

Conflicting Ideologies

By the time of the Revolution, the huge success and cost of the Seven Years' War had transformed the ideologies of Englishmen on both sides of the Atlantic. The removal of the French threat meant that the Thirteen Colonies no longer needed help from Britain to expand north and west on the continent on lands occupied by Aboriginal peoples. The colonists began to think of themselves as Americans destined to move to the lands they regarded as "empty." By the 1770s, these new "Americans" were blaming the British for the Seven Years' War, and objected to paying for it. In Patriot ideology, the huge war debt was placed firmly on the other side of the Atlantic.

The addition of New France and Florida to the empire meant that Britain was responsible for French Canadians, Spaniards, and Aboriginal allies in what was now a British North America, from Hudson Bay in the north down through the Thirteen Colonies to Florida in the south. The British insisted on controlling these new lands from across the Atlantic, yet also maintained that the colonists should help pay the new debt. Simply put, the English-Americans and the English-Britons were unable to share the cost-benefits of the Seven Years' War to their mutual satisfaction; the result, revolution.

The colonists evolved from Englishmen of the Thirteen Colonies into rebels of thirteen independent states, and finally into Americans of thirteen United States. What did the Scots have to do with this process? Well, the Scots, in fact, played a disastrous role in trying to keep the Englishmen of the Thirteen Colonies within the new post–Seven Years' War colonial system. Scots intervention in the Seven Years' War itself changed English perspectives. The Fraser's charge was linked in the public mind with the "Death of Wolfe" so that the British not just the English wept as they triumphed at Quebec. Partly as a result of the Scottish contribution to a sad but overwhelming victory, the English were beginning to slowly see themselves more as Britons. The postwar idea of "Britishness" meant that hungry Scots were given influential posts on both sides of the Atlantic: "In the uncertain aftermath of the Seven Years' War, Scots played a leading part in making British imperialism what it was."[21]

Progressive-minded Scots on both sides of the Atlantic were changing their world. In the 1760s, James Murray, first British governor of Quebec, implemented policies of conciliating French Catholics. This enraged the English colonists, who saw the Quebec Act passed in the British Parliament and which established Catholic rights as one of the "intolerable acts" right up there with the Stamp Act.[22] In England, the Somerset decision of 1772 by Judge William Murray (Lord Mansfield, a Scot) used habeas corpus to free fourteen thousand slaves without compensation to their masters.[23] Knowledge that Englishmen in England could no longer legally own slaves travelled across the Atlantic and alarmed "Englishmen" in America. The new idea that England was free of slavery, according to the *Virginia Gazette*, was "a notion now too prevalent among the negroes, greatly to the vexation and prejudice of their masters."[24] Another Scot, William Campbell, as the new royal governor of South Carolina, raised the ire of white Carolinians when he tried to save a possibly innocent freed black man from hanging and burning for planning a slave insurrection.[25] John Murray, Earl of Dunmore, the new royal governor of Virginia, provoked massive outrage among "Englishmen" in the colonies when he threatened to free the slaves held by rebel Patriots in 1775.[26] Murray's Proclamation, according to South Carolina Patriot leader Edward Rutledge, "was more effectual in working 'an eternal separation between Great Britain and the Colonies ... than any other expedient.'"[27] The rights of Protestants and slave-holders were being redefined by pushy Scots on both side of the Atlantic. Progressive Scots convinced many reactionary and religious colonials that they were Americans rather than Englishmen. By 1776 the revolutionaries had reasons to oppose the British legislature, British common law, the British King, and their British appointed governors.

In the Revolution, Highland redcoats undermined slavery in practice by treating African Americans as free, if not quite equal, people, and of course the British allied themselves with the Aboriginal peoples during the war. Consequently, the Patriots believed genuinely that the British had "violated their rights as Englishmen, and that this was part of a broader effort to impair their liberties and make them slaves."[28]

Duane Meyer, an American historian, writes about colonials: "But as Englishmen they did protest what they considered to be denials of their rights"[29] the most famous right being no taxation without representation. According to Jefferson, Englishmen in America had established a civil society under state legislatures free and independent of the British Parliament. The Patriots considered their actions justified because their elected assemblies followed the letter and spirit of the English Constitution every bit as much as the British Parliament.

We can then interpret the root causes of the Revolution by using the idea of original intent; that is, what the people of the time really meant.

Arguably, Jefferson's original intent was to say that Englishmen in the Thirteen Colonies were equal to Englishmen in England. The great slogans of the Revolution originally meant "We [Englishmen] hold these truths to be self-evident, all [Englishmen] are created equal," and "No taxation [of Englishmen] without representation [by Englishmen]."[30] Seeing the Revolution as a movement of Englishmen, for Englishmen by Englishmen in America, explains why the non-Englishmen in America (Scots, Aboriginal people, African Americans, French Canadians, Germans, Quakers, and Jews) by and large were not enthusiastic supporters of the Revolution.

At the end of the Seven Years' War, escaped slaves were returned to each side and the surrender terms in Montreal had a clause guaranteeing the right of French Canadians to keep slaves. Slavery in British North America continued unchanged until the American Revolutionary War (1776–83). British policy at this time allowed escaped slaves to be freed if they fought for the British. Those who fled their masters before the peace at the end of the war were treated as free people and were taken to Canada. The Revolution also involved a huge slave rebellion against the Revolutionaries. The British did not fight the Revolution to free the slaves, but unlike the Patriots, welcomed African Americans to their cause from the start of the fighting. By 1812, the British were even more anti-slavery. In brief, eighteenth-century Scots in the new British Empire moved against slavery too quickly for their ideas to be acceptable to the traditional English-American decision-makers of the Thirteen Colonies.

Why Move to Canada?

The rhetoric of the Revolution claimed that its cause benefited the common man; in reality, the common soldier fared much better under King George III than under President George Washington: "Loyalists generally... emerged in British North America [as] better off materially. Undoubtedly, this may not be true of many of the officer corps, but for the more numerous rank and file.... After the revolution they emerged as men of property."[31] The mercenary-minded Highland Scots gravitated to the paying side of the Revolutionary War, not to the winning side, and so received their promised land. In contrast, there were serious mutinies, riots, and hangings of former continental soldiers,[32] as the rebel soldiers were called, because they never did receive the money and land promised to them.[33] In the end, Highlanders fought for the old king and more land while continentals fought for no king and no land.

In their move to Canada, many Scots quibbled over their land grants and the insufficient compensation they received for losses. Yet, for the time, they were well treated. The Royal Highland Emigrants was the first to be recognized as a regular British regiment in the Revolutionary War. Being listed as a "regular" rather than a "provincial" regiment meant that the free commissions carried half-pay status or could be sold at the end of the war. As stated earlier, John Nairne of the 78th sold his commission as a major in the RHE for three thousand pounds — an immense sum in those days.

The Continental Congress, so called because it represented the Thirteen Colonies throughout the continent, gave its name to money as well as to soldiers. The famous phrase "not worth a continental" referred to the fact that the continental dollar being distributed to the Patriots was by then worth only a fraction of its pre-war value.[34] The plight of the continental soldiers is partly explained by the devastation of the continental currency. Nevertheless, the Highlander, with his King's Shilling, was worth far more politically and socially in the new British North America than was the continental with his continental currency in the new republican United States. Allan Taylor, an American historian, writes: "Although deemed the war's losers, the Loyalists in Upper Canada secured a lighter tax burden than that borne by either the pre-war colonists or the postwar citizens of the republic."[35]

The American Revolution was a turning point that failed to turn for its common soldiers, African Americans, and Aboriginal peoples. There was no sense of a lost cause among the Highland soldier-settlers who moved to Canada after 1783. They were proud of being Loyalist and had a sense of having fought well. Their attachment to upstate New York and Vermont was limited, as they had not been there that long, and Canada was not that different geographically. Catherine McCallum, daughter of a 74th Argyll

Sergeant James Thompson died at age ninety-eight and was one of many successful eighteenth-century Highland sergeants who settled North America. Thompson played a major role in rebuilding Quebec City, and in his long life met many famous people including Admiral Horatio Nelson. (Courtesy of Earl Chapman Archives.)

Highlander, described Scots Loyalists as those "who boldly stood out for British rule, and afterwards more boldly faced the dark forests of New Brunswick."[36] Patrick Campbell, a Scottish traveller,[37] eight years after the Revolution, described meeting a Thomas and William Fraser who settled in Glengarry, Ontario: "In America [they] entered into the royal cause ... by their own activity, alertness and merit, they raised themselves to the rank of Captain and got money and education by it."[38]

Scottish historians have noted the upward economic mobility of the Highland officers in Scotland at this time,[39] however, the upward economic mobility of the Scots Loyalists who were compelled to leave the new United States has been overshadowed by their compulsory geographic mobility. The veterans from the 78th did especially well. William Ross, the King's pilot on the St. Lawrence, received a large land grant for enlisting French Canadians to fight.[40] Sergeant James Thompson received large land grants, too, because of his highly successful efforts to fortify Quebec City.[41] Sergeant Sinclair of the 78th was one of several who were promoted to the rank of officer during the war and so received increased land grants. In Sinclair's case, he became a magistrate and respected citizen of Three Rivers. The officers did very well, and Sir Harry Seton, a Loyalist, even held on to his vast New York lands by signing them over to a Scots Patriot sympathizer and land surveyor, William Cockburn. Cockburn legally held the land and so the Patriot victors could not legally appropriate the lands after the Revolution.

As far as private soldiers in the Revolution, James Fraser of the 78th is probably typical. James was in Quebec City before the start of hostilities and joined the 84th RHE. He later claimed land in Nova Scotia when the 84th was disbanded, and his son, also named James, joined the army in 1805 to become a sergeant in the Newfoundland Regiment based in Halifax, Nova Scotia. This James Fraser, the son, returned to Quebec City as quartermaster in the Citadel there, and claimed land in 1823. Other sons of the 78th sergeant also claimed land in the Megantic, an area of Lower Canada largely pioneered by Scots. The army was a rather dangerous social security net for Scots in Canada for several generations after the 78th veterans.

The American Revolution was a vicious "civil war at home as well as a military struggle for national liberation."[42] The story of the 78th veterans puts the Revolution in a different light to what is often written.

The Scots benefited from the vast sums spent by the British fiscal military state on soldiers, bankers, and military supplies. While I have interpreted the Scots' stand during the Revolutionary War as enlightened and progressive, many people at the time did not. The judge Lord Mansfield, for example, had his London home burned because he advocated Catholic emancipation, and was accused of turning England into a magnet for destitute African Americans fleeing slavery. John Wilkes, an English radical and politician, objecting to the Scots presence in England from the Seven Years' War onward, initiated anti-Scots riots in London. He wrote that "the ruin of the British Empire is merely a Scotch quarrel with English liberty, a Scotch scramble for English property."[43]

The huge exodus of Scots from the old Thirteen Colonies is a reminder that as a percentage of the population, five times as many people fled the new United States as fled France after their revolution. Both revolutions had a dark side: the French Revolution had the guillotine and the Reign of Terror, while the Patriots turned to exile and property seizures to enforce conformity to their new regime.

The veterans of the 78th who settled between 1763 and 1775 had taken land in what was the former New France. Unlike the Scots at the time, modern historians remember the "Death of Wolfe," but not the death of New France. The removal of France meant that the Aboriginal peoples had no European alternative to supplying them with weapons and so they were unable to hold up settlement to the degree they could before the Seven Years' War. I pointed out in an earlier chapter, the 78th settled on land that only became upstate New York and Vermont because Highlanders had won it on the Plains of Abraham. They also pioneered land around Fort Ticonderoga, where hundreds of Highlanders had died in the battle over the fort. We could say of the Highlanders that "their own blood was spilt in acquiring lands for their settlement, their own fortunes expended in making that settlement effectual; for themselves they fought, for themselves they conquered and for themselves alone they have a right to hold."[44] In fact, this quote comes from Jefferson's writings about the Patriots. However, Highlanders also felt it was their land, and saw Ethan Allen and others from the Thirteen Colonies as interlopers who had done little to actually obtain this land.

The energetic military actions of Highland Scots to further their own interests under the King earned them animosity and expulsion to Quebec, New Brunswick, and Prince Edward Island — all part of the former New France. Unlike France, which remained united geographically after its revolution, the old British North America of 1763–75 was permanently divided geographically, politically, and culturally by revolution. The Thirteen Colonies separated not just from Britain but from Nova Scotia, Newfoundland, and Quebec. Curiously, the American Revolution is seldom seen as forcing Loyalist Scots from the former New France, nor is it seen as divisive, cruel, and bitter in the way, for example, that the Civil War between North and South is seen.

The Patriots claimed that they were just common men trying to establish their legitimate rights as Englishmen against a foreign king and aristocracy across the Atlantic. Patriots claimed they rebelled against those above them on the social scale and geographically outside America, an upward and outward struggle. However, Patriots also fought against "domestic foreigners" and "the internal enemies" — call them what you will, the people socially below them on the frontiers and slave plantations of America. Patriots valued liberation from the British, not the expansion of liberty at home. In fact, the really common men in the North America of the time were the Black Pioneers of Allan Stewart, the Aboriginals of Lieutenant Alexander Fraser, and the French Canadians who fought under Captains John Nairne and Alexander Fraser. The Scots advanced liberty substantially within the New World by fighting to retain their ties with the Old World, while the Patriots loosened the ties to the Old World by retaining the ties of bondage in the New. The Revolution was a reactionary victory downward and inward as well as a progressive victory upward and outward. We see later how those downward and inward who lost in the Revolution explain many of the differences between the United States and Canada after 1783.

Soldiers from highland regiments that served in the war, such as the Black Watch, the 71st, 72nd, 74th, 79th, and 84th, were given farmland in Canada, sparking a second mass migration of relatives from the Highlands. The 78th were the first in a unique chain migration of serving soldiers that took place between 1763 and 1812. Using land lists, I identified only a few dozen veterans of the 78th who re-migrated from Scotland to Canada after 1783. Some migrated to join John Stuart, a 78th veteran who helped pioneer the massive New Brunswick timber trade at Miramichi.[45] One veteran, Alexander MacKay, left the army and joined his two brothers who had emigrated on the *Hector* to Nova Scotia.[46] The five hundred Highland immigrants led by the Reverend Alexander MacDonell (1742–83) to Upper Canada may also have contained Fraser veterans. Highland groups, such as the MacMillans, who came to Glengarry, Ontario in 1803, included at least one ex-Fraser, a

John MacMillan. The case of the Glengarry Fencibles (militia), led by another Reverend Alexander MacDonnel (1760–1840), is interesting because they had not fought in North America, but they came to Canada anyway.

A second John MacMillan of the 78th is an example of the Scots' remarkable migratory flow. This MacMillan migrated to New York State in the 1760s, was repatriated to Northern Ireland with his family after the Revolution, then, in the 1790s, as a Late Loyalist, migrated to Glengarry, Ontario. This veteran of the 78th crossed the Atlantic at least five times in his lifetime, three times at the expense of the British government.

The evidence I have uncovered about the 78th Fraser's Highlanders and their relationship to North America during the Revolution clashes with many historians' ideas about Highlanders during this time. Here is a typical British historian's view:

> The strength of Highland loyalism is more surprising, for Highlanders had been the most conspicuous opponents of the house of Hanover in the Jacobite rebellion of 1745 ... the Highlander had simply followed the lead of his immediate landlord, to whom he owed similar obedience. In America he followed a similar course, fighting for the crown under the leadership of the tacksmen who had planned and led his immigration from Scotland...[47]

I argue that Highlanders not only fought for their own benefit, but, unintentionally perhaps, also fought for the rights of African Americans, French Canadians, and Aboriginal peoples. By the 1780s these Loyalist veterans and their families were in the modernizing capitalist vanguard of Canada.

9

Modernizing America: The Highland Scots' Heritage in the New World

> ... the plow is constructed to work with only two horses.
> — Excerpt from letter written by Simon Fraser (Scotland) to
> Malcolm Fraser (Lower Canada), 1792

Veterans of the 78th Fraser's Highlanders were "modernizers," people involved in "an ongoing process of change."[1] I have chosen to tell their story of modernizing up to the year 1830, the approximate end of their particular era. Sergeant Thompson, the last traceable survivor of the Battle of the Plains of Abraham, died at the age of ninety-eight in 1830. Two years earlier, Thompson had, along with Governor Dalhousie, laid the foundation stone for a uniquely modern war memorial in Quebec City, one dedicated to both Generals Wolfe and Montcalm.

Agricultural Heritage

Highland Scotland brought many agricultural improvements to the New World. In the military forts of the 1760s, Scots were conspicuous for using their gardening ability to help feed the troops and the families stationed there. General James Murray (1721–94) recorded that the 78th Fraser's Highlanders missed eating potatoes because no one was growing the tubers in New France. Consequently, one of Murray's earliest actions as governor of Quebec was to bring over several Scots agriculturists to set up field trials to find the potatoes best-suited to the Canadian climate. This is an important example of a government subsidizing scientific agricultural research, and one that would turn out to be advantageous, as potatoes provide more nutrition per acre than any other North American crop. One acre, in fact, produces as much nourishment as four or five acres of wheat. In addition, potatoes are a root crop, and far more protected from the elements than above-ground plants such as wheat, the main crop of New France at the time. *The Statistical Account of Scotland*, the parish-by-parish survey of everyday life in Scotland, notes that on the Fraser estates in the Parish of Kilmorack, near Inverness, in the 1780s, "new experiments are frequently made in the culture of potatoes" and that "the parish reaps more benefit from the culture of potatoes than from all other crops."[2] It seems that late-eighteenth-century Highlanders were improving the crop on both sides of the Atlantic.

An early Highland Loyalist remembers that "the men would get the ground ready for crop in the spring and leave the women and children to plant the potatoes."[3] The Columbian Exchange (the name given to the inter-continental exchanging of food products) had brought this South American produce from Europe, via the Scots, across to North America in the 1760s. However, the potato was not readily accepted in most areas of the world,[4] including in French-speaking Quebec.[5] But the Scots carried it throughout Canada, literally from coast to coast. Alexander Mackenzie, the explorer, mentions them being used by the NWC to feed its posts in regions far from European settlement. Arguably, this food carried the Nor'Westers across the continent first. It also fed the remote timber camps. Scots settlers migrated inland to areas unoccupied by the pre-conquest French, who had settled along the rivers and lived on wheat. These early Scots settlers survived mainly on potatoes until they had cleared and sold their timber or burned it and converted it into potash for sale as an ingredient for soap.

The grafting of the McIntosh apple is another example of the Scots' progressive approach to agriculture. John McIntosh discovered this first-rate apple on land he was working to clear in Upper Canada. The crop spread rapidly and soon dominated North American apple production because it was sold as grafted stems, not just as seeds. Today, approximately one quarter of the world's apple exports from both Canada and the United States bear the McIntosh name. John's father, Alexander McIntosh, was born in Inverness, Scotland, and emigrated between 1763 and 1775 to the area around Fort Ticonderoga in upstate New York.[6] There are records listing Alexander McIntoshes in the 42nd, 77th, and 78th regiments, all of whom claimed land in that area.[7]

Back in Scotland, James Small (1730–93) developed the world's first light metal plough around 1790. This new plough revolutionized farming because it was operated by only one man and not by teams of oxen. Malcolm Fraser, the 78th veteran, was sent one of these new ploughs in 1792. His cousin wrote that "the plow is constructed to work with only two Horses yoked abreast."[8] Malcolm Fraser was possibly the very first farmer in North America to use a light metal two-horse plough. His friend John Nairne apparently also received one of the new ploughs around the same time, according to a letter sent to his estate in 1805.[9] Nairne travelled back and forth between Scotland and Canada many times, so he was able to import new crops, machinery,[10] attitudes, and plants to North America. In contrast, well into the 1840s, New England farmers shared heavy wooden ploughs that could only be pulled by teams of oxen supervised by several men. It was not until the late 1830s that John Deere developed his metal plough in the United States.[11]

A scientific approach to agriculture helped Highland Scots to overcome many problems they had settling the New World. New understandings and knowing "how to go on" are important aspects of modernity.[12] The very first patent issued in Canada, in fact, was in 1791 to Angus MacDonnell, a Highland soldier garrisoned in Quebec City, who developed a process to convert wood into potash suitable for soap making.

Governor James Murray initiated another major innovation that updated life for the inhabitants of Lower Canada. Murray brought two Scots, William Brown (1738–89) and Thomas Gilmour (c.1740–72), up from the Thirteen Colonies to start the bilingual *Quebec Gazette/La Gazette de Québec* in 1764.[13] Prior to this, there were no printing presses in New France. Printing helped promote a modern, market-driven

The Scottish one-man, two-horse steel plough was a major agricultural advance, especially important for the growing of wheat in Upper and Lower Canada. The St. Lawrence River Valley became an important gateway between Europe and North America that changed the ecology of both continents. (Library and Archives Canada, Mikan 3029007 e008315506.)

capitalist economy. The distribution of the *Gazette* inside Canada gave notice of commercial interest such as auctions, contents of cargoes, and dates of ship arrivals and sailings — information of use to traders, farmers, and ordinary citizens. The *Gazette* was even sent to ports in Britain in an effort to create a market there for Canadian goods

Samuel Neilson, Brown's nephew and successor, printed journals in both French and English for the Agricultural Society in Canada, and sent the journals to educate English-speaking farmers and Catholic priests because, as said earlier, John Nairne (among other Scots) records that virtually all French-speaking farmers were illiterate then. One of the 78th, Donald MacLean from Fraserville, wrote in the journal that he "sowed Canadian wheat and early wheat supplied by the Society, measuring both," and found that "the Society's wheat was ripe ten days earlier than the other ... which must prove of infinite advantage to the farmer, as the ripening season is so short."[14]

The Agricultural Society in Canada, set up in 1789, was the first scientific society in the country, and at least two veterans of the 78th

— Malcolm and Alexander Fraser — were among the founding members. Other veterans, such as John Nairne, joined later. The Agricultural Society in Canada was not only one of the earliest in North America, but possibly the first to send out printed journals (in the 1790s).[15] The Society's journal stated that "the want of knowledge and the want of courage have hitherto retarded the improvement which the science of agriculture is capable of receiving."[16]

Scientific farming journals arose in Canada because, "the culture of the Scottish Enlightenment exerted a major influence ... through large numbers of immigrants.... This alliance between the practical and the theoretical unleashed the forces of science with new intensity upon the land."[17] The "Promised Land" for Loyalist Highland soldiers was also regarded as a "Land of Agricultural Promise."[18]

Captain MacDonald of the 78th was making whisky in Quebec around the end of the 1750s — the start of a massive Canadian whisky industry that still exists. In 1792, a man named Simon Fraser built a large whisky distillery in Beauport, near Quebec City. He hired skilled workmen from Scotland and built a fleet of schooners to carry the grain and deliver his whisky and beer throughout Lower Canada. Whisky became a major new feature of frontier life because of its high value and low volume and weight, which made it more profitable to export from remote areas than cheap and bulky agricultural products. By the early 1800s, Canadian whisky was being exported as well as being sold to the Aboriginals in the west. Imported French brandy and West Indian rum no longer destroyed First Nations society; homegrown Canadian whisky now did that.

Government revenue from spirits exceeded revenues from fur, wheat, or timber. Such was the profit from dealing in whisky that one wit claimed Canada as the first country in the world to drink its way to nationhood in 1867. To this day, Canadians use the Highland spelling of *whisky*, whereas in the United States, the Ulster Scots derivative, *whiskey*, is used.

Patrick Campbell, a former Scots mercenary who travelled in Canada and the United States in the 1790s, wrote that he was surprised to find that the farm of Captain Thomas Fraser, a prominent Scots Loyalist in Glengarry, did not look like a Highland farm placed in North America.[19] On Fraser's farm there was, for example, a Dutch barn, a building style Fraser possibly copied from the Dutch in New York, where he had lived before the American Revolution. Like their mercenary predecessors in Europe, these soldier-settlers copied and adopted what they had experienced on their travels.

Land was central to the eighteenth-century economy, as it provided some economic safety and independence in a harsh world. The crops produced on the farmland did more than feed the farmer and his family. Flax, for example, was converted to linen, which could be made into clothes and bedding. Wheat, oats, and potatoes nourished both animals and humans. The land supported draft horses and oxen and provided sustenance to migrant labour, such as timber workers and sailors hauling cargo. Consequently, increased crop yields ensured a healthy lifestyle for both man and beast, and in many cases a tidy profit for the farmer if he could sell the excess. Highland soldier-settlers saw agricultural land in much the same way we see oil wells and gold mines today — as a valuable resource central to the economy and worth fighting for. Highland Scots settlers strived for economic wealth, independence, and security.

In the newly industrializing Britain of the early nineteenth century, the thousands of horses and "hands," as the workers were called, needed fuelling every bit as much as the steam engines they served. Canadian food powered the British economy in much the same way that coal did. As C.E. Carrington, the British author and ex-army officer wrote: "The merchants of Montreal had prospered by shipping their surplus wheat from the St. Lawrence to Great Britain…. No one foresaw the day when England would depend for bread upon the harvest of the prairie."[20]

Highland Scots played a major role in converting the Canadian forests into farmland. As Canada expanded westward, crop yields increased at the same time. Ironically, George Washington's attempts to recruit Scots farmers to work his land demonstrate how valuable Scots had become. In 1796, Washington wrote to the Earl of Buchan: "Having seen several persons from the vicinity of your estate … one or two of whom I have employed … if there are persons on the move who may incline to associate and become tenants on such a plan … I had a well-founded hope of obtaining this class of men … where husbandry is well understood."[21]

By the 1800s, what was called "Scotch farming methods" in Lower Canada began to be copied by both French Canadians and New Englanders. Scots-Canadians continued the scientific farming tradition into the nineteenth century. For instance, Ontario farmer David Fife imported and developed the hardy Red Fife wheat, which became the standard across the country for years, and the Ogilvy family of Montreal was able to process the hard prairie wheat by using steel rollers. The Ogilvy's were the first flour millers in North America to replace millstones with steel rollers, a process that they had adapted from a Hungarian method. Canada soon became the largest flour and wheat exporter in the world. Scots intentionally sought out technological advances, then imitated and adapted them on both sides of the Atlantic.

Timber Heritage

A few years after the conquest of 1763, Samuel MacKay, the deputy surveyor of the Royal Navy, and Francis MacKay,[22] the surveyor general of the King's Woods in Quebec, collaborated to export timber to Britain.[23] These two soldier-settlers launched what would become Canada's massive timber trade.

The early timber industry was linked to agriculture as farmers made ready money by making up timber rafts to carry farm produce down the St. Lawrence and St. John Rivers (New Brunswick) to market.[24] Conversely, land cleared for timber could be sold as farmland.

Highland soldiers exhibited a scientific interest in planting forests in Scotland using seeds found in North America. Major Duncan Campbell of the Black Watch (Ticonderoga, 1758) sent seeds home across the Atlantic: "I sent from this Country ... two Barrels of the different kinds of Timber tree seeds etc. but I doubt they will be too late excepting the Pines which seed will do when two years old."[25]

Although the timber trade grew enormously as a result of the Napoleonic Wars, which gave rise to British fears that their Baltic timber trade would be cut off, it was already a trade in progress after the Seven Years' War. In 1778, Alexander Fraser, a major wood merchant at Chambly on the Richelieu River (which flows from Lake Champlain to the St. Lawrence River), sold timber to a Simon Fraser and John

Young for export.[26] James Dunlop was shipping oak to Leith, a port near Edinburgh, in the 1780s. John Nicol, an eighteenth-century Scots mariner on the St. Lawrence, wrote: "I was much surprised at the immense floats of wood that came gliding majestically down the river like floating islands. They were covered with turf, and [had] wood huts upon them."[27]

The small family farm as a source of timber became extinct, and in the new and expanded timber trade, "most of the positions of any consequence were filled by Scots or Scottish Canadians. A list of the great lumber families of Canada would almost sound like a roll call of the Scottish clans — Frasers, MacLarens, Gilmours, Gillies, McLaughlins, et al."[28] One possible explanation for the Scots dominance in the timber trade is that they brought the skills with them. Scotland had a wooden economy that was replaced by a stone and metal economy only in the nineteenth century[29] as Highland woods of the eighteenth century gave way to more profitable sheep pastures.[30] However, timber rafts, sawmills, dams, wood exports, and shipbuilding — features characteristic of early-nineteenth-century Canadian forestry — can be found throughout the eighteenth-century Highlands. The Fraser of Lovat Estates records indicate a substantial operation: "the saw-mill ... consists of three shades [sheds?] ... 7 saws are moved by different wheels ... and when the saws are in good order, they easily cut through a log of 10 or even 12 feet long in 4 minutes."[31]

The description continues: "After being cut into logs of 10 or 12 feet long, they are carried [dragged?] by horses to the water edge, and afterwards floated on the rivers Glass, Cannick, and Beauly, from 30 to 40 miles, before they come to the saw-mill.... They are afterwards floated in rafts, 4 miles down the Beauly and ... sold either in Leith or London."[32]

In the 1750s, the timber-fed furnaces erected at Inveraray, in Argyll, Scotland, home of Captain Archibald Campbell of the 78th, gave "employment and bread, to a considerable number of hands, both male and female who were annually employed to cut and peel the woods and make charcoal."[33]

The River Spey, a third area in the Highlands, was probably the most important centre of timber activity: "The planks, deals and masts are sent down the Spey in rafts .... The logs and spars are, for the most part, floated down the river loose, to the number, perhaps, of 20,000 pieces at a

Eighteenth-century Highland sawmill in Glenmore, Scotland. Wooden dams, millwheels, timber rafts, and log drives were features of the Fraser of Lovat lands and several other parts of Scotland. (National Library of Scotland, 74424914.)

time, with men going along the side of the river with the long poles, to push them on as they stick on the banks."[34] Child "clippers" worked with long poles and "Mary, the least active child I've ever seen, miscalculated the distance and fell plump into the stream, along which she was carried more rapidly than we could follow her, without a hope of rescue."[35] It seems some Highland men, women, and children had timber experience before emigrating.

While only about 5 percent of the Highlands were forested in 1750, much of this forest was distributed along ocean and loch shores, making it accessible and easily shipped.[36] A number of misconceptions cloud the history of Highland forestry.[37] One is that Highland forestry did not exist, and that Highland Scots did not bring timber-related skills with them. Although the Highland Scots in North America had the skills to operate

The job of "clipper," pushing logs using long poles with hooks, was as dangerous in the Scottish Highlands as it was in Canada. While conditions were very different in the two countries, experience in the timber trade prior to emigration may explain why the Scots initiated and dominated this industry in Canada. (National Library of Scotland, 74416570.)

a timber industry, Canada was remote. It took years to build up a tradition of British merchant ships calling in. Gradually, the industry expanded, especially after 1800 when Napoleon's boycott[38] forced the British to turn to Canada for timber: "There were 1,500 ships and 18,000 seamen employed in the Atlantic timber trade ... ships and shipmasters played no small part in the making of a maritime empire."[39]

There were few timber exports and no shipbuilding facilities on the St. Lawrence River in the 1750s, before the British conquest. The state-subsidized shipbuilding schemes of the French were very expensive and had died out before the British arrived. Besides, France in the eighteenth century had forests, so did not encourage a Canadian timber trade. Shipbuilding involved a great many skilled, highly paid trades such as rope-making, carpentry, and metal work.

The "timber-out, immigrants-in" situation reduced the cost of both timber and emigration considerably.[40] This relationship enabled mass migration to take place after 1815, with Quebec to Liverpool becoming the cheapest and busiest trade route between the Old and New Worlds at that time.[41] The timber-migrant trade impacted Atlantic freight and passenger rates, not to mention the interdependence of Europe and America.

The giant Gilmour operation is an example of cosmopolitan Scots transferring skills from mainland Europe to North America. Allan Gilmour (1775–1849) started out supplying local timber to Glasgow,[42] then shifted to importing timber from the Baltic. However, Napoleon's boycott forced Gilmour to turn to New Brunswick and Lower Canada (Quebec). By the 1820s, the various branches of the company owned 130 ocean-going vessels and employed fifteen thousand men in the woods and five thousand in shipyards.[43] Many settlers worked for the company over the winter months, returning with cash to work their farms in the spring. The timber camps also provided an important market for local food and whisky.

The Culture of Timber

There are far more Canadian folk songs about the timber trade than the fur trade for the simple reason that many more people worked in that industry. Curiously, Canadian history books and university theses about the fur trade far outnumber those about the timber trade. Given the group nature of the work, timber shanties were culturally important to those involved in the business of wood. The word *shanties* is derived from the Scots Gaelic for "old" (*sean*) and "house" (*tighe*) and the expression "shanty-town" grew from that. Some linguists also claim that the word *sea-shanty* arose from the St. Lawrence timber trade.[44] However the term is not actually that old, having come into use by the nineteenth century when shanties sheltered timber workers on the rafts. Gaelic work songs — shanty-songs — were transmitted by raftsmen to the sailors who worked on ocean-going ships stowing the timber from the rafts.[45] John Nicol, the Scots mariner who wrote about the eighteenth-century St. Lawrence River, said he "often heard the children sporting and singing in chorus upon these floating masses."[46]

The Highland Scots influenced the culture surrounding the timber trade because they dominated that trade. Well into the nineteenth century, lumberjack crews of Scots-Canadians, often Gaelic-speaking, from Ontario, Quebec, Nova Scotia, New Brunswick, and Prince Edward Island, were a feature of Western Canadian and American life. Ralph Connor's novel *The Man from Glengarry* portrays the lives of Highland Scots lumberjacks who followed the forests into the United States. Ian P. MacMillan noted that this novel broadly resembles the story of the descendants of John MacMillan, a veteran of the 78th Fraser's Highlanders who settled Glengarry, Ontario.[47] These MacMillans left Glengarry for Wisconsin and formed a lumber business that evolved into the MacMillan-Cargill Company, a giant corporation now based in Minneapolis, Minnesota. Scots Canadians took their timber expertise into the nineteenth-century United States, then to Western Canada. During the eighteenth century, their Highland Scots ancestors migrated to Lowland Scots farms at harvest time. In much the same way, nineteenth-century Scots Canadians migrated for seasonal work.

The timber they cut was sold in Britain, and the cheapest way to transport it there was to build ships to carry it. The *Columbus,* built in 1824 in Quebec City by the Scot Charles Wood, was the largest ship in the world up to that time.[48] The Gilmore timber company had probably the largest private fleet of ships in the world to carry lumber to Europe. Canadian ships became a part of the global carrying trade long before Canada became a country, and cheap transport over vast distances on rivers, lakes, and sea became a Canadian specialty. Mastery of the waters helped to settle Canada and to establish a market economy relatively quickly.

The Canadian Scots were then in the vanguard of modern shipbuilding developments. Their connections to modernizing Scotland and the British fiscal-military state interacted. For example, the first steamboat built in North America from local, as opposed to imported British, engines was Molson's *Accommodation.*[49]Jackson and Bruce, two Montreal Scots, built another Molson ship in 1811 using two of James Watt's steam engines — the first steamboat in history to be used in war. Using the *Swiftsure* to move men, supplies, and information efficiently and cheaply in the War of 1812 helped the British-Canadian side to ward off the

Built at Montreal in 1811 by two Scotsmen, John Bruce and John Jackson, the *Swiftsure* was the first steamboat in the world to be used in a war, specifically the War of 1812. (Courtesy of Sam Allison Collection.)

This print, *Rideau Canal at Kingston Mills*, illustrates both the military aspects and epic nature of the work required to tame the Canadian wilderness. Canals created towns in Canada whereas in Britain canals linked existing towns. (Library and Archives Canada, Mikan 2833777 c092920k.)

Steamboats on the early nineteenth-century Rideau Canal entered the Ottawa River at Bytown, named after Colonel John By, the army engineer who built the canal. It was an important geo-political military site. (McGill University, McGill Rare Books and Special Collections.)

much larger United States forces. Success in 1812 proved that steam worked, and led to the British government funding a massive Canadian canal system in the postwar years. Canals also opened up previously inaccessible frontier areas for settlement.

The canal system was to populating Ontario and Quebec in the early nineteenth century as railways were to populating Western Canada in the late nineteenth century, so the impact of the *Swiftsure* was enormous. The War of 1812 also resulted in many remarkable shipbuilding achievements on the Great Lakes.[50]

The Scots continued to pioneer shipping developments after the 1812 war. The journey up the winding St. Lawrence was slow for sailing ships, so, in 1823, John Torrance paid another Scot, John Munn, to build the *Hercules*, which had one of the most powerful engines in the world, to tow ships into the Montreal harbour. It was one of the first tugs built specifically to tow ships.

The very first ship built to tow larger boats was the *Tug*, built on the Clyde in Scotland in 1817. Charles (1790–1847) and John Wood, who

This twenty-first-century view shows that the Canadian Parliament Buildings in Ottawa occupy the spot where the Rideau Canal entered the Ottawa River. (Photograph by Robert Wilkinson, 2014.)

built the *Tug* and the *Comet* on the Clyde, emigrated to Canada and set up shipyards in Quebec.[51] The *Comet* is often regarded as the world's most technically advanced steamboat. The shipbuilder, Charles Wood, is regarded as "a genius in his way"[52] in Britain, but his achievements are virtually ignored in Canada. Also overlooked in Canada, but revered in the United States, is the Canadian shipbuilder Donald MacKay (1810–80). Born in Shelburne, Nova Scotia, MacKay moved to Boston to become the foremost builder and designer of "Yankee" clipper ships: the *Flying Cloud*, *Sovereign of the Seas*, *Great Republic*, and the *Glory of the Seas*. His grandfather came from near Tain, where Sergeant James Thompson and so many of the 78th originated, and had been in a Highland regiment at the end of the Revolutionary War. He definitely fits the Highland Scots immigrant profile as a soldier-settler whose descendant played an important role in modernizing the New World.[53]

The Scots pioneered shipping from Europe to the New World up until the 1950s. The *Queen Mary* and the *Queen Elizabeth* are world famous.

The *Royal William*, built in Quebec City in 1831 by the Scots-Canadian James Goudie, was the first ship to cross the Atlantic mostly by steam.

The transition from sail to steam was dominated by Scots on both sides of the Atlantic in the first half of the nineteenth century. Steamboats developed trade and commerce in a continent shaped by rivers, lakes, and oceans before the coming of the railroad. The Europeans from the sixteenth to the eighteenth century dominated the world with, what the historian Carlo Cipolla labeled, *Guns and Sails*, but at the start of the nineteenth century the Scots were using what I call *Guns 'n' Steam* to master their New World. The Scots had created a partnership of James Watt with James Wolfe by 1812, and so had a huge impact on North America.

Military Heritage

The military heritage of Highland Scots in the New World had been firmly established by 1830. Descendants of Highlanders like William Ross, who was the King's pilot on the St. Lawrence, and the MacKay brothers who helped start the timber trade, can be found in English and French-speaking military units from the War of 1812 through to the Second World War. By the time of the First World War, the Canadian Expeditionary Force was proving to be a remarkable army, and regiments with a Scots influence were an important part of that force.[54] Units with Highland Scots associations can be found throughout the Canadian military today, and even the Royal Canadian Air Force has its own tartan and pipe bands.

However, this military heritage is deeper than just pipe bands and kilted regiments such as the Black Watch of Canada. After the American Revolution, Canada was a long, thin population line just north of the hostile United States. Militarism influenced Canadian frontier life in a way that it did not influence the frontier in the United States or the outback in Australia.[55] For instance, membership in the local militia, even in urban areas such as Toronto and Montreal, was imperative for the Canadian elite right up to the First World War.

Attributes of Highland regiments passed into Canadian life in many subtle ways. Controlled violence was an attribute of Highland Scots soldiers. While it is difficult to prove, the controlled violence of the Canadian frontier versus the uncontrolled violence of the frontier in the United States is perhaps traceable to the former's Highland military heritage. Most Canadians trace their traits of controlled violence to their Loyalist heritage, and they are partly correct. The quality of controlled violence was characteristic only of the Highland Scots, who were a large and consequently influential proportion of the Loyalist mix.[56] Canadian habits of violence probably grew then from settlers from the many Highland regiments and Loyalist regiments manned and officered by Scots. Time has obscured the Highland regimental roots of such values, yet their influence remains.

The Royal Canadian Mounted Police is a regiment of policemen with token lances and red uniforms. Canadian frontier traits were well established long before the Mounties were formed in 1873 to police Western Canada. Although they were modeled officially on the Irish Constabulary, the Mounties became the symbol of Canada, partly because their token lances and red uniforms reflected so well the idea of controlled, directed violence.

Scots soldiers had steady and reliable incomes, which differentiated them from their French and American opponents between 1756 and 1812.[57] The strong Highland allegiance to the British Army is understandable when we look at how their opponents mishandled their fiscal responsibilities to soldiers.

Money also set Highland soldier-settlers apart from many other settlers of the time. Sergeant James Thompson often refers to his account books, in which he recorded details about the men's pay. The keeping of accurate financial records was apparently an important part of regimental life[58] at a time when most ordinary people still bartered.[59] Highland business success in North America can be, at least in part, attributed to their high level of financial numeracy: "Money is…. Associated with modernity" and "money proper is … an inherent part of modern social life."[60]

During the Seven Years' War the British used neutral Spanish or Portuguese ships, which were less likely to be attacked, to carry gold coins to pay the British Army. Sergeant Thompson writes about teaching French Canadians the value of what he called gold "portugueses," saying:

"These people did not, at that time, know the value of the gold coins, but egad before long they got to know them well enough."[61] While ordinary people are usually excluded from the financial story of the eighteenth century, soldier-settlers played a role in transforming Canada from a barter economy to a modern money economy.

By 1812, the British Army had begun printing its own system of paper money in Canada (using dollar denominations) and distributed it via Molson's ship, the *Swiftsure*.[62] The banking figure responsible for this exemplifies much of my argument.[63] A man named James Green, born in Sweden but apparently of British descent, was a sergeant-major in the American Revolution before purchasing a lieutenancy in the Cameronians and becoming the regiment's adjutant.[64] He later became director of the Army Bill Office during the War of 1812, where he printed bilingual paper currency with the support of the legislature in Lower Canada. Payments in paper dollars to British regiments and Canadian militia during the war shifted the Canadian economy to a more modern, capitalistic one. The success of paper money in Lower Canada led the Legislature to finally accept the need for banks — a measure they had previously blocked. When Green left the Army Bill Office in 1820, he helped start the Quebec Savings Bank and eventually became its president. Although Green had started out his working life as a private soldier, he eventually fused banking, migration, and upward social mobility with modernity in North America.[65]

The huge increase in Scots militarism in North America between 1759 and 1812 greatly benefited Scots bankers. Coutts, the Edinburgh bankers and goldsmiths used by officers such as Simon Fraser of the 78th, had established themselves firmly as a bank for aristocrats in London's West End during the Seven Years' War (1761).[66]Drummonds were the Black Watch paymasters during the Seven Years' War (1756–63)[67] and became the army contractors for much of the British Army during the Revolutionary War a decade and a half later.[68]

The Drummonds bank helped out many Scots entrepreneurs who were making their way in the New World, and these partnerships such as with the NWC, which operated to the Pacific and Arctic, helped to transform the continent. In the 1760s, Drummonds had begun accepting furs from Scottish merchants for bills of exchange (a form of cheque) that were used by the merchants to buy other goods.[69] Later, the Scottish agent for Drummonds bank in Canada, James Dunlop (1757–1815), was reputedly the richest man in the country at the time of his death. In 1800, he was purchasing bills of exchange valued at twenty-one thousand pounds.[70] He built one of Montreal's first shipyards in 1793. Dunlop was a key initiator of wheat and timber exports to Scotland from the start of the French Revolution in 1789 to the Battle of Waterloo in 1815. Dunlop's army and bank connections also won him the contract to sell Canadian provisions to the British soldiers fighting Napoleon in Portugal and Spain. He used his own ships built in Canada to ship the provisions to Spain. Canada had become a key component in the British fiscal military state by the 1790s.[71] Money is the sinew of war, and the pioneering role that the Scots played in the Canadian economy can be partly attributed to their duty as army paymasters and to their military connections.

After the 1812 war, Scottish capitalists created the Bank of Montreal, Canada's first bank. It quickly became the financial agent for the British Army and was charged with providing payment to the troops. The bank's military connections gave it enormous credibility and stability. What has been called "war capitalism" generated peaceful capitalistic enterprises because by controlling the Bank of Montreal, Scots were assured a central place in Canadian economic life. The main policies of Canada's banking system were created by a Highlander who came to Canada from upstate New York: Mr. John Richardson (1755–1831). Referred to as the "father of Canadian banking," Richardson had been a ship's captain of a Loyalist privateer, the *Vengeance*, during the American Revolution. So you could say that the man who devised the Canadian banking system graduated from piracy on the high seas to piracy on the high streets. Richardson was a product of the Scots Enlightenment[72] and wrote a brilliant outline of banking theory in 1808, which shaped the policies adopted by the Bank of Montreal in 1817.[73]

The advent of a banking system changed Canadian civil rights and how the Scots were perceived in Canada. In a complicated court case, Drummonds agent Adam Mabane, was prosecuted by a judge appointed by Governor Frederick Haldimand, for hoarding to speculate in wheat

Government Banker Works with the British Army, by Huntley Brown. A Mr. Brown of the Bank of Montreal, shown standing in top hat and coat (left centre), is paying British troops in the 1830s. British military expenditure gave the Bank of Montreal and Canada the financial stability that helped them weather the depression of the 1830s and the 1837 Rebellion. The United States experienced far greater and longer economic and political turmoil at this time. (Bank of Montreal Corporate Art Collection.)

prices.[74] The judge applied an obscure piece of medieval French law, and under that law, anyone else who owed even a small sum of money to the bank could have goods seized. The judge then seized a huge quantity of goods owned by Simon Fraser, who had nothing to do with the case. This was probably the Simon Fraser who was the son of Lieutenant Alexander Fraser of the 78th. Fraser was imprisoned only because he had legally borrowed a small sum of money from Drummonds bank.[75]

In those days, it was felt unjust to imprison innocent businessmen. Consequently, in the 1780s, the British replaced Quebec's medieval French commercial law with modern British commercial law. In addition, they introduced habeas corpus (a legal writ requiring that prisoners be given a court hearing to determine whether they are being legally imprisoned) and trial by jury in civil cases. Banking unintentionally played a role in modernizing civil rights in Canada.[76]

Canada is a vast country, and money was important because it "provides for the enactment of transactions between agents widely separated in time and space."[77] Public perception of Scots gradually improved after they introduced banking to Canada in 1819. Scots became trusted members of the community by 1830. Giddens believes that "trust is involved … in a fundamental way with the institutions of modernity. Trust [is] … confidence in the reliability of a person or system … bound up in trust in abstract systems."[78]

Today, Canada has a branch banking system, similar to the one pioneered in Scotland; a few large central banks with outlets which operate throughout the country. Scots-Canadian banking patterns were sharply different to the fragmented United States banking system. South of the border, branch banking was forbidden until the late twentieth century. Americans had many small local banks and many large failures in their banking history. Even in the twenty-first century, the Canadian banking system proves to be far more stable than its U.S. counterpart.

The Fur Trade Heritage

There are a great many Canadian books and articles written about the Scots who were involved in the fur trade because "a surprising number of … explorers [and] fur traders were either Scottish born or Scottish educated."[79] I do not attempt to write a history of the business as such and only write about those aspects of the trade that derived from the modernity of contemporary Scotland. American historians pay little attention to Highland Scots explorers such as James MacKay, William Dunbar, and George Hunter, who did so much to open up what is now the United States, and produced maps of unexplored areas and information on the Aboriginal peoples who lived there. While this book focuses on Highland Scots and their exploits in Canada, I want to stress that there was also a considerable Scots contribution to exploration south of the border. In the case of William Panton and John Leslie, they built a huge trading company in Spanish Florida after the American Revolution that was on a par for sheer size and importance with Montreal's much more famous NWC.

Highland officers were not prejudiced against those involved in trade, which may explain why so many Scots joined the fur trade. Other British officers, it seems, looked down on those who worked in business and preferred life as landed gentlemen. Lieutenant John McTavish's son,

Simon, was apprenticed in the fur trade and later became the founder of the NWC. It seems that the Scottish Enlightenment encouraged Scots at every level of society to acquire some sort of trade to further their lives.

The jump from the 78th to the fur trade was not as great as it might seem because military life was often good training for that trade. In addition, Highlanders were often trilingual (English, French, Gaelic), literate, numerate, well-travelled, and experienced frontiersmen who worked peacefully alongside the Aboriginal peoples and French Canadians. No other European group held these attributes. In fact, the Indian Department of the British Army, established in 1755 to conduct relations with the First Nations, employed many Highland soldiers.

Alexander MacKay, who accompanied Alexander Mackenzie across the continent, sent his children to live with his father Donald MacKay (78th veteran) in Three Rivers, where they would learn to speak French, English, and Gaelic for their future careers in the fur trade — practical education, it seems, was important to these soldier-settlers. Given the high level of literacy and numeracy among Highland Scots compared to other peoples on the frontier, it is no wonder that they dominated, expanded, and profited from a major economic activity such as the fur trade.

The Scots had a head start over the French and other British or British-American fur traders of the time. Scots bankers, after all, had been active in New France, charged with providing payments to the British Army, even before the British officially took over in 1763. The Scots were clannish, but so were most peoples in the eighteenth century. Approximately forty of the forty-six people who were partners in Montreal's NWC appear to have been Scots. Simon McTavish (1750–1804), the company's founder, brought many of his relatives into the business, one of whom was his nephew, and successor, William McGillivray (c. 1764–1825). William McGillivray was related to Lachlan McGillivray who much earlier engaged in the fur trade in what is now the south part of the United States.

In many ways, McTavish ran the NWC like an eighteenth-century regiment. Partners, called "factors" in eighteenth-century language, like military officers, had to buy the limited positions available, but it was possible to be promoted to a free partnership in return for outstanding work. Although this private company had no special connection to the government or its army, William McGillivray turned his NWC voyageurs into the Corps of Canadian Voyageurs. As their Lieutenant-Colonel, McGillivray led his voyageurs alongside General Brock to capture the American town of Detroit during the War of 1812.

Some Canadian historians claim that this company operated as the first joint-stock business in North America. The number of partnerships grew from approximately eight to twenty, and the men who worked at the NWC were hired under contract, but the work was hard and a few deserted their much-sought-after posts. The partners (factors) travelled in canoes paddled by voyageurs, but a social hierarchy was maintained throughout the trip. The factors dined first, whereas in Yankee fur companies, it was every man for himself with no regard for rank. Washington Irving, the author of "Rip Van Winkle," touched upon this aspect when he wrote about the NWC in his nonfiction account of the fur trade, *Astoria*: "Every partner who had charge of an interior post, and a score of retainers at his command, felt like the Chieftain of a Highland Clan."[80]

I explain later how Irving, under the influence of the romantic writer Sir Walter Scott, misinterpreted the actions of the fur-trading Scots. While the partners may have "felt like Highland Chieftains," the partners acted more like officers in a regiment. Prior to the formation of the NWC (1783–84), a number of Scots traders fought amongst themselves, and competition was literally cutthroat. These various competing traders at last decided to form the NWC, which would allow them to become more efficient and to cut costs. They were always switching allegiances and organizing rival groups for commercial gain. Profit ruled the day.

Highland Scots were more likely to fight each other for profit than they were to fight other peoples out of prejudice. While there was some rivalry and violence between the English-controlled Hudson's Bay Company (HBC) and the Scottish-controlled NWC, serious violence broke out only after a Scot, Thomas Douglas, 5th Earl of Selkirk, bought control of the HBC. Highlanders would transfer allegiances between the two companies, but would fight to the death for whoever employed them at any given time. In the district of Glengarry, in Upper Canada, some parents had sons in both the HBC and the NWC, much like the Highland families who had mercenary soldier sons fighting for opposite sides in a war.[81]

Nevertheless, as in Highland life, the fur traders believed that violence was to be directed and controlled. This set the tone for the Scottish exploration and exploitation of Canada. For example, the great explorers Simon Fraser, Alexander Mackenzie, and Alexander MacKay never killed an Aboriginal person during their thousands of miles of travel across the continent. Captain James Cook (1728–79) of South Seas and Battle of Quebec fame, also adopted such ideas about the Aboriginal peoples from the Scots Enlightenment of this time, but in the end was, unfortunately, killed by Aboriginals in Hawaii. Similarly, Alexander MacKay, a son of a 78th soldier, reluctant to fire upon the Aboriginals who attacked him, was murdered in 1811 while establishing the first English-speaking settlement on the Pacific Coast.

South of what is now the Canada–U.S. border, frontiersmen such as Daniel Boone, Kit Carson, Davy Crockett, and Buffalo Bill Cody were very different men in this regard. These men, mostly of Ulster Scots stock, had a history of violence and fighting, but unlike the Highland Scots, had little military background. Uncontrolled violence characterized the frontier in the United States, and even though Buffalo Bill was a remarkable businessman, he also made a fortune staging Wild West shows that glorified and stylized violence.

Alexander Mackenzie, possibly the best-known Canadian frontiersman, was also a remarkable businessman, highly literate, an international bestselling author that made him world famous, and a student of the First Nations of North America. He intentionally refrained from killing even those Aboriginals who threatened him. American president Thomas Jefferson (1743–1826) used Mackenzie's book *Voyages from Montreal Through the Continent of North America to the Frozen [Arctic] and Pacific Oceans* to instruct explorers Meriwether Lewis and William Clark, the first American citizens to cross the continent. Jefferson also provided them with the maps drawn by James MacKay, who had explored Louisiana while working for the Spanish government there. James was the son of Donald MacKay of the 78th and the brother of Alexander MacKay, who had crossed the continent with Alexander Mackenzie.

The endless portages between waterways linking the Atlantic, Pacific, and Arctic are captured in this picture. The sheer physical abilities of Alexander Mackenzie, Simon Fraser, Alexander MacKay, and other fur traders were remarkable. (Library and Archives Canada, Mikan 2836434 c040168k.)

President Jefferson used federal funds to promote William Dunbar and George Hunter's expedition to the southern areas of the Louisiana Purchase. Dunbar was a Highlander from Elgin near Tain, where many of the 78th had originated. He was also a product of the Scottish Enlightenment, a reluctant Patriot, and probably a Loyalist sympathizer.[82] Hunter was also a Scot. There were more than a few Highland Scots at that time who were instructing or leading Americans on their frontier expeditions.

Much about the North American fur trade culture can be traced back to the Scots. The famous Beaver Club in Montreal, where the NWC partners would meet to indulge in glorious drinking bouts, was perhaps modelled on the Edinburgh clubs of the time. And the culture of Scotland was even adopted by some of the Aboriginals as well, with a number taking up fiddle music and the wearing of tartan. Robert Cruikshank, the great Scots silversmith based in Montreal, probably initiated the tradition of selling Scots silver heart-shaped brooches to the Aboriginals.

Modern ideas from the Scottish Enlightenment were applied to the fur trade and helped make the NWC a profitable enterprise. McGill University's website, *In Pursuit of Adventure: The Fur Trade in Canada and the North West Company*, describes Mr. Roderick Mackenzie's survey of the Canadian west. He was a cousin of the explorer Alexander MacKenzie and one of the partners in the NWC:

> In 1806 he had printed a circular letter that he sent out requesting information for his survey. He was interested in geography, longitude and latitude, mountains, rivers, the weather, the soil; flora and fauna and methods of hunting; the Natives and their history, culture, morals and government; and the history of the fur trade.... Mackenzie had as his model *The Statistical Account of Scotland* published in the 1790s.

I believe that conventional historical wisdom about the capitalist fur trade is very different from the reality. For example, the following observation by Washington Irving has stood virtually unchallenged since its writing: "Such was the Northwest Company in its powerful and prosperous days, when it held a kind of feudal sway over a vast domain of lake and forest."[83] The fur trade helped to reflect and mould both Canadian and American stereotypes. A very different cultural tradition developed north of the border from that south of the border, where the "Wild West" was the norm. Canadian fur traders, such as Alexander Mackenzie, have been largely forgotten and ignored, but could be described as quiet yet adventurous, literate yet physically tough, respectful of legitimate authority, peaceful (but remarkably fierce soldiers), highly successful but modest, and conscious of tradition while embracing modernity. In many ways, the Canadian motto "Ad mari usque ad mare" — from sea to sea — reflects the explorations and legacy of these Highland fur traders.

Capitalism is usually treated as an abstract impersonal process by historians, but the evidence I have found about the 78th Fraser's Highlanders illustrates and explains the many individuals involved in implementing this process. The Scottish Highlanders were much more than simply the first to navigate North America in a geographical sense; Highland Scots were also the intellectual vanguard of North American modernity. Theirs is obviously a victorious, revolutionary, and capitalistic epic, not the medieval, reactionary, and defeated clan tragedy it is sometimes assumed to be. The Scots in Canada were receptive to revolutionary ideas and able to develop them in many aspects of life from the Atlantic to the Arctic and Pacific. They had something to prove to themselves and to the rest of the world after the failed but bloody rebellion in 1745. By bringing new crops and new industries — such as whisky distilling — they expanded the ecological possibilities of North America. The "notion of overcoming"[84] is central to the idea of modernity, and the Scots overcame many obstacles as they laid the foundation for much of the North American economy, political system, and society.

10

The Scots' March to Modernity

Scotland was home to a creative surge whose mark on western culture
is still clearly discernible.
— Alexander Broadie, *The Scottish Enlightenment*

The mass migration of Scots to eighteenth-century America grew
from militarism. However, this migration also coincided with an
extraordinary explosion of practical creativity in many aspects of Scottish life, which became known as the Scottish Enlightenment. There is
dispute about the start and end of this Enlightenment, but I have dated
it from 1750 1800. Historians have focused on the sheer intellectual
brilliance of thinkers such as Adam Smith and David Hume, rather
than on the rise of a creative, entrepreneurial Scottish middle class and
the start of a highly skilled working class that operated and created new
agricultural, financial, and industrial activities. Eighteenth-century
Scotland was on the move to America and modernity at the same time.
As the Scots became conscious of their backwardness and poverty after
the bloody 1745 Rebellion, they were determined to improve themselves and their country. This chapter explains how the modernization
taking place in Scotland united with Scottish militarism and migration
in the New World. In turn, Scots success in the New World sometimes

promoted modernization in Scotland, and so the flow of ideas and innovation went both ways.

The Scottish Enlightenment

As the term *enlightenment* suggests, Scots were "throwing light" on their traditional ways of life in order to change them. Enlightenment in Scotland was not just an intellectual movement as in France, but also a series of down-to-earth changes in the lives of ordinary people, including the abolition of the Highland clan system. Some of these fundamental changes were: Adam Smith's development of economics as a science (*The Wealth of Nations*); David Hume's groundbreaking ideas on morality and politics (*Enquiry Concerning Human Understanding*); John Sinclair's and Lord Kames's scientific agriculture and the same John Sinclair's use of statistics in the census; Joseph Black's discoveries of carbon dioxide, latent heat, and chlorine; Robert Adam's revolutionary approach to architecture; Alexander Mackenzie's extensive and peaceful exploration through Aboriginal lands; James Lind's idea of using fruits and juices to prevent scurvy; and James Hutton's advances in the science of geology relating to the earth's crust. The Universities of Glasgow and Edinburgh were the world's best in the areas of medicine, chemistry, agriculture, and possibly also history and philosophy. The Scots Enlightenment was the spark that helped generate what we now label the Industrial and Agricultural Revolutions in Britain, a period that produced some of the most significant changes ever to take place in human history. However, ordinary people seldom regarded factory work, coal mining, and the clearing of small tenants from rented farms, as much of an improvement.

This remarkable knowledge explosion converted Scotland into a modern country by 1812, and Scots played a major role in the wider European Enlightenment sometimes called the "Age of Reason." A possible impetus for the Enlightenment is a religious one: Presbyterianism required the individual and the minister to read the Bible in order to reach God, so literacy and learning were encouraged among individuals to an unusually high degree. A poverty-stricken Scotland developed a materialistic philosophy that valued possessions. They were an outward-looking

James Watt. This great inventor modernized steam engines and revolutionized production and transportation
all over the world. Watt sent several
mechanics to Montreal in the early
1800s to install his engines there. In
turn, the St. Lawrence River Valley
became a centre for steam power.
(McGill University, McGill Rare Books
and Special Collections.)

country, internationally minded rather than nationally minded, and
adopted many worthwhile ideas, features, technologies, and machines
from all over Europe. Adam Smith, for instance, adapted and perfected
many economic ideas learned when he lived in France. Being cosmopolitan "counted for much with the enlightened Scot."[1] Indeed, Scottish
intellectuals often displayed disdain for Scotland, and were, by and
large, completely opposed to the Jacobite Rebellion and the American
Rebellion: "The spirit of the age," as David Hume called it, led Scots to intentionally seek out and imitate ideas and techniques from many sources, but unlike the French and American enlightenments, the Scots chose
to reform, not to rebel against, the established government.

Scotland from 1750 to 1800 was similar to late nineteenth-century
Japan or twenty-first-century China, countries determined "to catch
up" to the best of the world. Scotland, Japan, and China copied many
things, and made some things their own in their contemporary worlds.
For example, the great architect Robert Adam (1728–92) went to Italy,
adopted and modernized the neoclassical Palladian architecture of the

Italian Renaissance, and then made a fortune expressing the style. He drew from the past and the present. Adam was probably the most influential architect in the eighteenth century, and his ideas radiated from St. Petersburg in Russia to the new United States.

The eighteenth-century Scots had a global impact far in excess of their numbers, yet their part in many achievements is often ignored, and the credit given to others. For instance, Peter Kennedy and Charles Maitland, Scots doctors working in eighteenth-century Constantinople, wrote about the Eastern practice of inoculation against disease. Maitland returned from Turkey to perform the first ever inoculation against smallpox in Britain. Smallpox was a major killer in the eighteenth-century world, and the idea of inoculating someone provoked a great debate. For example, anti-inoculation riots broke out in Virginia in 1768–69 after a Scottish doctor, John Dalgleish, inoculated some slaves: "The Scots immediately became the focus of considerable antagonism whipped up by prominent Virginians who would later support the Revolution."[2] Progressive modernity made the Scots unpopular in the Thirteen Colonies, as well as in England. By the end of that century, the great English doctor Edward Jenner had developed the much safer technique of vaccination with cowpox to guard against the more lethal smallpox. It is Jenner who is remembered for this accomplishment, while the two Scots who prepared the way are now largely forgotten.

The Scots themselves developed many important inventions, ideas, and techniques. The Carron ironworks, for example, which were founded in Falkirk, Scotland, in 1759, grew to be the biggest in Europe, employing over two thousand people by 1812. The company developed a naval cannon, the carronade, which it exported all over the world, including the United States in the War of 1812. This iron factory, in turn, gave a great boost to the manufacture of machine parts and to the coal mines nearby; my grandmother's ancestors were coalminers at Carronshore, producing coal for the factory. James Watt, the brilliant inventor, started out by supplying the Carron Ironworks with a vastly improved steam engine that radically changed factories, shipping, and rail transport all over the world. And then there were Charles Tennant and Charles Mackintosh (of waterproof fame) of the St. Rollox Chemical Works, who patented chlorine bleach, and revolutionized the cotton industry by making dye much cheaper because of mass production, safer processes, and drastically reduced production time. All of these innovations were of global importance, and all had their beginnings in the previously unimportant Scotland.

During the late eighteenth century, Britain replaced the Netherlands as the world's banking centre, and London, rather than Amsterdam, dominated global finance by 1812. George Watson (1645–1723), who became chief accountant of the Bank of Scotland, had been sent to train as a bookkeeper in Rotterdam, then a global financial centre. He introduced Dutch ideas to the Scottish banking system and revolutionized the keeping of financial records and account books so important in every business. Accounting first became a profession in Scotland, and the term *chartered accountant*, or *CA*, comes from nineteenth-century Scots accountants who were members of a society that held a Royal "Charter."

At this time, Scotland's financial institutions also became world leaders in banking innovations. The idea of overdraft, coloured bank notes, branch networks, banks that accepted and exchanged each other's notes, and limited liability ownership of public banks, were developed in eighteenth-century Scotland. The intellectual and economic climate of Scotland in the latter part of that century encouraged practical originality, especially where money was concerned. Unlike the Bank of England, which was the British government's bank (so was given a monopoly), Scotland had three competing, publicly chartered banks: the Bank of Scotland, the British Linen Company, and the Royal Bank of Scotland. These were commercial, not government, banks. As stated earlier, private Edinburgh banks such as Coutts and Drummonds elbowed their way into London's West End, where they remain today.[3] In the nineteenth century, Karl Marx wrote that bank crises were a consequence of capitalism, except in Scotland.[4] I think Marx over-stated the situation, however. Scottish banks did have crises, but the innovative soundness of the Scottish banking system did much to overcome the poverty of Scotland, and is a major reason why an industrial revolution began in that country. Scots charted Canada's economic course during the eighteenth and

John Richardson, the Highland Scot who founded the Canadian banking system and initiated many progressive changes, is an example of the dual nature of the eighteenth-century Scottish mind. Although an establishment figure and key member of the Château Clique, he promoted far more progressive causes in Lower Canada than his American Revolutionary and Patriot opponents. (Library and Archives Canada, Mikan 4399116 c-138080.)

nineteenth centuries partly because a steady stream of highly skilled banking staff transferred the innovative soundness of the Scottish banking system from Scotland to Canada.

The adage that Edinburgh at this time was like Renaissance Florence, or like Athens in Ancient Greece ("The Athens of the North") fails to reflect the more cosmopolitan nature of the Scottish Enlightenment. Athens and Florence blossomed locally in their time, but Edinburgh flourished internationally in its time. The Scots were connected to people and places all over Europe and its colonies, in a huge number of different fields, playing a major part in what we call the "knowledge explosion." In our world, New York and London are major airplane hubs, connecting and dispersing international and national traffic. Rather in the same way, Edinburgh and Glasgow in the eighteenth-century world were both international and national hubs, connecting and diffusing people with intellectual ideas. One example is the Scots' adaptation of the encyclopedia first produced by the French between 1750 and 1780. This first major attempt to catalogue human knowledge was a success. Consequently, Edinburgh produced the *Encyclopaedia Britannica*, whose first edition took from 1768 to 1771 to complete. The *Encyclopaedia Britannica* proved an even bigger success than the French original as it sold more copies, lasted longer, and was imitated worldwide. Scotland's two major cities became world printing and publishing centres, selling books, magazines, journals, prints, and newspapers. Scots law at that time did not allow for copyright to be held in perpetuity, and in 1774 a famous legal case was decided in favour of allowing Scottish printers to reprint English books no longer covered by copyright. This legal decision led to a much more liberal approach to printing than was allowed in most countries at the time.[5] Scots books became much cheaper than English books, and readership soared. Printers became important tradesmen in Scotland, reflecting the advanced nature of the trade in Scotland, and through emigration, they became a feature of Canadian and American life well into the nineteenth century. A demographic lightweight, Scotland nevertheless punched for the intellectual heavyweight championship of the world from approximately 1750–1800.

The Scottish Enlightenment also sparked social and legal breakthroughs of particular importance to the New World of the eighteenth century. Scots-Irish philosopher Francis Hutcheson (1694–1746), source of the idea of "the greatest happiness of the greatest number," was the first modern thinker to advocate the abolition of slavery. Another great thinker during this period of change was Adam Smith, who also wanted to end slavery and was an advocate of the Scottish Enlightenment's philosophy of sympathetic, benevolent feeling toward all human beings. William Murray, Lord Mansfield (1705–93), the man who finally put an end to slavery in England in 1772, "was the first Scot to become a powerful English lawyer, legislator, politician, and judge."[6] Scotland soon followed suit and abolished slavery after the decision rendered in the Wedderburn case of 1778.[7] Mansfield's decision eventually led the courts of Lower Canada (Quebec) — despite the protests of the colonial legislature — to effectively end slavery there.[8] In 1798-99, a situation occurred that almost mirrored Mansfield's case. Two African-Canadian slave women, Charlotte and Jude, who had escaped their owners, were initially imprisoned but later freed, "the Chief Justice declaring at the same time, in open Court, that he would, upon Habeas Corpus, discharge every Negro, indent[ur]ed Apprentice, and Servant, who should be committed to Gaol under the Magistrates Warrant in the like cases."[9]

The climate of opinion during the Scots Enlightenment also urged respect for the Aboriginal peoples of the world. The idea of sympathetic understanding of all people, regardless of race or religion, was fundamental to Scottish thinking at that time.

Scots soldier-settlers, including those who served in the 78th, were imbued with a modern outlook on farming — for profit rather than for subsistence or for social status — and hence were motivated to improve the farming methods employed in North America. They were equipped with the knowledge of great changes that were being implemented and invented in their mother country, which led them to prosper in the New World. The Scottish Enlightenment was not just a series of intellectual ideas promoted by the elite, those ideas "spilled over [into] the habits of the mind and the habits of the heart that make up the whole moral and intellectual state of a people."[10] Ordinary people used practical knowledge to improve Scotland and to advance their own personal fortunes. The phrase that I chose as the title of this book — *Driv'n By Fortune* — was coined by an ordinary Scottish product of this period: the ploughman poet Robert Burns. I think that the phrase reflects both the soldier-settlers *and* the spirit of the Scotland that created them.

Highland Scots soldier-settlers had adopted the practical economic perspective of the Enlightenment. They were as firmly on the side of the Agricultural Revolution as they were on the side of King George in the American Revolution. Scottish migrants blended their old mercenary-migratory land relationships with the new agricultural and capitalistic ideologies of the times. In the American Revolution, Highland soldier-settlers fought to win even more farmland, while in the Agricultural Revolution they sought to win more *out of* that farmland. These Highland masses resisted the American Revolution and promoted an economic and Agricultural Revolution with equal vigour and for much the same reason: profit for themselves.

While much has been made of Yankees fighting for freedom in the American Revolution, I suggest it is time to make more of the Scots who fought for other types of revolutionary change in the New World. We need to cut through the misconceptions and rhetoric from both sides in the Revolutionary struggle, explained more fully in chapter 12. The Scots were a major military pillar of a constitutional monarchy in the Thirteen Colonies, and then founders of many of Canada's capitalistic enterprises. They built bridges to overlooked peoples, and were the glue of social peace. Highlanders were not just the best frontier soldiers in the Empire, nor were they simply peasant workers who transferred to peasant work in North America. These soldier-settlers reflected a "New Scotland" and wielded swords, ploughs, and pens to make their fortunes in eighteenth-century North America.

Historians have emphasized eighteenth-century Highland poverty, thus overshadowing the fact that these soldier-settlers brought the Scottish Enlightenment to America. Indeed, some historians ignore that the Scots challenged, changed, and modernized both groups of original European settlers — the French and the English. In fact, "Peace, order and good government," arguably the most memorable lines in the Canadian Constitutional Act of 1867, can be traced to the Scots. Unlike the lofty ideals in the Declaration of Independence, Canada's founding Constitution remained firmly grounded: The Scots "imagined no ... utopias crafted by man. They believed instead in ... common sense ... the pursuit of happiness. A perfect society was impossible...."[11]

"New Frontiers" Produce a "New Alliance"

The Fraser's Highlanders who trooped west from a modernizing Scotland in the eighteenth century were similar to but not the same as the mercenaries who once travelled from what was considered a backward Scotland east into Europe. The "Auld Alliance" of Scotland and France generated a military-migratory land relationship in the Old World where Scottish soldiers took up land and stayed there. What I call a "New Alliance" of militarism, maritime activity, and modernizing capitalism radically transformed the Scottish part of the New World. Maritime technology, such as the steamboat *Swiftsure*, generated a great many unintended changes — paper currency seemingly unrelated to river travel by steamboats became accepted in Lower Canada. Modernization in Canada was a process where fundamental change in one part of everyday life sparked off unintended changes in other aspects of life.

This New Alliance meant that kilted redcoats settled as progressive farmers, banker paymasters, fur traders, pioneer lumbermen, whisky distillers, shipbuilders, and the fathers of some of the world's great explorers. Highland Scots carried the Enlightenment with their broadswords to late-eighteenth-century America, and became formidable but unifying settlers in what became Canada. Scots were at the forefront of western civilization in the Old World and on the frontiers of settlement in the New World — possibly the only people in history ever to be in that position. John Nairne made approximately eight journeys back to Scotland and developed a highly successful seigneury because of knowledge of the most modern agricultural machines and techniques of the Old World. John Fraser, a sergeant in the 78th, became the first and most respected English-speaking schoolteacher in Quebec. Scots militarism and Scots education were, in this case at least, blended. William Ross of the 78th became a highly respected King's pilot for ships on the St. Lawrence River. In many ways, Nairne, Ross, and Fraser represent a microcosm of the eighteenth-century Scots response to the challenges they faced in America. There was a new alliance of modernity, militarism, migration, and maritime activity, which I have summed up with the term Guns 'n' Steam. That new alliance of very powerful forces operating among the Scots explains how the poverty and tribalism of 1745 evolved into the wealthy, peaceful Canadian capitalism of 1812. The New World shaped the Scots as much as the Scots shaped their New World.

Impact of the New Alliance on the New World

This New Alliance was very much a process that happened over time, changing mercenary-minded soldiers into modernizing settlers. In the American Revolution, many Scots had to re-migrate to Canada, which at the time was much more Celtic Scottish as opposed to English than

The Gibraltar of North America, by Don Anderson. North America's first steam powered railway hauled stone to rebuild the Citadelle at Quebec City for the British Army in the 1820s. The steam engine, not seen in this twentieth-century print, was located to the left of the rail line. (Bank of Montreal Corporate Art Collection.)

was the United States. The American Revolution forged two countries in North America. There was a republic and a new colony with its own dream of Celtic modernity created in North America.

Under the cloak of a wider British Empire, the New Alliance played a major role in creating a modern economic, intellectual, and political infrastructure that stretched west to the Pacific coast and north into the Arctic. Consequently, the colonies that became Canada were in many ways a New Scotland of the Enlightenment. One traditional view — that the Scottish Enlightenment influenced the Patriot side but not the Loyalist Highland Scots side of the American Revolution — is, in fact, only revolutionary rhetoric. In reality, modern North America owes much to those who *opposed* the Revolution.

This leads us to a second related point; British North America by the late eighteenth century had become viable and valuable because the New Alliance had developed a new colonial economy, one that was more global in scope and more or less independent of the new United States. This had a great impact on nineteenth-century Britain, especially with regard to diet, as large quantities of cheap Canadian wheat were imported.

Subsequently, the Highland consumption of oats and barley steadily de-clined, and wheat, which was thought of as "dainty" in 1800, had become the major staple of the Highland diet by 1900. Canada played a major role in this dietary revolution in Britain during that time.[12]

Cheap Canadian timber also caused the Highland forestry industry to virtually disappear in the nineteenth century. As the remaining Highland forests were no longer profitable, landowners cleared their forests to make way for sheep. It is ironic that the agricultural modernization brought to Canada in the eighteenth century should contribute to large-scale landscape changes in nineteenth-century Scotland. However, there is no doubt that many other environmental changes were brought about by this "globalization" of trade, as we would call it. Indeed, the transport of cheap food and wood to Britain was a major step toward globalization. Historians have noted the mass European migration to North America after 1815, but often fail to remember the transport of vast amounts of cheap food and wood heading the other way. The Scots soldier-settlers in Canada at that time did not just create the first transcontinental trade in furs; in many ways, they initiated the mass intercontinental trade route of timber-out and people-in from ports such as Quebec City and Liverpool. In fact, the export of people from Liverpool became the major activity in what was the world's largest port in the nineteenth century. As stated, Scots on both sides of the Atlantic played a role in the shipping develop-ments that conquered the ocean frontier at this time.

The third point I wish to make is that the New Alliance of the British fiscal-military state and the Scots Enlightenment were important forces acting upon ordinary soldier-settlers. I write cautiously in this section because I am aware I am dealing with the nature of ordinary people and the broad forces that influenced them during the eighteenth century. This is a highly contentious argument for many reasons. Even modern Scottish historians attribute deep conservatism, not capitalist modernity, to Highland Scots. According to Scottish historian James Hunter, "they remained deeply attached to clanship's traditional values, which, because of the stress those values placed on inherited position, were hopelessly at odds with the ideals motivating the makers of the United States."[13]

The Scottish Enlightenment is usually seen as a force influencing the elite supporters of the American Revolution, men like Benjamin Franklin and Thomas Jefferson. Two Scots who signed the Declaration of Independence were John Witherspoon, an influential president of Princeton University, and John Wilson, one of the first members of the U.S. Supreme Court. In contrast, I maintain that the Scottish Enlightenment also influenced those elites who opposed the Revolution, such as John Richardson the founder of Canadian banking, and John Nairne, who imported steel ploughs and promoted the Agricultural Society in Canada.

Scottish intellectuals such as Adam Smith, Lord Mansfield, Lower Canada's John Richardson (the banker) and John Nairne (seigneur) were conspicuous opponents of the American Revolution and promoters of progressive causes, such as the abolition of slavery.

However, the Scottish Enlightenment influenced the ordinary Highlanders in North America to oppose the Revolution. I will remind readers that many private soldiers of the 78th Fraser's Highlanders were working around Dundee in the modernizing Scottish Lowlands when they were recruited. Many of the 77th Montgomerie's Highlanders were recruited from the industrializing towns of Glasgow and Edinburgh. In addition, the Annexed Estates that operated lands confiscated from Jacobites in the 1745 Rebellion were in the forefront of rural moderniza-tion in Europe. Consequently, these ordinary soldiers who migrated to the New World were precisely those Highlanders most exposed to the mod-ernization process in the world's most advanced agricultural-industrial areas. It would be surprising if these migrants had *not* pioneered modern ideas, techniques, and machines in North America.

I argue that the officer class *and* the rank and file soldier-settlers transmitted much of the capitalistic modernity in Scotland to the New World. The Scottish Enlightenment was also a mass or bottom-up af-fair supporting opposition to the Revolution among Highland Scots. While it is difficult to prove as such, the Scots Enlightenment trans-formed the ordinary Highland people who fought the Revolution as well as the powerful people who debated the philosophical merits of that Revolution. Gun 'n' Steam helps to explain why ordinary, kilted redcoats

Highland soldiers were prominent figures on the Canadian frontier and in towns such as Montreal from 1760 to 1870. (McGill University, McGill Rare Books and Special Collections.)

accepted and disseminated modernity while repelling and resisting republican revolution in America. Arguably, Scotland was Europe's most progressive and modern-minded country and its most enthusiastically counter-revolutionary country from 1776, through the defeat of Napoleon in 1815, to the American Civil War in the 1860s.

The broad political support for the King in the American Revolution maintained the Highland military-migratory tradition and helped maintain the British Empire in North America. In moving to the Thirteen Colonies, and then to Canada, these soldiers were not merely collecting their wages: land. I argue there was a land rush from Scotland and a rush for more land by the Scots who settled before the American Revolution.

As said, there was also a rush by the Scots to improve that land while ordinary people are usually excluded as an influence in eighteenth-century history, the popular experience of the land-hungry Highland masses from 1750–75 determined their course in America.

Many of the Scots who emigrated during the years 1763 to 1775 and 1783 to 1790 *were* the sad victims of a clan system disintegrating in the face of a relentless modernity. However, Highlanders as the victims of modernity in Scotland has overshadowed Highlanders as the initiators of modernity in America. As a group, these Highland soldier-settlers were formidable agents of change. John Nairne wrote that "the winters are getting colder, not milder, as had been predicted with the clearing of the land."[14] The eighteenth-century view was that clearing trees would warm up the winters. It was said at the time that the Highland Scots in Canada were responsible for clearing more trees in twenty years than the French in Canada had in two hundred years. While there is obviously bombast in their claim, the "agro-forest" trade in Canada cleared a vast area from Nova Scotia through to Ontario for settlement.

The agri*cultural* psychology of late eighteenth-century Highlanders in Canada was associated with Protestantism, patriotism, practical improvement, and prosperity. Canada's landscape was altered dramatically because the Scots brought zeal to clearing the woods. "Clearing away" was important to Scottish Enlightenment thinkers. Catholic religious trappings were "cleared away" and enthusiastic conversions to Protestantism left few Catholics in Scotland. The clan system was, of course, also cleared away, and Adam Smith cleared away economic restrictions. The Scots became fanatical in their desire to improve. These people thought they had a duty to clear away and throw light upon many aspects of life, a "Let there be Light" philosophy derived from the Bible. The Church of Scotland was split into the "Auld" and "New Lichts" (Old and New Lights), conservatives and liberals.

Prints of Canada often reflected this aspect of enlightenment, and popular prints featured sunlight streaming down through a clearing in the high trees onto a log home, glowing as a beacon in the dark. The Scots were not at war with nature and did not hate trees or the woods. They wanted to improve upon nature. These settlers saw progress in terms of co-operating scientifically with nature to obtain God's bounty. At that time, nature existed to be reined in to the benefit of hungry humans. In hindsight, some modern thinkers fault them for that. To eighteenth-century Scottish settlers, the wealth that grew from a good farm showed that God loved the good Protestants of that family. As I stated, enthusiastic tree clearances derived from the same broad agri*cultural* psychology that led to the clearance of Highlanders from the Highlands itself by landlords, one of the great tragedies of British history. The wet hills of the Highlands had become very profitable for sheep that supplied the new Lowland wool factories on a large scale. However, sheep required only a few shepherds to look after them, and so entire districts were evicted and sent to North America or Australia. The potato famine of the 1840s made small holdings impossible, and by the 1850s there were not enough people left to clear off the land. These clearances destroyed the Highland population base itself and it was claimed that there were more Highlanders abroad than in the Highlands by the late nineteenth century.

The Fading of the New Alliance

The years between 1745 and 1812 were a short golden age for the Scots. Few nations pioneer settlement across continents, transport technology across oceans, and spread new knowledge throughout the world, and the Scots marched in the vanguard of modernity at this time, but could not maintain such energy indefinitely.

First, the American Revolution had an enormous economic impact on Scotland and the Scots living in the New World. It caused, for example, the collapse of Glasgow as the world's largest and richest tobacco hub. The city's wealth had been centred on re-exporting American tobacco to Europe, but after 1783, the United States no longer needed a middle-man and began shipping their tobacco directly to the European continent. Less obviously, the American Revolution also ended the military-migratory landholdings established by the Scots who usually had to relocate to Canada. The British Empire that grew after the Revolution flourished in places like India, South Africa, and Australia, as well as Canada. It is interesting that Scots attitudes toward migration to Australia blossomed only after Scots soldiers were stationed there and had written letters home to attract their countrymen, just as Scots had done after the Fraser's Highlanders had written home from North America.[15]

Second, the French Revolution, which began in 1789, generated a narrower, nationalist ideology within Scotland. The Scots became unable and unwilling to draw upon Europe, in general, and France, in particular, for military employment or for ideas and techniques. Scotland gravitated to England, not Europe, after 1800–15 and the Scots became less cosmopolitan as they became more British.

These two major revolutions contributed to the inevitable end to Scotland's brief role as the world's intellectual hub. After 1812, Scotland was still intellectually dynamic, but it was not as dominant or as cosmopolitan as it had once been. The Scots' cosmopolitan tradition of European mercenary service also died completely. The New Alliance disappeared after the War of 1812 and the Napoleonic Wars, and there was no need for the British to recruit and reward Highland soldiers with free land in such numbers.

The new economic ideas put forth by Adam Smith during the Enlightenment period about natural, human, and capital resources can be used to summarize the Highland impact on the New World. Thanks to their military role, the ownership of natural resources characterized Highland Scots in North America. These soldier-settlers often had first access to good river frontage and farmland in New York, Vermont, North Carolina, and, especially, in Canada.

As well, these people brought the human and financial resources that could develop their natural resources. Scottish bankers and highly skilled labour from Scotland pioneered large-scale enterprises such as the fur trade, timber trade, and shipbuilding. The British fiscal-military state, the richest in Europe, provided much of the capital used by Highland soldier-settlers who had access to free land as wages. As I pointed out in the Introduction, military service was to the Scots what indentured service was to the English and Irish of the time and was a cheap way of migrating to the new World.[16] The army was basically an economic if dangerous ladder up for these soldier-settlers in that they could re-enlist in 1776–83 or even in 1812 for more land. These people were driven by fortune as settlers every bit as much as they were driven as soldiers of fortune. By "fortune," I mean that hard work leading to individual prosperity has the unintended consequence of also enriching the community, circumstances that Adam Smith labelled the "Invisible Hand."

Unintended consequences characterize the story of these people. Military service led to land ownership and attracted thousands of emigrants to North America. Land hunger and modernity led them to oppose the American Revolution, which in turn led to their expulsion to Canada. Consequently fortune, in the sense of chance circumstances, also determined their story in America. They happened to be: the right soldiers, bilingual at Quebec and frontiersmen in the American Revolution; the right settlers, practical scientific farmers and able to convert dark forests into timber reserves; at the right time in history, the end of New France and the birth of Canada; and in the right place, the New World, which was expanding at a huge rate.

While the musket and the broadsword symbolize the Highland heritage in the New World, the Scots brought much more with them than kilts and bagpipes. Mention has been made of such modernizing features as the metal plough, the McIntosh apple, potatoes especially suited for Canada, new strands of wheat, clipper ships, steamboats, whisky, maps of previously unexplored areas, banking, printing, the Mounties, peaceful commerce between Aboriginals and newcomers, and the multicultural construct that is Canada.

11

Past Fiction: Sir Walter's Scott-Land

Scott, as the first great romancer, made an impression on social ideas
that lasted for decades and decades.
— Hamilton James Eckenrode[1]

In this chapter I will trace many of the misconceptions surrounding the
78th Fraser's Highlanders back to the fictional tales written by authors
such as Sir Walter Scott, Robert Louis Stevenson, Washington Irving,
and James Fennimore Cooper. American historian Lee Holcombe wrote
of the 1745 Rebellion, "Historians ever since have been hard pressed to
retrieve the realities of Highland life which lay behind all the romantic
and patriotic stereotyping."[2]

Sir Walter Scott's Times, 1771–1832

I think it can be agreed that Sir Walter Scott's nineteenth-century pen
changed the Highland image forever. Scott romanticized Highlanders,
mists, lochs, islands, and castles, and invented the Highland legend in
works such as *Rob Roy*, *The Lady of the Lake*, and *Lord of the Isles*. Sir
Walter was a product of the cosmopolitan, cultural traffic that characterized Scotland at the time.[3] He also met and influenced important
American writers who absorbed his ideas to start their own national

A signed page from one of the hundreds of thousands of books sold by Sir Walter Scott. Although plagued by lameness from a bout of polio, Scott's achievements in law and literature earned him the name, "The Wizard of the North." His magic still lives on. (Library and Archives Canada, Mikan 4310468 e010966202.)

literature. Although his stories such as *Ivanhoe* and *Robin Hood* have entered popular culture, the author himself is largely forgotten and underestimated in the popular imagination.

Cultivated eighteenth-century people who set down the attitudes of the time were not at all taken with the Highland landscape. A typical comment about the Highlands appears in John Brewer's *The Pleasures of the Imagination*, a study of eighteenth-century high culture: "accustomed to flowery pastures and waving harvest … astonished and repelled by this wide extent of hopeless sterility."[4] Colonel Simon Fraser was aware of this perspective when he wrote, of Halifax, Nova Scotia: "The country round the Town affords as Disagreeable, a prospect to an English eye as any part of old Scotland."[5]

Sir Walter Scott used real historical events in his writing. One example is the accidental wounding of Magdalene Nairne (sister of John Nairne of the 78th) by Highland Jacobites. When Scott had met Magdalene, she told him how Bonnie Prince Charlie had come to see that she was well and had given her a miniature portrait of himself. John Nairne later hung that same portrait in his own manor house at Murray Bay in Lower Canada. Scott included this incident in his book *Waverly*. He used other real people as characters in his fiction, as well, including Rob Roy and Alexander Stewart (brother of Allan Stewart of the 78th). He showed how decent, fictitious figures, with whom we can identify, were involved with real historical events such as the 1745 Jacobite Rebellion.

Novelists throughout the world copied Scott's technique of portraying the strength of ordinary people caught in extraordinary historical events. His techniques produced some of the best-loved stories ever written.[6]

Scott's works also inspired some great musical talents.[7] *Lucia di Lammermoor* by Donizetti (1835), *The Fair Maid Of Perth* by Bizet (1867), and *The Lady of the Lake* by Rossini (1819) are just a few of the dozens of operas inspired by Scott's books.[8] Several verses from *The Lady of the Lake* were set to music around 1812 by the songwriter James Sanderson, and the resulting anthem "Hail to the Chief" is still played to introduce American presidents. And so Scott still marks the cultural life of the American Republic.

The cultural explosion triggered by Scott had an impact quite on a par with the influence Hollywood moguls or television producers have on our world today. Painting, architecture, tourism, and clothing were all deeply influenced by his work. Because printing had become dramatically cheaper with the invention of new processes, a new mass readership had been born by the nineteenth century. Scott was the world's first living, international literary star.

Rather in the same way that many grumble about television's influence today, Mark Twain complained about Scott's pervasive influence in the late nineteenth century and labelled it "the Sir Walter disease." Much modern romantic fiction written in North America and Britain today is still set in the Highlands of Scotland, indicating the virulent nature of this "disease." The Highland legend indeed lives on.

Scott also believed that romantic Highland men sprang from romantic Highland scenery.[9] Highlanders were claimed to be in a "natural state," "wild," rather than domesticated, and began to be admired as "noble savages." Highlanders were also portrayed as rooted to their beautiful clan homeland. As I stated earlier, the reality was often quite different. Highlanders were a pastoral people who fought over their countryside.

Life was hard and placed them among the most migratory, mercenary people in Europe. By Scott's time, the Highlands were modernizing rapidly.

Scott, through his writing, hoped to counter the adverse effects of the Industrial Revolution, and he viewed the Highlands as a cultural anchor holding out against these waves of change. The new science of geology proved that the Highland hills were exceptionally ancient. Scott believed that Highland clansmen were naturally rooted to their ancient landscape, and to their chiefs and monarchs. In the nineteenth century, the new urban industrial masses were regarded as major threats to social order. Sir Walter's vision of Scotland provided comfort to many who were anxious about the future. The Highlanders in Scott's fiction exhibited the key virtue of "the absolute devotion of a follower to his master"[10] and "each clan bore to its chief all the zeal, all the affectionate deference, all the blind devotion, of children to a father."[11]

Scott portrayed the clan system as a one-way, top-down relationship where obedient clansmen faithfully followed their chiefs. However, real Highland social bonds were far more reciprocal than Scott painted them. The real Highlanders transferred to other clans, adopted new names, and sought the protection of a new chief if the old one was unsatisfactory.[12] Highland chiefs had to heed clan opinion, if only to retain their clansmen. Scott's notions also countered the evils of the French Revolution and the Napoleonic Wars. France was the centre of European civilization and education at the end of the eighteenth century, yet it was in 1789 that the Paris mob erupted and guillotined thousands. Later, the Napoleonic Empire killed millions in war, re-introduced slavery, torture, and the secret police, and extorted vast wealth from conquered peoples. Such was the devastation of the Napoleonic Wars that the British worried about the social implications of France in much the same way they would worry about the social implications of Germany during the Second World War. Scott's world was haunted by the example of France, and asked, as we did about the Holocaust after 1945, "Could it happen here?"

Scott wrote, in effect, that the French revolutionaries were nothing compared to the Scottish clansmen, for their militant nationalism let alone their militarism. Books such as *Waverley* transformed the rebels of 1745 into misguided, softhearted Jacobites who fought because of a devoted loyalty to their "rightful king." But approximately fifty thousand Highlanders fought in the Napoleonic Wars, and were the military backbone of the British forces that eventually destroyed Napoleon and neutered France's leadership role in Europe. In much the same way that Europeans admired and were grateful to North Americans after 1945, Europeans admired and were grateful to Scotland after 1815: "When the Scottish regiments appeared in Paris, in their kilts and tartans, Scott's writings linked them with the historical imagination of Europe."[13] The Highlands, and what it meant to be a Highlander in previous centuries, were reinterpreted dramatically because of Sir Walter Scott's fiction.

The Scots mercenaries in previous centuries were now seen as "nominally entering the French service as mercenary troops ... among the Italian and German hirelings, the Scots alone had a cause at heart. France was the field on which they could meet and strike the Norman invaders who had dealt so much oppression on their paternal soil."[14] Scots soldiers were thought to have fought the English (Normans) in France for a patriotic cause, not for money.

As for the many wars in which the Scots fought for both sides, it was claimed by some Victorian intellectuals that they "enjoyed the respectability of being engaged in their own quarrel. They were fighting for a party, not a country."[15] Sir Walter's Scots were so patriotic and loyal to Scottish causes that they found foreign wars to continue their political quarrels. In many bizarre ways, romantic writers glossed over the uncomfortable fact that Scottish Highlanders fought mostly for money throughout Europe from 1250 to 1783.

Scott's work made it popular to identify with Jacobite Highlanders. Approximately 4,500 Scots emigrated or were exiled because of the Jacobite Rebellion, with about seven hundred of them going to North America. Jacobite exiles were also portrayed as tragic figures in sentimental Scots folk songs about Bonnie Prince Charlie, such as Lady Nairne's "Will Ye No Come Back Again?"[16] Jacobite migrant numbers were also exaggerated into the thousands, especially by North American historians. In many cases, fiction defeated fact, and the Jacobite Rebellion acquired a prominence in emigration far beyond its actual importance. As was stated earlier, in *The Statistical Account of Scotland*, a survey conducted in the 1790s, there is no mention of the 1745 Rebellion or Culloden in the many references to Highland emigration. In many history books, the 1745 Rebellion was labelled as the motor of Scots migration only after Scott's books of fiction appeared in the nineteenth century. In novel, poetry, and song, Highlanders were so anchored to their homeland that no mercenary pull for land in Europe, let alone English colonies, could prompt them to migrate.

The very idea that Highland soldier-settlers were pulled to Europe, New York, North Carolina, and what is now Vermont and Canada has vanished from popular memory in Britain, the United States, and Canada itself. Reality clashed with the new myths: "We mistakenly think that memories are like carvings in stone; once done they do not change."[17] False memories based on fiction grew, and by his poetic interpretation of the old Highland life, Scott created a picture that has in many cases superseded history.[18]

Auld Scott Land and Loyalty to Royalty

In 1822, Sir Walter Scott and Colonel David Stewart, the romantic historian, orchestrated King George IV's visit to Edinburgh — the first reigning monarch to come since Charles II in the middle of the seventeenth century. Scott and Stewart staged the event as a national clan gathering. Highland chiefs and their followers arrived wearing kilts and tartans, as did King George. This started the craze for tartans, and soon "the whole land was tartanised."[19] The chief of the MacGregors, whose name by that time had been legalized, was chosen to give the symbolic toast: "The Chief of Chiefs —The King."[20]

Such was the public enthusiasm for this singular event that the British monarchy came to be identified with the Highland chiefs, and the chiefs with the monarchy: "[C]hiefs themselves, recently so dangerous by reason of their incorrigible treachery, now became romantic warrior-princes."[21] Before the emergence of Scott and his writing, unless an unusually large army accompanied them, most Scottish and English kings alike had avoided the Highland chiefs.

Scott's poem "Hail to the Chief," from *The Lady of the Lake*, was written during the time of the British King George III, who was opposed to the American Revolution. It was then set to music during the reign of George IV, and played during his visit to Edinburgh. Ironically, the song is now regarded as an American republican tradition linked to presidents such as George Bush and George Washington. Even the British and Canadians today associate the anthem with presidents, not monarchs.[22] Auld "Scott Land" has become Americanized.

Loyalty to Royalty: The Victorian Years

When Queen Victoria came to the throne in 1838, she boosted the myth of Highland loyalty to the monarchy even more. After their third visit to Scotland, Victoria and Prince Albert fell in love with the Aberdeenshire scenery around Balmoral Castle, and the estate and its lands became the personal and private property of the Queen in 1847. The old castle was demolished in 1856 after a new larger house was built on the site — in the Scottish architectural style and decorated with tartans, of course. Thus began Queen Victoria's love affair with the Highlands — and, it is rumoured, possibly with the Highlander John Brown (after Prince Albert's death).[23]

Details of Victoria's Highland life were spread widely by the new mass media, and Highlanders were identified with the Queen as much as she was with them. Victoria was arguably the most famous person of the nineteenth century, and her stamp of approval transformed the Highlands into a major cultural anchor in the minds of Victorian Britons, Canadians, and perhaps even Americans. The Highland identity was rather like Victoria's identity in the public mind: a permanent force in the changing British and Canadian societies. In much the same way that Balmoral Castle was rebuilt to suit Victorian tastes, the Highland image was refashioned to suit the tastes of the time. While the seeds uniting the Highland image to royalty were sown in the time of George IV, the flowering of the myth occurred in the Victorian era. That myth has persisted to this day, and members of the modern royal family still don kilts and tartan on occasion.

Even Highland animals were imagined to have royalist leanings in nineteenth-century British art. One of the most successful landscape paintings ever created captured the spirit of the times by labelling the

The Monarch of the Glen, by Sir Edwin Landseer, 1851. Landseer's famous painting helped to establish the monarchy, the British aristocracy, and rich foreigners as patrons of Highland hunting and fishing estates. It is still widely used as a commercial logo by many corporations.

painting of a Highland stag *The Monarch of the Glen*. The title is brilliant, and connects the Highlands, nature, and royalty. Thousands of prints were made of Landseer's painting and the phrase lives on today.

Colonel Simon Fraser's eighteenth-century assertion that Highlanders were unusually loyal to the Hanoverian monarchy, which I discuss later, echoed even more powerfully in the Victorian era. Rather than realize that the association of Highlanders and British royalty started in the mid-nineteenth century, historians assumed wrongly that it started in the late eighteenth century. For example, the great American historian D.H Fischer, in his Pulitzer Prize-winning book *Washington's Crossing*, describes Scottish soldiers in the American Revolution as bound together by "a fierce sense of loyalty that flowed through family, clan and chiefs and upward to the king himself."[24] Hence, loyalty to the British Crown became a fundamental part of the Highland character in the eighteenth century according to prominent historians.

The idea that Highlanders had an emotional attachment to the British monarchy through their chiefs is misleading, however. The real Highland soldiers had been loyal to monarchs in the past, but this had been built up over time and owed to French, Swedish, Russian, Prussian, Austrian, and Polish royalty. The flood of printed romantic, nationalistic myths that backdated the association of kilted warriors to British royalty overwhelmed the historical reality of Scots service with foreign royalty. Fiction replaced fact even among the great historians.

Lowland Scotland, one of the most advanced industrial regions in the nineteenth-century world, began adopting and internalizing a medieval Highland past. Colonel David Stewart's book *Sketches of the Character, Manners and Present State of the Highlanders of Scotland* became the origin of "the new orthodoxy concerning the antiquity of the kilt and distinctive clan tartans."[25] While tartans were originally of regional and local design, Stewart wrote that tartans had always been woven in distinctive patterns for the different clans, tribes, families, and districts.[26] In 1842, the then Lord Lovat, chief of the Clan Fraser, helped the two "Sobieski Stuart" brothers publish their book *Vestiarum Scoticum*, which they followed up with *The Costume of the Clans*.[27]

Although the tartan designs in these books were as bogus as the brothers, who were really Welshmen named Allen, their designs and ideas were accepted with enthusiasm. "Tartan fever," as the *Scotsman* newspaper of the time called it, broke out. Literature invented new tartans, new family groupings, and indeed new clans for the nineteenth-century Lowland Scots.[28] Scotland as a whole identified with the Highlands: clans, tartans, kilts, (Highland) games, and all. Scott's misreading of history in the early nineteenth century had moved from books into real life by the middle of that century. Scott and his disciples evoked false memories, and Scotland yearned for a tartan past that it never actually had. The tartan kilt became a powerful symbol of Scottish heritage because it combined the individual with a clan family, nostalgia with fashionable modernity, rural with urban, royalty with commoners, men with women, and the ordinary with the powerful. Clans and kilts, symbols of backwardness in the eighteenth century, by the nineteenth century were transformed into major cultural symbols of a modern Scotland.

Lowland Scottish regiments became tartan-clad, too. The Scots Guards created a pipe band in 1870.[29] The Cameronians, initially formed to fight the Highlanders in 1689, adopted tartan in 1881.[30] The Royal Scots, disregarding its past in the service of other European countries, adopted tartan in 1882.[31]

By the late nineteenth century, the Highland soldier became treasured as an ancient, royal national symbol of Scotland, not because of what had happened in the past, but born of the false assumptions of books and newspapers. Clans, tartans, and Jacobite images, not those of the eighteenth-century Scottish Enlightenment, were adopted by Scotland. As a key part of the British Empire, the Scots occupied a central place in the new world power structure. The intense nationalism generated by Scotland's success in the nineteenth-century British Empire motivated collective amnesia, invention, and pretence about the Scottish past. Brand new traditions from "Auld Scott Land" cloaked Scotland in general and the country's soldiers in particular. The Highland soldier became a British icon and played a major role in forging a new British identity.[32]

Scott's devoted son-in-law, J.G. Lockhart, was taken aback by what he called a "collective hallucination"[33] that identified all of Scotland with the clans that had formed only a portion of the Scottish population. This misinterpretation of that time evolved into the "false collective memory syndrome" of our time. Scott's fiction of the early nineteenth century became Scottish fact, and today clans and family tartans are a fundamental part of popular Scottish heritage at home and abroad. Scotland became stereotyped as romantic, but untouched by modernity.

Auld Scott Land in the New World

Thanks to a fictitious "Scott Land," American history books also portrayed eighteenth-century clansmen in North America as royalist and medieval. For example, Scott was remarkably wrong in his assumptions about the similarities between Highlanders and North American Aboriginal peoples. Scott wrote that "the whole north of Scotland was under a state of government nearly as simple and patriarchal as those of our good allies the Mohawks and Iroquois."[34] In fact, the Iroquois tribes lived under a complex federal system of government and were very much matriarchal, not patriarchal. Nevertheless, Highland Scots in the literature about the North American frontier were often portrayed as successful because of a romantic kinship to Aboriginal peoples.

The actual Highland experience on the frontier was coloured by hardheaded attitudes from the Scottish Enlightenment. The Highland Scots *were* comparatively enlightened and humane for the times. Highland frontiersmen united money with morality, and concentrated on trading with Aboriginal peoples. It was a profitable benevolence that explained their co-operation with Aboriginal peoples, not some sort of romantic, softheaded kinship with them. However, Scots in the United States and Canada found themselves reinvented as Sir Walter's vision dictated.

While it is now forgotten, the United States had its own nineteenth-century reasons for accepting Scott with great enthusiasm. For "the young United States, Scotland served above all as a political and cultural role model. Scotland was the land of perpetual rebellion against England."[35] In the years following the American Revolution, England and Scotland, not the United States or France, were the world leaders in virtually every field of endeavour. The revolution in the United States had encouraged the bloody French Revolution, which was followed by the even bloodier career of Napoleon. However, "Scott Land" was eternally opposed to England. Fiction gave the Protestant United States the intellectual confidence that it had done the right thing in uniting with Catholic, reactionary France to break away from a hateful England. "Scott Land" served as an intellectual justification for rebelling against the richest, most advanced, and most progressive Protestant nation in the world. Nineteenth-century America ignored that Scotland was even more opposed to their revolution than was England, and that states such as Georgia had gone so far as to outlaw the Scots.

In the place names of the United States there are: 11 Lady of the Lakes, 22 Rob Roys, 52 Kenilworths, 89 Ivanhoes, 171 Woodstocks, and 210 Waverleys.[36] While Washington Irving inspired 7 places called Rip Van Winkle and 128 named Sleepy Hollow, no other writer appears to have had the same cultural impact as Sir Walter Scott had on United States place names. It's ironic that an enthusiastic royalist is arguably the most significant novelist in the history of the "Republic."

Scott sold incredible numbers of books in the new United States, and thousands saw musicals such as *The Lady of the Lake*. The cultural impact of Scott's ideas upon Americans was far more lasting than the sales of his own works. The first full-time writers produced by the United States — Washington Irving (1783–1859) and James Fenimore Cooper (1789–1851) — went separately to Europe with introductions to meet Scott. Cooper's subsequently successful novels, *The Last of the Mohicans*, for example, describe Scots soldiers as settlers, and include references to real regiments such as the 55th (raised in Stirling) as a background to the stories. Scott, who suggested German folk tales to Irving as a source of inspiration, directly encouraged Irving to write "Rip Van Winkle" and "The Legend of Sleepy Hollow."

Despite being of recent Highland Scots descent, Washington Irving reflected Scott's distorted perspective and was probably typical of nineteenth-century American writers. He wrote of Scott: "His works have incorporated themselves with the thoughts and concerns of the whole civilized world for a quarter of a century, and have had a controlling influence over the age in which he lived."[37] Irving also wrote about the Highland Scots on the frontier in ways deeply influenced by Scott. In *Astoria: Anecdotes of an Enterprise Beyond the Rocky Mountains* (1836), Irving penned descriptions of Highlanders that are still widely quoted despite being remarkably wrong. For example, he wrote that: "they ascended rivers in great state, like sovereigns making a progress, or rather like

Highland chieftains navigating their subject lakes. They were wrapped in rich furs, their huge canoes freighted with every convenience and luxury, and manned by Canadian voyageurs, as obedient as Highland clansmen."[38]

This statement has passed down unchallenged into the twenty-first century; even the part about being wrapped in rich furs. In reality, the canoes travelled in the summer. Irving associated terms like *royalty*, *luxury* (in canoes), and *obedient clansmen* with Highland chiefs. Even nature is subordinate to these Highland chieftains, who navigate "subject" lakes. The idea of a huge social gap between chiefs and their docile clansmen is emphasized. The social distance created by Southern plantations was far more exacting. In reality, the "Nor'West Company" was almost certainly more socially cohesive than most contemporary organizations in the United States. There is a poetic truth in Irving's great line that the Scots were "the Lords of the Lakes and Forests" at this time because Scots were very successful in the fur trade. However, it is important to state that Irving ignored that, poetically, Scots were also the "Lords of Modernity."

The point is that American writers such as Irving and Cooper were writing under the influence of what Mark Twain labelled the "Sir Walter disease." They were the first Americans to write fiction about the frontier, and, arguably, they stamped the image of "Auld Scott Land" into American minds.

By the end of the nineteenth century, Mark Twain was complaining of Scott's influence on U.S. architecture, clothing, education, and, of course, literature. Twain wrote that Scott did more lasting harm than anyone who had ever written. He was serious when he made his famous but exaggerated assertion that "Sir Walter had so large a hand in making southern character, as it existed before the war that he is in great measure responsible for the war." [39]

Scott had not only romanticized war and created the bizarre notion of Southern chivalry through works such as *Ivanhoe*, but had unintentionally solidified slavery where people were considered "property." Sir Walter wrote that masters were owed total allegiance by their inferiors and had an absolute right to their own property.[40]

In much the same way that nineteenth-century Scotland invented a tartan and clan history that it never had, the nineteenth-century South invented a Scottish past that it never had. Indeed, while "the rest of America read Scott with enthusiasm … the South assimilated his work into [its] very being.… Scott was incorporated into the Southern people's vision of themselves."[41] Plantation owners in the "Old South" saw themselves as clan chiefs with a military as well as a social role to play, and Scotland's flag — the St. Andrew's Cross — became the war flag of the Confederacy, the Southern Cross. This flag still represents defiance and resistance in the United States, and is still quoted in twenty-first-century newspapers as a symbol of protest.[42] The failed 1745 Rebellion inspired the post–Civil War South to adopt the idea of the Lost Cause, that they fought nobly although they knew from the start they could never win.[43]

Ku Klux Klan was the name given to those who resisted Reconstruction after the Civil War, and there is no doubt a Highland heritage has been tagged onto that organization. An American, Hamilton James Eckenrode, blamed Scott for the undemocratic and racist character of a South he labelled "Scottland."[44] This phrase is a measure of the popularity of Scott's fiction in North America, not of the actual influence of Scottish immigrants in the South.

The 1905 novel *The Clansman: An Historical Romance of the Ku Klux Klan* by Thomas Dixon is dedicated to "the memory of a Scotch-Irish Leader of the South. My Uncle, Colonel Leroy McAfee."[45] The book describes how "the young South, led by the reincarnated souls of the Clansmen of Old Scotland, went forth."[46] According to Dixon, the Ku Klux Klan is a reincarnation of the Highland clans. The United States first full-length film, *Birth of a Nation*, was based on this bestselling book. Originally called *The Clansman*, this racist film was a smash hit, and helped to revive the Ku Klux Klan in the early 1900s.[47]

Scott misrepresented and may well have invented the idea of the "fiery cross" to summon the clans in several of his books, including *The Lady of the Lake*. Some doubt whether the Highland clans actually did operate with a fiery cross. Nonetheless, Dixon wrote in *The Clansman*, "dispatch your courier tonight with the old Scottish rite of the Fiery Cross. It will send a thrill of inspiration to every clansman in the hills."[48] There is a print entitled *The Fiery Cross of Old Scotland's Hills* included in Dixon's book. The film *Birth of a Nation* also perpetuates this idea, and depicts exciting, dramatic scenes of the Klan rallying to a fiery cross.

The idea of burning crosses arose *after* the book and film of the early 1900s revived the Klan. The burning of such crosses apparently did not take place among the original KKK formed after the Civil War in the 1860s.[49] The revived KKK reflected Dixon's literary imagination, not the past reality. I find it difficult to see how the "reincarnated souls of Old Scotland" defended the South, partly because comparatively few Highland Scots ever settled there. Even in North Carolina, the Highland influence was very much a minority one. A Highland South was a figment of the Southern literary imagination. If the name "Leroy McAfee" is the closest the South could come to a Highland name, nobody could suggest that the roll call of a Klan gathering was like that of clans gathered at Culloden. Scottish regiments in Poland, Sweden, France, and so on display more Highland names than the Klan mobs of the South. The Ulster Scots who formed a part of the Southern population tended to be of Lowland Scots stock, not of Highland stock. In brief, identifying the Klan with "the clan" is historical fiction overpowering reality and is part of the Americanization of Scott's work.

Waverley, a novel about the 1745 Rebellion , was one of the many books and popular songs that created the idea that the rebellion was a glorious, if lost, cause and that it "was perfectly suited to be the national epic for the South."[50] Jacobite sympathizers in the nineteenth century cultivated the false idea that Highlanders fought a rebellion to free Scotland against overwhelming numbers of Englishmen; it was a lost cause to begin with. Apologists for the South saw clannish, high-spirited aristocrats defending the traditions of the "old plantation South" against interfering hordes from the North. Films such as *Birth of a Nation* and *Gone with the Wind* reflect these sentiments very well.

Other Americans have interpreted Scott's stories about freedom and rebellion very differently. To justify the African-American struggle for freedom and defiance of tyranny in the South, Frederick Augustus Washington Bailey (c. 1817–95) adopted the name of a heroic character, "James Douglas" from Scott's *The Lady of the Lake*. The original James Douglas, a great warrior for Robert the Bruce, was nicknamed "The Black Douglas," and helped win freedom for the Scots at the Battle of Bannockburn against the English. Frederick Douglass also became known as "The Black Douglass" and went on to become an influential journalist and abolitionist trying to win freedom for slaves. Both African Americans and whites in the Old South turned to Scott's fiction to help them show defiance and resistance. However, the Southern mind absorbed Scott to such a degree that the American mind then placed Scott's books with the whites and the South rather than with the Black Douglass and the North.

Frederick Douglass visited Scotland in the 1840s and was sympathetically received. He claimed that freedom, not slavery, was Scott's message, and quoted both Walter Scott and Robert Burns to his Scottish audience to prove his point.[51] The overwhelming number of racist interpretations of Scott in the United States reflects the literary power structure, not the inherent content of the author's work. However, Scott's ideas about what Scotland represented lasted well into the twentieth century in the United States.

These fictions about the country appealed to the ruling American elite in both the North and the South. Romantic writers such as Irving, Cooper, and the racist Dixon stated that Highlanders were defeated and exiled, but still showed defiant support for the correct social order and hierarchy. Scott was the right novelist for the elite in the United States and Canada in the wake of nineteenth-century problems.[52] His Scottish vision provided hope in dangerous times. By the early twentieth century, American books identified Highlanders with elitism and royalty, order and deference, Southern defeat and defiance. According to one Scottish historian, Highlanders in North Carolina "have consistently had a raw deal, whether as defeated Jacobites, defeated Loyalists or defeated Confederates."[53] American historians believe that Highlanders were "remarkably consistent in choosing the losing side,"[54] were Americanized and identified with "lost causes." This is in marked contrast to the actual eighteenth-century reality of Scots on the frontier — adventurous, progressive, and capitalist — that I have outlined. Historical fiction partly explains why it is difficult for historians to identify Highland Scots with the progressive modernity of the Scottish Enlightenment. Unfortunately, Scott "was able to have his view of history accepted" on both sides of the Atlantic.[55]

Literary Myths and History

Links between literary myths and history are also evident when we look at Colonel Simon Fraser (1726–82), the 78th's colonel. Fraser was the first president of the aristocratic Highland Society of London (HSL) — renamed the Highland and Agricultural Society — which stated as its mission to "diffuse knowledge" and to preserve the "martial spirit, language, dress, music, and antiquities of the Caledonians, and rescue from oblivion the valuable remains of Celtic literature."[56] The HSL became an "organ of propaganda" for Celtic literature, including the story of Ossian.[57] Stories supposedly told by the bard Ossian about his father Fingal were published in the 1760s by James MacPherson and purported to be based on ancient Gaelic oral ballads and manuscripts. By placing Ossian on a par with Homer, Scottish culture was transformed immediately from irrelevant to a fundamental part of European heritage. MacPherson was a skilled writer and his work, like so many aspects of the Scottish Enlightenment, was absorbed by the rest of Europe and the Thirteen Colonies; President Jefferson was apparently fond of Ossian.

MacPherson was rather like Scott, who used Scottish folk tales in his work, except that Scott never claimed that his stories were true. Colonel Simon Fraser and most other Scots used Ossian as a national Scottish symbol to feed the "noble savage" view of Highlanders. Ossian became "an article of faith"[58] for the Scots who insisted for a long time that the poetry was genuine and that the events actually happened.[59] According to the historian Trevor-Roper, the pretence that Ossian was genuine was part of "a chain of error" that constantly "falsified the national past" of Scotland.[60] Colonel Fraser had no part in the forgery of the Ossian poetry, but did use it to feed the enormous appetite for things Scottish that was growing in the Britain and Europe of his time. In many ways, Colonel Fraser of the 78th used Scottish writing as much as he used Scottish fighting to promote himself and other Scots in the forging of Britain.

Simon Fraser was again caught up in a major literary falsification, this time in the Appin murder of 1752, one of the most dramatic trials in Scottish history. Colin Campbell was the Crown's rent collector on the Appin Estate seized from the Jacobites. Campbell had allowed

James Stewart to collect the official rent plus extorted amounts that were sent to the former Jacobite owners. The arrangement was ending because Campbell planned to evict many of the Clan Stewarts and replace them with Campbells. Allan Breck Stewart, a Jacobite recruiter for the French Royal Scots, was accused of shooting Campbell in the back, but had to be tried in absentia because he had fled. James Stewart was tried for being an accessory to the assassination because he had sent clothes and money for Allan to escape. The result of the trial was by no means a foregone conclusion because thirty-one witnesses gave evidence for the prosecution; eighteen were used by both sides, and ten for the defence. James Stewart had three lawyers and Jacobites had contributed large sums for his defence. Simon Fraser, the future colonel, gave a balanced, but powerful performance as the chief prosecutor who not only successfully rebutted the many arguments for the defence but proved that James Stewart helped Allan Breck escape immediately after the murder. James Stewart was executed as an accessory-after-the-fact, but Allan Breck Stewart escaped to France, fought in North America for the French, and died an old man protesting his innocence. Although many Appin Stewarts were involved in the murder, only James Stewart was hanged. Simon Fraser and the Duke of Argyll, the Hanoverian political leader in Scotland, made it clear to Highlanders and London that justice, not clan vengeance, was the new norm in the Highlands. Fraser was of course rewarded for his work in the trial by receiving the colonelcy of the 78th in 1757.

However, Robert Louis Stevenson, best known as the author of *Treasure Island*, falsified the events surrounding the murder and the trial in two of the most popular books in the nineteenth and twentieth century, *Kidnapped* (1886) and *Catriona* (1893). Stevenson has the fictitious David Balfour witness the murder, when in reality there was no clear view of the ambush. In *Kidnapped*, Stevenson has Fraser order the fictitious David Balfour killed because he could prove that James Stewart was innocent. In fiction, the villainous Simon Fraser intentionally prosecutes an innocent man, which converts the execution of James Stewart into "an exercise in clan vengeance, Campbells against Stewarts, and an example of military tyranny."[61] Sir James Fergusson, the prolific Scottish author, wrote about the popular view of the murder, stating "how much dearer to the popular mind in Scotland is the preservation of legend rather than the desire for historical truth."[62] Tourists from both sides of the Atlantic still flock to Appin to see where the fictitious David Balfour "witnessed" the murder and statues of Balfour and Alan (Stevenson's spelling) Breck can be found in Scotland.

Robert Louis Stevenson placed the Clan Campbell, the Hanoverian party, and Colonel Simon Fraser of the 78th among historical fiction's great villains, with the Jacobite Stewarts of Appin as their victims. The hero of *Kidnapped*, David Balfour, describes Simon Fraser as "a man whom I distasted at the very first look, as we distaste a ferret or an earwig."[63] Nineteenth-century books such as *Kidnapped* invented Highland myths, but in the real life of the eighteenth century, Lieutenant Allan Stewart of Appin (possibly related to Allan Breck Stewart of Appin) recruited among his clan and joined Simon Fraser's 78th to fight for King George.[64]

In brief, the 78th in general and Colonel Fraser in particular are very much on the wrong side of prominent fiction and modern Scottish "heritage" sites. In Highland fiction, only rogues changed sides. In the pop culture and the tourism of the nineteenth to the twenty-first centuries, the Appin Stewarts were loyal Jacobites who would never join a redcoat regiment under Simon Fraser, the evil prosecutor of the innocent James Stewart. The 78th violates the Highland identity forged by nineteenth-century fiction and modern tourism. Much of the "Highland identity" described in today's history books is, in fact, the product of nineteenth-century pop culture.

This is not to forget the role played by Colonel Simon Fraser himself in reshaping the literature of the regiment he raised. He asserted that Highland soldiers had enthusiastically flocked to enlist in the 78th Regiment for love of their king and gentlemen such as himself (clan chiefs). He exaggerated the speed at which his regiment was raised, stating that "such a number of men as I raised in the year 1757 in four weeks could not have been processed so speedily for any sum of money, without the concurrence and aid of friends, Gentlemen of the country with proper connections."[65] Fraser fails to mention that he recruited from all over Europe, the Highlands, the Hebrides, and amongst Highlanders working in the Lowlands. Fraser also inflated his local influence as a clan chief and the royalist fervour of Highland clansmen.

After returning home as a wounded war hero from America, Colonel Fraser became a key political figure as a reformed Jacobite who had suffered for the Hanoverians. A fine speaker in Parliament and in public, Simon Fraser overstated his own importance for personal glory and also for the return of the Lovat title and lands that had been lost after the 1745 Rebellion.

Colonel Simon Fraser *was* a brave Highland chief of long lineage who re-invented himself as a loyal British subject, leading one of the most spectacularly successful regiments in the British Army. Yet he also started the fiction that only clan chiefs could recruit in the Highlands because they were "properly connected" to clansmen. By the nineteenth century, the much-quoted friend of Sir Walter Scott, the Highland Romantic historian Colonel David Stewart of Garth, dismissed the importance of money, and reinforced the idea of clan loyalty even more. Stewart wrote of Fraser: "Without estate, money or influence, beyond that influence which flowed from attachment to his family, person and name, this gentleman in a few weeks found himself at the head of 800 men recruited by himself. The gentlemen of the country and officers of the regiment added more than 700."[66]

Colonel Stewart's statements and omissions evolved into the twentieth-century belief that "more than half of the thirteen companies were raised in Fraser country"[67] and that "Fraser alone found it easy to raise a regiment[68] … the Highland gentry … raised them as clan levies by threat and persuasion, by enticement and appeal to traditional loyalties, calling upon men of their own name and from their own districts."[69]

In reality, of course, mercenary habits were still strong, and as was shown earlier, "the King's Shilling" was a major factor in explaining why so many enlisted from so far away. Rather than analyze the solid recruiting achievements of Colonel Simon Fraser, the young British soldier at Quebec, historians have chosen to repeat and believe his statements as an old Highland parliamentary politician on the make.

History books over two centuries have transmitted the myths generated by "Sir Walter's disease." Despite this, many scholars still "overvalue the influence of historical truth as against historical myth."[70] For instance, families of Highland soldier-settlers fought conspicuously for the British Crown throughout the eighteenth century and well into the nineteenth. Veterans such as John Nairne who had prominent Jacobite relatives would arguably be surprised, perhaps even insulted, by the sheer weight of songs, books, films, and websites emphasizing those Highlanders who took part in the rebellions against King George.

The Battle of Culloden in 1746 was written about in history and in fictional works such as *Kidnapped* as one of the really bitter, divisive battles of the British past. In fact, Hanoverians such as Sergeant Sinclair, and Jacobites such as Lieutenant Allan Stewart, who had fought against each other at Culloden, fought together very successfully in the Fraser's Highlanders. In many modern history books, Jacobites hate the Hanoverians just as they did in *Kidnapped*. Alexander Stewart, brother to Lieutenant Allan Stewart of the 78th, both of whom fought at Culloden, wrote a letter in 1746 that suggests that Highlanders "viewed rebellion not as an act of treason or bitter conflict of ideologies, but as a rather rough sport of gentlemen and sometimes a family squabble."[71] Whatever the reason, Highland soldiers disregarded many of our ideas about warfare so that Culloden was more of a temporary rift than it was a permanent divide.

Two centuries of Sir Walter's disease afflicted historians on both sides of the Atlantic. As Thomas Sowell points out, "whole nations can be given fictitious characteristics in furtherance of a prevailing vision" and "a whole fictitious country can be created, totally different from the real country it is said to be."[72] Scott's myths are also updated to reflect modern prejudices, and Highlanders are sometimes seen as colonial conscripts, Britain's first "ethnic soldiers."[73] Highland soldiers are placed on a par with other British Empire "warrior peoples" from Africa, India, and North America.[74] This view ignores the great social mobility experienced by Highland Scots in the Empire and the fact that the Highland Scots aristocracy became colonial governors, generals, administrators, businessmen, and settlers in a way no other "ethnic" peoples did.

Whatever the reasons, Highlanders are not generally identified with either the modernity of Scotland that took place between 1745 and 1812 or with the renewal and modernity of British North America after 1783. North American historians tagged Highlanders as victims rather than as agents of modernity in Canada, Britain, and the United States. Whose Enlightenment do historians think it was?

In our time, we debate how countries like Japan, China, and India shifted to modernity and economic prominence. In the nineteenth century, the explanation for Scotland's Industrial and Agricultural Revolutions often came from fictional accounts — and Scott's answer was the wrong answer. Chiefs, kilts, and tartans had little to do with Scotland's march to modernity, but the people of that time were unaware of this fact.

Scott's imaginary past won out completely, transforming the 78th into a state-sponsored clan levy fighting for the Hanoverian monarchy out of loyalty to their chiefs. "Often fictitious individuals and nations have characteristics that are not merely different from, but the direct opposite of, those flesh-and-blood people to whom they are supposed to correspond."[75] However, Scott's literary legends passed into reality because of our failures, not his. It is hardly Scott's fault that the world transformed his historical fiction into historical fact. By many accounts, Scott was a fundamentally decent human being concerned with the adverse effects of his time. Scotland did much to invent our idea of the modern in the eighteenth century, and Scott did much to invent our idea of the past in the nineteenth century. In many ways, our views of the past and the modern are two sides of the same Scots coin.

This chapter is a tribute to the remarkable literary powers of Scott. Canada, Britain, and the United States are culturally indebted to him because he invented the hero as an ordinary person forced to fight evil, the basis of much of our pop culture, good and bad. He also made the world aware that the past can speak to the present and his stereotypes are still media blockbusters. However, identifying eighteenth-century Highlanders through the pop culture of Scott, Stevenson, Irving, Cooper, or Dixon is about as reliable as viewing the past through Hollywood's vision in films such as *The Last of the Mohicans, Gone with the Wind, Kidnapped, Braveheart, Ivanhoe, Robin Hood, The Patriot, Brave,* or *Rob Roy.*

12

The March of the Highland Men Through the History Books

I've a grand memory for forgetting.
— Robert Louis Stevenson, *Kidnapped*

According to historian Hugh Trevor-Roper, "the whole history of Scotland has been coloured by myth."[1] History is the written story of the past, and myths are wrong ideas that people believe to be true. After marching for two hundred years through history books, the 78th's story has also been coloured by myths — and the national ideologies of the United States, Britain, and Canada.[2] National myths, which glue countries together, are patriotic beliefs that omit or invent significant aspects of the past, but which are more often than not assumed to be true.[3] Myths are not so much lies but credible, false beliefs about the national past that the public enjoys because it separates "us" from "them." And many of the unspoken assumptions made about the 78th Highlanders, such as that they had no military experience other than that of clan warfare, are simply wrong.[4]

Historiography — the ways history is written — partly explains why some of these misconceptions exist. History writing has become very specialized and narrow in focus. For instance, military history of the

American Revolution often ignores the Highland soldier-settler experience from the Seven Years' War, while migratory history tends to undervalue the impact of Highland soldiering on migration.

I suggest that the birth of British, American, and Canadian national imaginations — the often chauvinistic notions these nations create about themselves, especially in times of war — also led to imperfect histories. National histories in Canada, the United States, and Britain also have amnesia about some races, times, and places. Highland Scots, African Americans, and Aboriginal peoples are often left out of these national histories.

1745–1812: The Births of Three Nations

The peaceful intervals between wars are often overlooked, although they are times of great change. The importance of some places in eighteenth-century North America, such as those parts of New France absorbed into the Thirteen Colonies after 1763, is often forgotten by historians. Between 1745 and 1812, Canada, Britain, and the United States were shaped by wars [5] that created their geographic and intellectual borders.[6] Bagpipes played conspicuously in the births of the United States, Canada, and the United Kingdom, fuelling three nationalistic sentiments over the next two hundred years. Benedict Anderson, author of *Imagined Communities*, first published in 1983, defines a nation as a historically "imagined political community with borders that are as much intellectual as geographic."[7] How these three nations imagined their origins — Canada from the Seven Years' War, the United States from the Revolution — spills over into how they imagined their Highlanders who played a central role in these wars. Highlanders were a force to be reckoned with in the United States, Canada, and Britain in ways they were not before and after.

An eighteenth-century Scots mercenary grace went: "Lord. Turn the world upside down that Christians may make bread of it."[8] Their prayers were answered as the Atlantic world was "turned upside down" by war several times and Highlanders "made bread" of the situation as soldiers, as settlers, as friends, and as foes of three nations. Were these soldiers from the 78th Scottish, British, or Canadian? They can claim all three nationalities. Were their children American, because many, such as Simon Fraser of Canadian river fame, were born in the Thirteen Colonies but did not live in the new United States? Were they Jacobites or Hanoverians? They fought for both. Were they reactionary and medieval as so many historians claim — when they freed slaves, saved many Aboriginals, and brought a capitalistic modernity to much of the New World? Consequently, it is very difficult for historians to place them accurately in a national history.

Nation-Centred History Writing

It is important to emphasize that "the simplest thing that can be said about historical writing … is that it remains conspicuously national in character."[9] Each nation has a historical canon containing the fundamental beliefs the intellectual elite wish to transmit. Each national grand narrative is widely believed. Stories such as that of the 78th, which cross the borders of three nations, are seldom told in full. Grand narratives usually turn a blind eye to the Highland story that took place in the other two nation-states under discussion. Indeed, the American historian David Lowenthal points out that "falsified legacies are integral to the exclusive purpose of group identity."[10] Highlanders are seen through the national identities of Britain, Canada, and the United States, so the very same Highlanders acquired different national images. Nations are also imagined and then re-imagined to meet the circumstances of the time, and, as the British historian Eric Hobsbawm commented, "forgetting is an essential factor in the formation of a nation."[11] Accurate historical information about these Highland soldier-settlers in Canada, the United States, or Britain did not travel well into the grand narrative of the other two nations mentioned.

Be that as it may, the proper role of history is "to challenge and even explode national myths."[12] Three sets of national myths create problems: George Orwell's selective memory, Margaret MacMillan's historical amnesia, and Eric Hobsbawm's invention of tradition are important concepts when looking at the Highland story in three nations. Pretence, and the enjoyment of that pretence, is the problem tackled by Clive Cheesman, Jonathan Williams, and Walter A. McDougall. Their ideas form the basis for the following:

Table 8: Faith in a National Identity Motivates

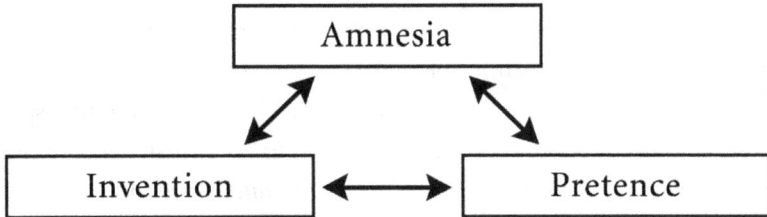

```
                    ┌──────────────────┐
                    │     Amnesia      │
                    └──────────────────┘
          ↗                                    ↖
  ┌──────────────────┐              ┌──────────────────┐
  │    Invention     │  ←──────→    │     Pretence     │
  └──────────────────┘              └──────────────────┘
```

Faith in the nation meant that "nationalism became ... a new secular religion."[13] Extravagant self-praise and excessive criticisms of outsiders are features of history writing about nations and wars. Historians in three countries wove their three national attitudes towards the same soldier-settlers into a complex pattern that sometimes blended but often clashed.

Orwell defines a nationalist as someone who applies a belief to his own nation and a contradictory belief to those on the outside. Orwell's observation about nationalists believing two contradictory assumptions at the same time is evident in many history books. For instance, historians often write that Highland soldiers fought valiantly for England in North America, but then claim that these same Highlanders fled to America and became settlers there because they hated England.

Selective memories ensured that Highlanders were portrayed in contradictory ways when perceived as national foes as opposed to founders of that nation. This situation is similar to the changing perceptions of Sir Walter Scott's song "Hail to the Chief." Exactly the same tune evokes very different meanings depending on the time, place, and individual.

Selective memory also applies to the 78th Regiment of Foot and how it is described in three sets of national history books. In British history books, before his success at the Battle on the Plains of Abraham, Simon Fraser, the ex-Jacobite trying to win back his place in Hanoverian Britain, is portrayed as a reactionary turncoat. As the new colonel of the 78th, he is denigrated as someone who "raised the regiment in hopes of buying his way back into the good graces of the British government with the lives of his fellow Scots."[14] But after the success of the 78th on the Plains of Abraham, British history then described Simon Fraser as "a leading general in the Seven Years' War and fervent opponent of American independence ... an extreme example of ... the increased integration of Scots into the British community in the aftermath of the 'Forty-Five and in response to war and its conquests."[15] It seems that even today British history regards the 78th Fraser's as both "Scotland the Brave" *and* "Scotland the Knave."

Britain's Nationalistic Myths

Prime Minister William Pitt claimed in the British Parliament that he was the first to enlist Highlanders in military enterprises. Probably because Pitt was the first to use Highlanders to extend the British Empire, his statement had an impact on the British historical imagination, and the Seven Years' War became regarded as the first time Highland soldiers were "called forth" to fight. Rather than analyzing Highland soldier-settlers in eighteenth-century America as a work in progress for over five hundred years, British historians made the unspoken assumption that these were the first Highland soldiers to ever fight and settle abroad.

British history, until recently, has exhibited a collective amnesia about the Highland Scots mercenaries and migrants who served many European countries and their colonies overseas. The following was written in an 1899 edition of the *Scotsman* newspaper: "In popular memory, and in military histories, the Scots Brigade, which for fully two hundred years marched under the flag of the United Netherlands, has not fared so well."[16] Since that statement, this author could only find one book written about the Scots Brigade in the Netherlands, but more than ninety books about the British Black Watch Regiment.[17]

In the histories of these three countries, there are not just missing pages, but whole chapters have been left out. Historians have built vast intellectual frameworks upon highly imperfect assumptions about Highlanders in Canada, Britain, and the United States. Scots mercenaries in North America such as Captains Nairne and MacDonald became the Unknown Soldiers of three national histories.

United States Nationalistic Myths

Amnesia, invention, and pretence[18] motivated the national narratives of the United States as well. American historians were remarkably attentive to the few Scots who signed the Declaration of Independence, but, remarkably forgetful of their many Scots Loyalist foes: "Until the 1970s ... the Loyalists were a neglected lot in early American historiography."[19] Ezra Stiles of Connecticut perhaps sums up the American attitude at the time of the Revolution when he wrote, "History will say it, that the whole of this War is so far chargeable to the Scotch councils & to the Scotch as a Nation."[20]

The history of the United States does *not* say that, and the progressive Scots' ideology that opposed the Revolution is still surprisingly untouched by modern historians, who assumed Loyalism was uniformly reactionary rather than a broad tent containing both progressive and reactionary elements.

In order to illustrate the Orwellian nature of American national history writing, I examine the viewpoints surrounding the important idea of the "new American man."[21] The Frenchman, Hector St. John de Crèvecoeur, penned a much-quoted perspective of immigrants in the Thirteen Colonies in *Letters from an American Farmer*, first published in 1782. According to Crèvecoeur, himself an immigrant farmer, the various European peasant-migrants (but not African Americans) became a "new American man" because they were "regenerated" by life as freehold farmers in the frontiers of the Thirteen Colonies. According to Crèvecoeur, the peasant farmer created newness on the frontier. Crèvecoeur asked a famous question that has echoed down to modern times: "Who was this new American man?"

I suggest that the new American man was, in fact, an enlightened Scot who brought scientific farming and new values to the American frontier as he had in Canada at that time. Indeed, Crèvecoeur did identify Andrew the Hebridean from the Island of Barra in Scotland as typifying the "new American man."[22] Crèvecoeur had settled in frontier New York among numerous Scots, and he became a scientific farmer and a great supporter of potato farming.[23]

"Andrew," in my view, represents the type of soldier recruited on the Island of Barra by the eldest son of the clan chief, Lieutenant Roderick MacNeil of the 78th; many Barra MacNeils became soldier-settlers.[24] However, I was unable to find out if Andrew, the "new American man" from the Island of Barra, was actually in the 78th Foot.[25] Some historians have even suggested that Crèvecoeur created Andrew from a composite of multiple Highland Scots.

National history, *before* the American Revolution, identifies "Andrew the Hebridean" as being in the very vanguard of progress as a new self-reliant American. However, in true Orwellian fashion, *after* the Revolution, history endows these same Highland Scots who opposed the Revolution with an opposite identity. For instance, the famous American historian Franklin Folsom wrote that "these clansmen … were trained to respect authority, whether that of the king or their clan chiefs…. Such medieval hearts and minds had little in common with patriot rebels, so it was small wonder that they joined Tory efforts to support King George."[26]

Bad history about Highlanders in America travelled to Britain. Maldwyn Jones writes "Effective though the American environment could be in most cases in transforming Europeans into new men, it was evidently incapable, in so short a time, of eradicating deeply ingrained habits of feudal subservience."[27] In the same vein, Tom Devine, the distinguished Scots historian, claims that "some Highlanders supported the Revolution. In the Carolinas most, but not all, were loyalist…. Their role in the notorious loyalist militias of the back-countries of North Carolina and New York is well documented."[28] Highland Loyalists are "notorious" even to the best of Scots historians. In reality, Andrew the Hebridean, fighting for the king, was as much a product of frontier America as was the New England Whig Patriot who fought against the king.

American historians recognize that many Highlanders were not remotely obedient in 1745, but, as regards 1776, "Because the Highlanders were more accustomed to obedience than to self-assertion, they had to take their medieval values to Canada…." Franklin Folsom, who wrote these lines, was a Rhodes Scholar, author of eighty books, secretary of an anti-Fascist Society, and sympathetic to the poor and African Americans.

He was no flag-waving American chauvinist; yet, even historians such as Folsom assumed that Highlanders were medieval because they supported King George in the Revolution. Medieval qualities of "hierarchy and obedience" are attributes pinned upon Highland Scots by historians of the political left and right, but not upon Patriot slave owners such as Benjamin Franklin.

Michael Kammen, a Pulitzer Prize winner, writes about the American historical imagination that,

> Professor Bernard Bailyn of Harvard University had an immense impact upon Revolutionary scholarship.... He has stressed certain psychological transformations that took place in the Whig mind ... the colonial sense of social and cultural inferiority gave way to a belief in their moral superiority.... Bailyn also sketched out features of the Tory mentality — its concern for rank, hierarchy, deference, order, obedience....[29]

Bailyn states that the Whig Patriot mind progressed, whereas the Tory Loyalists who opposed the Revolutionary War retained regressive traits. In reality, Highlanders were not only forced into new geographic boundaries, but into new alliances that led to new social boundaries. Highlanders were transformed as well as transferred by the American Revolution.

Wars often lessen prejudice against people outside the mainstream of society.[30] The diverse peoples who were the Loyalists won new rights as well as new lands in Canada that were not given in a republican United States. The loss of the Revolutionary War forced the British — perhaps more accurately the English — into a more inclusive society. The English Loyalist population base in British North America (Canada) was too small anyway to establish an independent country. African Americans, Aboriginal peoples, French Canadians, and Highland Scots were needed to establish a viable Canada, and then to win the moral high ground in the peace that followed.[31]

After the Revolution, in many ways, the British mind under the influence of the Scots became more progressive, while the Whig Patriot mind became more reactionary. Despite claims to the contrary by Bernard

Bailyn, the North Carolina historian Jeffrey Crow points out that "to re-build the social structures which had prevailed before the war, southern whites moved quickly to redefine the status of blacks. This was accomplished in part by the escalation of the slave trade.... The black population of North Carolina grew faster during the 1790s than any other decade in the antebellum period."[32]

Much more than Patriot society, Loyalist society was forced to become the innovator in race relations after 1783. Both sides after the Revolution were new, but in different ways. The Declaration of Independence created an idealistic breakthrough in human rights, while Loyalist Canada created a practical breakthrough in human relations. In turn, these two results came about because I interpret the Revolution as a conflict of two enlightenments: the Scottish and the American.

The Loyalist "new American men," as Crèvecoeur called those with frontier experience, were forged by war into a nation of British North Americans who eventually evolved into what I call the "new Canadian men." It is no historical accident that Protestant Highland Scots and French Catholic Canadian canoe men, with First Nations peoples as their guides, were *First Across the Continent*, as Barry Gough called his biography of Sir Alexander Mackenzie. The "new Canadian men" were the first to bridge various ethnic and religious groups as well as the North American continent itself.

The historian Frederick Turner (1861–1932) advanced Crèvecoeur's ideas about the frontier to say that the experience generated self-reliance, individualism, ingenuity, and resourcefulness. None of this is to suggest that Turner's frontier thesis, Crèvecoeur's idea of the "new American man," or my idea of "the new Canadian man" are correct interpretations of the past. American historians have, in fact, severely criticized the frontier thesis and the "new American man" on the grounds that African Americans were omitted from the ideas. The inclusion of many different peoples in the Highland Scots narrative is fundamental to my understanding of the new Canadian man.

As for the "new American man," arguably, he is still assumed to be white and a Patriot in Canada, Britain, and the United States. The frontier and the Revolution are also assumed to be exclusively American.

In reality, frontier expeditions, such as that of Lewis and Clark, were preceded by Highland Scots frontiersmen. William Dunbar and George Hunter, who led the southern frontier expedition equivalent to Lewis and Clarke's northern expedition, *were* both Scots. The complete Highland Scots story in many ways challenges the historical pretensions of three nations. "What happened to Crèvecoeur's new American man after 1783?" American historians have tried in vain to trace Andrew the Hebridean, so perhaps the answer is that this Gaelic-speaking Highland redcoat went to Canada to pursue a new capitalist modernity there.

As I mentioned, several states, such as Georgia, banished the Scots after the Revolution. History continued this exclusion by ignoring Highland Scots' achievements on the frontier. George Orwell brilliantly describes this pretence when he writes: "Every nationalist is haunted by the belief that the past can be altered. He spends part of his time in a fantasy world in which things happen as they should ... and he will transfer fragments of this world to the history books whenever possible."[33] For instance, world achievements such as the first crossing of the North American continent by Mackenzie and MacKay and the epic explorations of Simon Fraser go unrecognized by many, perhaps by most, American school histories. Yet MacKay and Simon Fraser were born in upstate New York/Vermont to Highland soldiers, and Mackenzie lived there. In U.S. school history books, it was Whig-Patriot supporters of the Revolution, such as Lewis and Clark, who successfully explored the frontier, not Loyalist Scots Americans such as Mackenzie, MacKay, Simon Fraser, William Dunbar (possibly a Loyalist), and the Scots Loyalist traders in the Spanish borderlands of the southeastern United States.

According to nineteenth-century American nationalists, the United States had a "manifest destiny to overspread the continent allotted by Providence."[34] Frontier history was interpreted patriotically to match political history, and Simon Fraser, the MacKay brothers and so on were driven from their birthplace and from history books to become the unknown frontiersmen of U.S. history.

Canadian Nationalistic Myths

The rise of French-Canadian nationalism partly explains the amnesia, invention, and pretence about the Highland Scots in the Canadian grand narrative. This is explained partly because there is a Francocentric aspect to present-day Quebec history that overlooks and underestimates the impact of eighteenth-century Highlanders in Canada in general, and Quebec in particular. This spirit of Francocentred history is illustrated in Quebec City. Sergeant Thompson, diarist of the 78th Foot, as deputy-overseer of (Public) Works, played a major role in rebuilding and redesigning Quebec City after Wolfe's siege in 1759. Yet he was virtually forgotten by historians until the twenty-first century. Thompson's own house in the "Upper Town," occupied over the years by four generations of Thompsons, still stands, though it was given an official French name, but the "Lower Town" fell on hard times, and the magnificent stone Georgian buildings had fallen into disrepair by the mid-twentieth century. At this time there occurred a modern assault on Thompson's city every bit as destructive as Wolfe's eighteenth-century assault. There were no surviving pictures, maps, or blueprints of pre-conquest Quebec City, and speculation about the size, shape, appearance, and design of the original buildings of New France was shadowy. Nevertheless, municipal, provincial, and federal governments in the 1970s and 1980s intentionally destroyed Thompson's authentic eighteenth-century British-styled stone buildings in the Lower Town, to be replaced with imaginary French-styled stone buildings. What is being preserved in Quebec City? What past is being resurrected?

Canadians assumed that Thompson's buildings were not worth restoring. Why? Using Orwell's idea of "non-persons," Thompson's creations became "non-buildings" and were no longer significant in the national memory. Canada spent huge sums on a Francocentric heritage that was not a reality and destroyed much of the two-centuries-old Highland heritage. As D. Lowenthal suggests: "Amnesia is central to [Canadian] national heritage."[35]

The military effectiveness, frontier abilities, innovativeness, and the sheer number of Highland Scots in Canada have all been downplayed over the years. As I have said, the bilingual role of two Highlanders at

This French-only plaque is the official acknowledgement of Sergeant James Thompson's life, and omits his many accomplishments in Quebec City. It says that the house was constructed in 1793, he was in King George's army, and his descendants lived there until 1957. It ends by pointing out that he was born in Tain, Scotland, and died at the age of ninety-eight in 1830. (Photograph by Sam Allison.)

the Battle on the Plains of Abraham has been forgotten by "bilingual" Canada. The actual battle lasted approximately fifteen minutes, with eighteen dead Fraser's Highlanders to the literally hundreds of enemy French soldiers. Yet, Canadian books consistently state that the Highlanders suffered huge losses in the battle.

Canadian history books do not mention the huge impact the eighteenth-century Scottish Enlightenment had on this country. No Canadian school history text known to this author has ever illustrated the effects of Murray's introduction of the potato and printing to New France-Quebec. Even these two incredibly important aspects of modern life are excluded from Canada's Francocentric heritage.

In 1819, John Richardson, the Highland "founder of Canadian banking," outlined the framework for Canadian banks. *The Quebec Mercury* of May 2, 1808, reprinted his views, which included the view that "the utility of Banks cannot perhaps be better illustrated than by a reference to Scotland." At least a quarter of Richardson's speech referred specifically to Scottish banks, including the statement that the three Scottish charter banks had "in all, in the different towns of Scotland, above thirty branches." Yet, the widely quoted *Canada's First Bank* claims that "the Canadian

General James Murray, a former Scots mercenary, became the first British governor of Quebec (Canada). He promoted French-English relations and population growth for both linguistic groups. He wanted to settle in Canada after his time as governor but his wife did not, so they returned to Britain. (Library and Archives Canada, Mikan 2837238 c002834k.)

system derived directly neither from Scotland nor from England, but from the United States."[36] It even claims that "branch banking, later to become a distinctive feature of the Canadian system, was an indigenous and necessary invention, wholly unrelated to Scottish precedent."[37]

Richardson was also involved in a host of other progressive changes in Lower Canada[38] and held progressive views about Catholics, slaves,[39] Jews, African Canadians, and women.[40] For example, the Protestant[41] Richardson supported Catholic emancipation in Lower Canada (1791), then Jewish emancipation (1807–09).[42] Although Catholics and Jews were not allowed to vote in Britain, an exception was made for Lower Canada's Catholics. Richardson then sponsored a bill supporting Ezekiel Hart's battle for Jewish emancipation.[43] However, Papineau, the leader of the Catholic Patriotes, opposed the bill on the hypocritical grounds that Jews were not allowed to vote in Britain.[44] It was another enlightened Scot, John Neilson (1776–1848), who introduced the final Jewish Emancipation Act[45] because Richardson had died. But the role of the two enlightened Scots in Jewish emancipation has been ignored, and Canada even issued a postage stamp to commemorate Papineau because, as Speaker of the Assembly, he *had* finally agreed to the emancipation in 1832.

Other oversights in the Canadian national narrative about Highland Scots involve forestry. Credit for starting the timber trade was often given to Americans like Philemon Wright in the nineteenth century, rather than to Highland Scots such as Alexander Fraser, the MacKay brothers, or William Davidson in the eighteenth century.[46] There is neither a modern study of the St. Lawrence timber-migrant trade nor a Canada-wide study of the timber and shipbuilding industries in the eighteenth and nineteenth centuries.

The first Scots immigrants to Canada are identified in virtually every Canadian history book with the *Hector* and its voyage to Nova Scotia in 1773. The coming of the Fraser's Highlanders in 1759 and their disbanding in Quebec in 1763 are a forgotten part of the national memory. American and British historians adopt false Canadian assumptions too. In his excellent book, *Voyagers to the West*, the American Bernard Bailyn describes the *Hector's* landing as "The scene which would prove to be a vivid moment in the collective memory of Scottish Canada."[47]

The ability of Highlanders to range the continent was often attributed to French-Canadian voyageurs or to members of the First Nations, so that the Highlanders' frontier expertise with the land and its peoples were ignored. *The Beaver*, a magazine of Canadian history, carried an article in April-May 1989, written by one of Canada's finest historians, entitled "Conducted Tour." Mackenzie's thousands of miles of canoe and foot trips to the Arctic and to the Pacific and then back were labelled "tours" because he used many Aboriginal guides and French-Canadian voyageurs. Mackenzie, a devout Protestant, respected North America as the inhabited territory of Aboriginal peoples and employed French Catholics in ways few of his non-Scottish contemporaries did. Yet, he is demeaned rather than praised for his adaptability.

Canadian secondary school history books, such as *Close-Up Canada* by Oxford University Press, have pages devoted to French and French-Canadian fur trade explorers, but omit Scots explorers such as Alexander Mackenzie, arguably one of the most important explorers of inland North America. Textbooks reflect and shape the collective memory, and once again I point to the Francocentric nature of Canadian national history.

The idea that Loyalism pulled Highland Scots to the "Promised Land," as Highlanders referred to it in their letters from the time, did not enter into Canadian historical thinking. Land was assumed to have been compensation for losses rather than a promised part of the King's Shilling. It was common in Canadian history narratives to assert that the Loyalists were losers psychologically, intellectually, economically, and militarily. The idea that Canadian farmland was an economic springboard that helped launch the new Canadian men into the vanguard of North American life was not explored. The very presence of Highlanders among Loyalists was understated, so those Highland Scots characteristics — controlled violence, deference to legitimate authority, mercenary outlook — were seldom recognized as such.

Failure to recognize the demographic existence of Highland Scots is perhaps the most important part of this historical amnesia. Here is but one example:

> In Upper Canada there were perhaps 35,000 people, 2,400 French-speakers along the St. Clair River opposite Detroit ... 3,000 Gaelic-speaking Highlanders just established ... some 2,000 Indians, and perhaps 23,000 Loyalists, late Loyalists, and their descendants, most of whom had come from upstate New York.[48]

The three thousand Gaelic-speaking Highlanders described as "just established" were probably members of the Glengarry Light Infantry Fencibles and their families who had just arrived from Scotland. However, many of the "23,000 Loyalists" from upstate New York were also, in fact, Scots and their families from the 78th and other Highland regiments. Simon Fraser the explorer was a Gaelic-speaking Scots Loyalist from New York who went to live in Upper Canada. He became one of the most famous people in the world, yet this survey gives no recognition to such settlers. Indeed, there were thousands more Scots living in Upper Canada (now Ontario) than were recorded in the above survey.

As with studies of Scots mercenaries in European wars, Canadian and American demographers fail to realize there were large communities of Scots abroad. Scots were a highly mobile people within Scotland and between countries in the eighteenth century. Canadians assumed that the Loyalists were Yankees, and often stereotyped them as reactionary Tories who lost to the democratic Whig Patriots. Identifying some of the Loyalists — such as John Richardson the banker, and Alexander Mackenzie the explorer — as progressive Scots of the Enlightenment more accurately explains Canada's story. United States historians often assume that those who migrated to Canada after 1783 were republican Yankees rather than re-migrating Scots or their grown children. Historians then wonder why such migrants from the new United States were often loyal to Canada in the War of 1812.

Few history books connected the 78th Foot who climbed the Plains of Abraham with the Scots Loyalists who migrated to Canada from New York and Vermont after the American Revolution. History forgot that the 78th Foot was a mobile, multilingual, multicultural bridge in a pluralistic Empire. As a consequence of their bilingual role, the Highland Scots made New France's transformation into a British colony more palatable to the inhabitants. Highlanders converted as well as conquered the French Canadians, and were cultural brokers, go-betweens with other "internal enemies" as the historian Alan Taylor labels them — peoples such as African Americans and First Nations peoples. The British Empire was often said to have existed by dividing and conquering people. The exact opposite seems to be the case for the 78th Foot, who conquered then united diverse peoples.

For instance, 78th soldiers who owned seigneuries (John Nairne, Alexander and Malcolm Fraser, James Murray, Sergeant Lachlan Smith) encouraged hundreds of Scots to work in Quebec. Many came, but were mobile and failed to stay in those seigneuries partly because they intermarried with eighteenth-century French Canadians and wanted to become landowners themselves. Modern clan societies, including the Clan Ross Society of Quebec, are composed of "French" Canadians, but

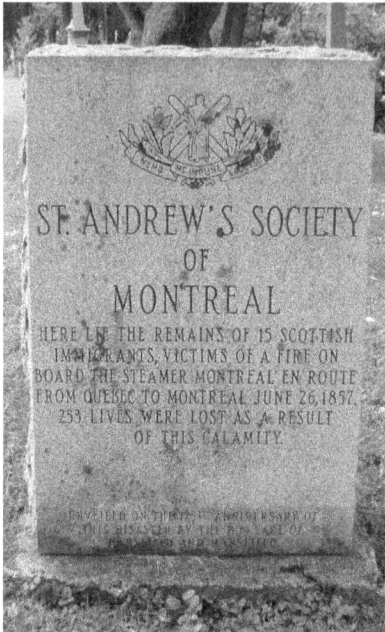

At one time it was thought that immigrants were safe once they survived the Atlantic crossing. This tombstone in Montreal's Mount Royal Cemetery reminds us that literally thousands of eighteenth- and nineteenth-century immigrants died during the St. Lawrence River/Great Lakes leg of their journey. It was Scottish charitable organizations, not the government, that gave temporary food and shelter to their migrants. (Photograph by Bruce Bolton, MacDonald-Stewart Foundation, 2015.)

are below the radar of official Canadian history.[49] The Parti Québécois, a Quebec nationalist political party that advocates separation from Canada, had a minister by the name of Robert Burns, and a leader, Premier Jacques Parizeau, who had Munro ancestors. There are hundreds of thousands of French-speaking Canadians descended from Scots. However, Canadian history writes about "two solitudes" and "two founding peoples" — the French and the English. This attitude ignores the fact that both the English and French were often Scots. The Canadian concept of two founding nations is a false dichotomy that fails to reflect the complexity of Canada's past, and turns the Scots into the unknown soldier-settlers of both English and French Canada.

Defeated Races, Disputed Places, and Shadowed Spaces in History Writing

National narratives play down minority peoples, remote places, and the spaces of time regarded as unimportant in their national imaginations.

For instance, the Scottish Lowlands monopolize the story of the Scottish Enlightenment and the Highlands and Highlanders are portrayed as playing a small role (if any role at all) in that narrative.[50] As regards non-races, "American historians … have often sought to construct an intellectually plausible lineage for the nation, while until recently excluding those such as Indian tribes, African Americans or the Spanish and French…."[51]

Spanish soldiers who defeated the British in Florida are considered "non-persons" in the American memory of the Revolution. Scots explorers such as MacKay (son of a 78th soldier-settler), who explored what is now the United States for the Spaniards, are also viewed as "non-persons." As regards time, the era after the Seven Years' War is studied mostly for the causes of the American Revolution rather than for the consequences of that war, one of which was mass Scottish immigration mostly to what was the former New France.

Table 9: Orwell's "Non-Persons" in Nationalistic History

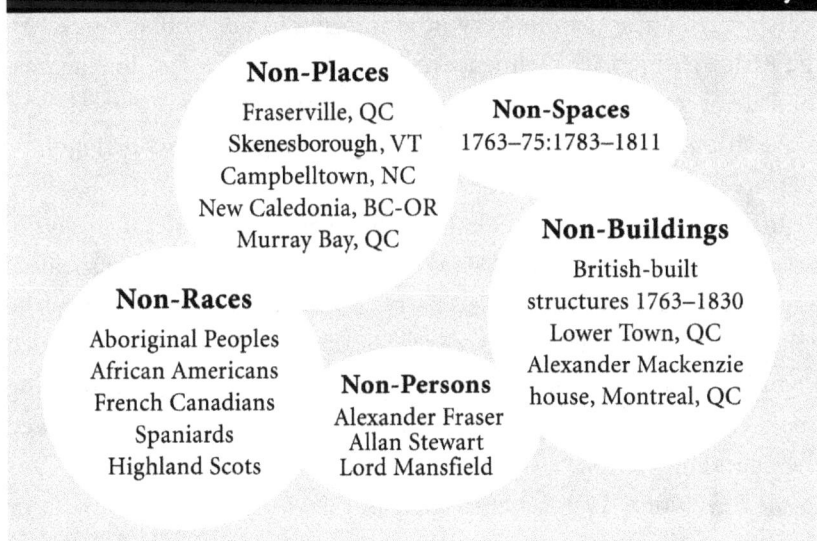

Non-Places

Fraserville, QC
Skenesborough, VT
Campbelltown, NC
New Caledonia, BC-OR
Murray Bay, QC

Non-Spaces

1763–75:1783–1811

Non-Buildings

British-built
structures 1763–1830
Lower Town, QC
Alexander Mackenzie
house, Montreal, QC

Non-Races

Aboriginal Peoples
African Americans
French Canadians
Spaniards
Highland Scots

Non-Persons

Alexander Fraser
Allan Stewart
Lord Mansfield

In many parts of North America, evidence of a Scots presence was erased by changing the original names that acted as signposts to their Scottish past. In the *Dictionary of Canadian Biography*, for example, many of the entries about the descendants of the 78th state incorrectly that these settlers were born in Rivière du Loup, when, in fact, it was called Fraserville at the time. Campbelltown in North Carolina was re-named Fayetteville to remember the French general of the Revolutionary War. Highland soldiers settled in forgotten places with forgotten names that indicated their Scottish origins.[52]

Two veterans illustrate how nationalism has downplayed their ac-tivities with the domestic foreigners, neglected times, and overlooked geographical places. Lieutenant Allan Stewart, mentioned in chapter 6, recruited for Jacobites, Hanoverians, and then Loyalist forces in North Carolina. He also recruited migrants in Appin for North Carolina, Loyalists in North Carolina for Nova Scotia, then in Appin, for emi-grants to his new lands in Nova Scotia. The sheer geographic diversity of his activities makes it difficult to track him, as does the fact that the Loyalist presence in North Carolina has often been obliterated and his lands in Nova Scotia are now in New Brunswick. To add to these re-search difficulties, there is very little information or public interest in the African-American regiment Stewart led to fight for freedom against the Patriot forces in the Revolution. In contrast, there is a great deal of research and interest in the African-American regiments who fought for their freedom in the U.S. Civil War.

In a book that won the 1968 Pulitzer Prize, *The Ideological Origins of the American Revolution*, Bernard Baylin dismisses Lord Mansfield as one of the "corrupt, Frenchified party in the nation"[53] and ignores the epic Mansfield decision. It was, of course, Mansfield's decision that freed English slaves. It was not until Allan Taylor's 2014 Pulitzer Prize–winning book, *The Internal Enemy*, that mainstream academic history recognized the important role played by Colonel Allan Stewart's African Americans in the Revolution. Popular films such as *Twelve Years a Slave* now show slavery very differently to popular films such as *Gone with the Wind*.

The second veteran whose remarkable adventures are absent from patri-otic history is the French-speaking Lieutenant Alexander Fraser. His activi-ties took place 1763–65 and 1776–83. The time 1763–65 is ignored because it took place after the Seven Years' War and long before the Revolutionary

War. The Ohio Valley was inflamed because the French had lost the War and ceded the area to the Spanish and British, who had not yet occupied the vast area of the Mississippi Valley. British troops had been killed and their units repulsed in a vain effort to transfer the French forts to the British and Spanish. Fraser was sent with the Indian trader Croghan and only two or three companions (accounts vary) with valuable wampum, a symbol of peace, to establish friendly relations with the Aboriginal peoples in the Mississippi region. He was separated from Croghan, and paddled in disguise with a companion approximately two thousand river miles, then donned his uniform to officially take the surrender of the French forts between Fort Pitt (Pittsburgh) and New Orleans at the mouth of the Mississippi. After the massacre of British civilians at Fort William Henry, British soldiers held a grudge against French soldiers and would execute those who harmed a British officer after the peace treaty ended the war.

This was the largest land transfer in history, with the eastern half of the region going to the British and the western part to the Spanish. Fraser's life was in constant danger from the French traders who wanted to sell their goods to the Aboriginal peoples before British traders arrived, and many of the Aboriginal peoples still supported the French. Fraser's account puts the Aboriginal peoples in a good light, and says that Pontiac "has saved my life twice since I came here."[54] He paddled into British-held New Orleans still in disguise because the French traders were pursuing him. The British Army, not known for its generosity, awarded him six hundred pounds, an immense sum in those days. He joined the Canadian Indian Department, which negotiated with the Aboriginal peoples on behalf of the British Army. In 1776, he formed a very formidable British ranger unit, the British Marksmen (they used rifles and muskets) composed of British soldiers, French Canadians, Aboriginals, and American colonials. This was a highly effective unit that was feared and hated by the American rebels.

Although he was the instrument of a huge land transfer among colonies, Lieutenant Alexander Fraser is more or less forgotten. In marked contrast, President Jefferson's role in the 1803 Louisiana Purchase of just the western part of the Mississippi is regarded as a major turning point in history.

Jefferson did not need to leave his office to be lauded as a hero. As George Orwell wrote, "All nationalists have the power of not seeing resemblances between similar sets of facts.... Actions are held to be good or bad, not on their own merits but according to who does them."[55] National history celebrates leaders' extending national territory, but not a Highlander in a canoe who enabled the largest land transfer in human history.

Why does it matter that the United States, Canada, and Britain have amnesia about Allan Stewart and Alexander Fraser? It matters because their stories help us to understand what really happened in the past. One soldier brought African Americans, and the other, Aboriginal peoples to Canada after the Revolution. The Underground Railroad for African Americans is well-known. Less well known is that thousands of Aboriginal peoples, starting with Joseph Brant and others in the 1780s and continuing through to the 1870s, tried to find sanctuary in Canada. How is the movement of these domestic foreigners related to the two Highland officers? History presents the Underground Railroad as a product of New England in the pre-Civil War era (1860s) but excludes those African Americans who came to Canada during the Revolutionary and 1812 wars. In fact, defeated domestic foreigners sought refuge in Canada from 1783 onwards. While it is difficult to prove, I suggest that their desire to reach Canada was a product of the Scottish Enlightenment, and that to link both groups, we should call this movement an "Enlightened Railway." This is a demographically tiny movement, but it tells us that the United States was freedom for oppressed Europeans and Canada was freedom for the oppressed internal enemies of the United States.

Telling the story of the 78th Fraser's Highlanders is an occupational hazard for even the best of historians because three vigorous nationalisms share this story. The eminent British historian Eric Hobsbawm is quoted by the equally eminent American in the field, Eric Foner, as saying that "historians are professional remembrancers of what their fellow citizens wish to forget."[56] Indeed, Scots have difficulty recalling that Jacobites and Hanoverians joined forces in the 78th soon after Culloden. The British opt to ignore the fact that Highlanders fought loyally in the American Revolution for more land as well as for the monarchy. The Americans forget that they were supported by Spain and Holland and opposed in the Revolution by the most modern mindset in Europe rather than by a medieval one. Canadians assume that Highland Scots Loyalists were losers in the Revolution, when, in fact, the Scots did very well afterward.

The Highland image differs among countries, and it takes dramatic changes to alter each perception. For example, the Scots had a collective amnesia about their own mercenary service until Scotland joined the European community. Suddenly, they remembered that their soldiers had once enjoyed a vibrant presence on the Continent. And across the sea, the Americans not only kept the thousands of African Americans who opposed the Revolution out of historical sight, but their "historians have tended to lionise the few black patriots such as Crispus Attucks, slain at the Boston Massacre in 1770."[57] However, when Barack Obama became the first black president, the Americans suddenly remembered that the "internal enemy" was an important ally of the British during the Revolution.

It takes a dramatic new present to change deeply held national beliefs in order to reinvent a nation's past. What becomes important to the citizens today is suddenly regarded as significant in history. Far from being "professional remembrancers," national historians are an essential part of what I call a system of national checks and biases. The country provides the money to research what is now regarded as important, and the historians provide the biases to explain why previously ignored people are significant in the new national narrative.

The idea of one people with one national history has died, but the idea of one nation still forms the framework of most history writing. In my opinion, national histories have to become even more inclusive if we want to see them become the historical canons they claim to be. Nations also need to accept the influence of other countries in their stories, but historians in the U.S., Britain, and Canada seem to agree that each country has ownership of its own past. The much-talked-about "history wars" in these three countries, which involve internal fights usually to do with school curriculums, are watched with interest from the outside. Perhaps understandably, then, there seems to be a pact of accepting one another's amnesia when it comes to the Highland Scots. In addition, national histories should appreciate complexity more and should not be so certain about differences. It is foolish to demonize the losing side and eulogize the winning side in eighteenth-century wars. Dichotomies such as Jacobites and Hanoverians, soldiers and settlers, Tories and Patriots, or even victors and vanquished are blurred in the story of the Fraser's Highlanders.[58] History writing is changing, but it has still a long way to go, and to quote Scott, Scottish soldier-settlers are still marching "unwept, unhonoured, and unsung" through the history books of all three countries.

Epilogue

If you should wish to find peace,
Go north to the land of redcoats.
— Sitting Bull, 1877

This biography explains who the 78th Fraser's were, what they were not, and why there was so much misinformation recorded and perpetuated about them. The story of these soldier-settlers provided the material for a multi-faceted study of the interaction of militarism, migration, and modernity within the evolution of Britain, Canada, and the United States. I tried to place a human face on soldiers of a particular regiment within the general histories of three eighteenth-century countries.

The eighteenth-century population explosion in the Highlands created a huge surplus of young men available to the British Army. Previously, Highlanders had travelled as mercenaries to Europe, but now larger numbers would fight in North America's wars between 1759 and 1812. Highland military-migratory activity was encouraged by events in Britain and in British North America.

The Fraser's Highlanders are important in history for several reasons besides marking the shift in Scottish military-migratory activity from

Europe to North America. The 78th Foot's conspicuous military abilities brought Highland soldiers into the front ranks of the British Army and British life. Military success caused Highlanders to identify with Britain and caused the British to embrace Highland traditions. The Highland success at Quebec helped remove New France as a barrier to American settlement because France could no longer help Aboriginal peoples resist British expansion westward. The subsequent expansion of the Thirteen Colonies westwards led to the largest mass migration to North America from Europe up to that time.[1] Approximately 215,000 Europeans migrated between 1763 and 1775, including about forty thousand from Scotland. New England's population increased by 59 percent, New York State's doubled, and Georgia's tripled during this time. This huge demographic boost to the Thirteen Colonies, combined with the removal of the French Empire in North America, changed the colonial outlook because they no longer needed the British to protect them from the French, and it increased colonial numbers able to fight the British in the Revolution.

Following the publication of the fictional novels and short stories by Sir Walter Scott in the nineteenth century, defeat at Culloden rather than victory at Quebec in the eighteenth century was widely believed to have been the motor of Highland migration. Scott's stories still colour conventional history to this day to a remarkable degree. A distinguished British intellectual shows the power of Scott's fiction when he wrote in 2011: "Jacobite refugees who had settled in America almost unanimously rejected the revolution and fought for the king who had crushed them at Culloden."[2] In fact, Highland settlers were not Jacobite refugees as a consequence of Culloden, but landowners as a consequence of victory at Quebec.

Despite what Scottish intellectuals may write, Culloden, clans, and clan chiefs are seldom mentioned in the numerous writings left by members of the 78th Foot. These soldier-settlers were led by widely experienced professional soldiers, some of whom happened to be clan chiefs. Veterans from the 78th were professional soldiers who proceeded to raise other Highland regiments from the American Revolution onwards. Highland regiments were highly effective units not only because they contained clan chiefs, but because they had a cadre of highly experienced officers who ran the regiments.

Highland military service and migration were intertwined because free land was awarded where the soldiers had served and often worked. Although the declining clan system was a factor that spurred emigration, military relationships gave that migration a co-operative, capitalist, and family touch that is often ignored.

In 1745, Scotland was at the edge of European civilization, but by 1812 the New Scotland had pushed itself to the geographic, economic, and modernizing centre of the Atlantic world. Highland guns at Waterloo[3] and Scottish steamboats being used in the War of 1812 signalled that British power overseas was to be built around these two forces: guns and steam. I believe the impact the Scots had in North America is a mosaic traceable to those two forces, James Wolfe and James Watt.

It is important to emphasize that the Fraser's Highlanders were above all a highly effective military unit and used force with deadly effect. Later historians were to claim that Highlanders were victims of Empire, but ignore that for the times, they did well from their empire experience. In the American Revolution they fought to a man for the King, but in their own interests, even more land. An aura of "moreness" clung to the Scots that made them unpopular on both sides of the Atlantic. Land hunger drove Highland military activity in North America. As in the twentieth century, eighteenth-century wars radically changed those Highlanders who spent many years participating in them. Highland soldiers were changed into frontiersmen by the end of their service in North America and were able to adapt quickly when they became settlers. Perhaps, as some claim, Scots at this time "invented" modernity, but I think this overstates the situation. Modernity was "invented" by many different peoples, some of whom happened to be Scots. Obviously, the Scots who were living in the New World were implementing what they had learned in the Old World. Modernity matters because the eighteenth-century Scots, perhaps the most progressive people in Europe at that time, rapidly formed a formidable culture of Loyalism in the face of the American Revolution; the Enlightenment had inoculated the Scots against the American Revolution.[4] Progressive modernity and counter-revolutionary feelings marked the Scottish mind, and so Scottish intellectuals opposed rebellion, clanship, and slavery.[5]

Even during the American Civil War of the 1860s, it is no historical accident that the Scottish Duke of Argyll was arguably the most prominent politician and intellectual who opposed both slavery and secession vociferously.[6] The Scots had been both the strongest advocates for reform and the strongest opponents of revolution since the late eighteenth century and up until the mid-nineteenth: a curious mix.[7] The Scots stood against the American Revolution's social ideals in the same way the Patriots stood for its political ideals. Both sides fought a vicious civil war armed with the highest of Enlightenment principles. Arguably, these Highland Scots fought for the right reasons — their self- interests as well as other, more principled interests.

Highland modernity matters in the story of the battles for America. The Patriot rebels did not, in fact, fight reactionary, sword-wielding Jacobite refugees, but actually faced a much more daunting task: they overcame confident, professional Highland soldiers who fought hard for their own version of America. The Patriots won decisively, and caused the transfer of these Scots geographically to what is now Canada, while Scottish philosopher Adam Smith's "invisible hand" of the Scottish Enlightenment transformed them intellectually between 1745 and 1812.

The nationalist "spin" of U.S. history fails to acknowledge that the Scots Enlightenment helped to stoke opposition to the Revolution in the thirteen English colonies. Adam Smith, David Hume, and others opposed the Revolution precisely because the new Scottish ideas about capitalism advocated the freeing of people such as African Americans from slavery. Abolition of slavery, respect for First Nations, and toleration of French-Canadian Catholics were ideas that pushed American colonists to rebel against the Crown; forces that even the best of American historians ignore. Slave-owners, after all, provided many early presidents — surely no historical accident.

Not only do three nations believe their own false historical assumptions, they adopt each other's false assumptions. For example, although it was true that Highland Scots lagged behind the achievements of Scots from the Lowlands, Highlanders were not the backward barbarians that Lowlanders and American Patriots claimed. The Highland Scots were in fact deeply influenced by an intellectual spirit centred in the Lowlands. Historians of the American Revolution often label Highland Scots as "medieval" because of their clans and chiefs. They ignore the fact that the unpopularity of these Scots in the New World derived more from their new ideas than their old ones.

The wars in the Atlantic world from 1745–1812 created peoples who were regarded and treated as defeated domestic foreigners. The Highland Scots after the 1745 Rebellion, French Canadians after the Seven Years' War, and Loyalists in the wake of the American Revolution became regarded as foreigners in their own country and were written out of history until recently. I have tried to write these peoples back into mainstream history by showing their relationships with Highland Scots. These neglected Highlanders have important stories to tell. The 78th had Jacobites and Hanoverians who once fought each other, making one wonder at the cohesiveness of the regiment. Their incredible actions on the St. Lawrence River, their cleverness at the trailhead, and the effectiveness of their charge are epic. The Highland relationship with the Mississippi, scientific farming, timber and shipbuilding industries, African Americans and Aboriginal peoples are absent from three national memories, a telling criticism of history writing.

The complete stories of many remarkable eighteenth-century Highland individuals have yet to be told. Similarly, the collective stories of the colonies that became Canada have also yet to be told. In fact, the new Canadian colonies at the time looked down — geographically, economically, and intellectually —on the new English Republic to the south. Even Canadian historians find it hard to accept that domestic foreigners — namely First Nations and African Americans — in the new United States may have looked north to colonial Canada for a better life well into the nineteenth century.

Within the Thirteen Colonies, approximately 20 percent of the population were slaves, 20 to 30 percent were Loyalist, and only about 60 percent were republican Patriot. This was no universal uprising, but rather a prolonged conflict and a remarkable victory for a clear but not overwhelming majority. Harsh measures had to be taken against these internal enemies, a minority large enough to be regarded as a dangerous to the new order. An old Loyalist poem explains why domestic foreigners continued to flee the new republic for the next seventy-five years (if they could): "The cry was for Liberty. Lord what a fuss. But Pray. How much liberty left they for us?"

Is it justified to claim that the 78th and other redcoats had established a Canadian refuge for Aboriginal peoples as well as for African Americans? After defeating Custer at the Little Big Horn in 1876, Sitting Bull and the U.S. Cavalry certainly thought Canada was a refuge. This famous warrior escaped the pursuing cavalry by crossing into Western Canada in 1877. Sitting Bull and his band were then met by Major Walsh and three other red-coated Mounties. Sitting Bull showed Walsh his grandfather's George III medals received for service with the British redcoats during the War of 1812. According to Walsh, Sitting Bull said that his grandfather told him, "If you should ever wish to find peace, go north to the land of redcoats."[8]

The presence of the four Mounties also impressed the pursuing U.S. Cavalry, who, though in hot pursuit, respected the border and Canadian law. In 1877, redcoats symbolized power, law, and controlled violence to both the victors and victims of the Declaration of Independence of 1776.

The nationalist "spin" in Canadian history is that the British conquest by and large brought great hardship and misfortune to New France. For instance, Canada did not even hold an official remembrance ceremony on the 250th anniversary of the Battle on the Plains of Abraham. A small Quebec nationalist group threatened violent protests about an event thought to be too traumatic for most French Canadians. There is a touch of Orwell and Monty Python to this. We can ask what modern features the British conquest brought to Quebec after 1763. Well, apart from new agricultural products such as whisky, printing, a parliament, banking system, steamboats, freedom of religion, habeas corpus, trial by jury, the abolition of legalized torture, the abolition of slavery, and the abolition of compulsory military service, I suppose the conquest modernized — nothing. Curiously, only in the fur trade are the Scots universally recognized in Canadian history for their modernizing capitalism. Yet, a capitalist ideology drove the

Scots to constantly adapt North America to global needs. Canadian timber and wheat were as much intercontinental enterprises as was American cotton, yet are virtually ignored on both sides of the Atlantic.

To be fair, the Orwellian side to history writing about Highland Scots is partly explained by the contradictory nature of Highlanders themselves. They are difficult to write about. These people were formidable soldiers *and* settlers. They were a paradox, and often changed "identities" created by historians — from rebels to Loyalists for instance. Captain MacDonald, who spoke French on the trailhead, had recruited in Scotland for the French in the early 1750s, but then played an important role in fighting them in the late 1750s. Malcolm Fraser and John Nairne wielded medieval swords at Quebec, then wielded what was probably North America's first modern steel ploughs *in* Quebec. Fraser and Nairne were important counter-revolutionaries in the American Revolution, but were important environmental, social, economic, and institutional revolutionaries there, too. The unique Highland Scots' combination of brains and brawn challenges many unspoken and unjustified historical assumptions so that historians have to be nuanced when writing about these people.

The 78th Fraser's and other Scots had the motivation and the means to change the military, political, economic, environmental, and migratory face of both Europe and the New World. There is nothing ambiguous about their story in North America. They marched from poverty to prosperity and from the Atlantic to the Pacific and Arctic within one generation. They were the first to link the Atlantic by steam and the first to cross the continent by land. They were also the first to connect many of the social groups on the continent to mainstream political society. Political stability, economic development, and enlightened social progress across a vast geographic space are their legacies in the New World.

The significance of these overlooked eighteenth-century soldier-settlers can be appreciated by the fact that 118 lakes, rivers, mountains, and towns in Canada and eighty-two in the United States include "Fraser" as part of their name. Simon Fraser University in British Columbia and two Canadian world-champion pipe bands named after the 78th Fraser's Highlanders are, after all, significant memorials to those "driv'n by fortune."

Notes

Abbreviations:
AO: Archives Ontario
LAC: Library and Archives Canada
NAS: National Archives of Scotland
SAS: Statistical Account of Scotland
SFEP: Scottish Forfeited Estate Papers

Introduction

1. F. Parkman, *Montcalm and Wolfe* (New York: Collier Books, 1966), 552.
2. T.C.W. Blanning, *The Pursuit of Glory: Europe 1648–1815* (London: Penguin Books, 2007), 586.
3. Ibid., 92.
4. Margaret MacMillan, "History Belongs to All," *Montreal Gazette*, July 19, 2008, B7.
5. Stuart Macintyre and Anna Clark, *The History Wars* (Melbourne, Australia: Melbourne University Press, 2004), 20.
6. M. Morgan and J. Adams, "How Well Do FACTS Travel?" *LSE Magazine* (Summer 2008): 14–15.
7. "Jacobus" is Latin for *James*, hence "Jacobite."

8. Bernard Bailyn, *Voyagers to the West* (New York: Alfred A. Knopf, 1986), 26.

9. T.M. Devine, *Scotland's Empire, 1600–1815*, 98.

10. R. Clyde, *From Rebel to Hero: The Image of the Highlander, 1745–1830* (East Linton, Scotland: Tuckwell Press Ltd., 1998), 182.

11. Devine, *Scotland's Empire, 1600–1815*, 178–81.

12. K.J. Duncan, "Patterns of Settlement in the East," in *The Scottish Tradition in Canada*, W. Stanford Reid ed. (Toronto: McClelland & Stewart, 1976), 52, 56.

13. K. Phillips, *The Cousin's War* (New York: Basic Books, 1999), 137.

14. Devine, *Scotland's Empire, 1600–1815*, 181.

15. D. Meyer, *The Highland Scots of North Carolina, 1732–1776* (Chapel Hill, NC: University of North Carolina Press, 1961), iv.

16. A. Taylor, *The Civil War of 1812: American Citizens, British Subjects, Irish Rebels, & Indian Allies* (New York: Alfred A. Knopf, 2010), 88.

17. Duncan, "Patterns of Settlement in the East," 52, 56.

18. *Dictionary of Canadian Biography*, vol. 4 (Toronto: University of Toronto Press, 1979), 276.

19. I.M. McCulloch, in *Sons of the Mountains*, labels him "McDonell" (page 84) while R. Harper in *The Fraser Highlanders*, labels him "MacDonald" (page 42).

20. Lists of Clan Appin Jacobites; Fraser's Highlanders; North Carolina immigration records, half-pay lists and New Brunswick–Nova Scotia land records 1790s. He signed as Allan Stewart.

21. E.F. Curtis, *The Organization of the British Army in the American Revolution* (New Haven, CT: Yale University Press, 1926), chapter 3, footnote 23.

22. *NY Land Lists* identifies *two* Sergeant Alexander Frasers. Surveyor William Cockburn's map has *three* (companies of Colonel Fraser, Captains Alexander Wood, and Hugh Fraser).

23. There were at least five Simon Frasers in the ranks plus several among the officers.

24. The kilted Colonel Simon Fraser is to the left of the dying Wolfe in the portrait.

25. F. Maclean, *Highlanders: A History of the Highland Clans* (Woodstock and New York: The Overlook Press, 1995), 243.

26. Simon Frasers: the explorer (1776–1862) of the river in British Columbia who was born in Bennington, New York (now Vermont); the merchant in Quebec City whose fortified house was attacked by Benedict Arnold and Montgomery during the American Revolution; a different fur-trading Simon Fraser (*circa* 1757–1839) who built a famous house that can still be seen occupying the very tip of Montreal Island at Ste Anne de Bellevue (1769–1844); the physician and surgeon (1769–1844) who corresponded with his nephew, John McLoughlin, the "Father of Oregon." All (*perhaps* not the merchant) were related to soldiers in the 78th.

Chapter 1: Mercenary Migration Through Europe

1. Stephen Wood, *The Auld Alliance* (Edinburgh: Mainstream Publishing Co., 1989), 32, 34.
2. Ibid., 23–24.
3. G. Simpson, *The Scottish Soldier Abroad* (Edinburgh: John Donald, 1992), viii–x, 17.
4. Ibid., viii–x, 17.
5. D. Catteral, "Scots Along the Maas, c. 1570–1750," in *Scottish Communities Abroad in the Early Modern Period*, A. Grosjean and S. Murdoch, eds. (Boston: Brill, 2005), 170.
6. J. McCaffrey, "Historical Sources, 1750–1900" in *Oxford Companion to Scottish History*, M. Lynch, ed. (Oxford: Oxford University Press, 2001), 315.
7. Allan Patrick, a Scots Canadian, made a Canadian television program in the 1980s, *The Thistle and The Lily*, extolling the Auld Alliance.
8. Simpson, *The Scottish Soldier Abroad*, 17.
9. K.P. Walton, "Scottish Nationalism Before 1789: An Ideology, a Sentiment or a Creation?," *International Social Science Review* 81 (September 22, 2006).
10. Wood, *The Auld Alliance*, 42.
11. J. Hunter, *Scottish Exodus* (Edinburgh & London: Mainstream Publishing, 2005), 51.
12. The Chateau De Ramezay is Montreal's oldest house and a De Ramezay surrendered Quebec City to the British after Wolfe's victory in 1759.
13. Words such as *ashet* (*assiete*) for a cooking dish are still used in Scotland, but not England.
14. See Paul Reiter, "From Shakespeare to Defoe: Malaria in England in the Little Ice Age," in *Emerging Infective Diseases* (January 1, 2000), wwwnc.cdc.gov/eid/article/6/1/00-0101.htm. See also Fred Page, "Between 1550 and 1700 Britain Suffered a Little Ice Age," *The Independent* (February 18, 2000); and Michael Telzrol, "Climatic Golden Age," in *The New American* (February 18, 2008): 35–39.
15. R.J. Knecht, *The Rise and Fall of Renaissance France* (London: Fontana Press, 1996), 298, 299.
16. J.H. Burton, *The Scot Abroad*, 3rd ed. (Edinburgh: William Blackwood & Sons, 1881), 34.
17. M. Brown, "Franco-Scottish Relations to 1513," in *Oxford Companion to Scottish History*, Michael Lynch, ed. (Oxford: Oxford University Press, 2007), 246.
18. A. Stewart, *The Cradle King: The Life of James VI & I* (London: Pimlico, Random House, 2004), 318.
19. Danzig was a German city, independent of Poland, and in 1577 hired some seven hundred Scots to fight Poland. The town guard became Scots. From T.A. Fischer, *The Scots in Germany* (Edinburgh: Otto Schulze & Co., 1902), 71–72.

20. E. Hortling, "The Stuarts in Sweden and the Royal House of Scotland," in *The Stewarts,* vol. 16, no. 4 (1983): 178.
21. A. Francis Steuart, *Papers Relating to the Scots in Poland, 1576–1793* (Edinburgh: University Press, Scottish Historical Society, T. & A. Constable, 1915), XXI–XXII.
22. Fischer, *The Scots in Germany,* 179.
23. Ibid., 32.
24. Ibid., 39–40.
25. A. Francis Steuart, *Papers Relating to the Scots in Poland, 1576–1793,* IX.
26. T.C. Smout, N. Landsman, and T. Devine, "Scottish Emigration," in *Europeans on the Move,* N. Canny, ed. (Oxford: Clarendon Press, 1994), 85.
27. In 1564, Poles imposed a tax on Scottish peddlers, classifying them with Jews and gypsies.
28. Devine, *Scotland's Empire, 1600–1815,* 12–13.
29. Patrick, his son-in-law and an Admiral Peter were some of the "Gordons" in Russian service. Ian Anderson, *Scotsmen in the Service of the Czars* (Edinburgh: Pentland Press, 1990), 40, 51.
30. Patrick Gordon (1635–99), a Catholic, served with various Scottish units in Germany, Sweden, and Poland. He kidnapped European nobility for ransom, fought alongside John Sobieski, the Polish warrior king, and established a blackmail scheme for cattle in Germany.
31. Rupert was the son of the deposed King of Bohemia and of Elizabeth his "Winter Queen." Elizabeth was Scottish, the daughter of James VI of Scotland and I of England and sister to Charles I of Scotland and England.
32. Burton, *The Scot Abroad,* 326–27.
33. Walter Leslie became a landowner in Poland, Germany, the Czech Republic, and Slovenia; count of the Holy Roman Empire; and the ambassador to the Turks in Constantinople.
34. R. Gillespie, "An Army Sent from God: Scots at War in Ireland, 1642–9," in *Scotland and War, AD 79–1918,* Norman MacDougall, ed. (Savage, MD: Barnes & Noble Books, 1991), 122.
35. Burton, *The Scot Abroad,* 320.
36. See W.S. Brockington, Jr., ed., *Monro, His Expedition with the Worthy Scots Regiment Called Mac-Keys* (Westport, CT: Praeger, 1999).
37. M. Glozier, "Scots in the French and Dutch Armies," in *Scotland and the Thirty Years' War,* Steve Murdoch, ed. (Boston: Brill, 2001), 128.
38. Murdoch, "Introduction," in *Scotland and the Thirty Years' War,* 18.
39. Smout, Landsman, and Devine, "Scottish Emigration," in *Europeans on the Move,* 85.
40. A. Grosjean, "Royalist Soldiers and Cromwellian Allies?" in *Fighting for Identity: The Scottish Military Experience c. 1550–1900,* Steve Murdoch and A. MacKillop, eds. (Leiden, Netherlands: Brill, 2002), 62.
41. Burton, *The Scot Abroad,* 316.

42. Blanning, *The Pursuit of Glory*, 118.
43. F. Pearce, "It Bites, It Kills, It's Coming to Essex," *The Independent* (London), February 18, 2000.
44. J. G. Stedman, *The Journal of John Gabriel Stedman: 1744-1797*, Stanbury Thompson, ed. (London: The Mitre Press, 1962).
45. R.C. Alberts, *The Most Extraordinary Adventures of Major Robert Stobo* (Boston: Houghton Mifflin Co., 1965), 28-30, 42, 45, 49. B.G. Seton, *The Prisoners of the '45* (Edinburgh: Scottish Historical Society, T. & A. Constable, 1928), 210.
46. James Keith enlisted in France and Spain, and Russia, where he was Colonel of Empress Anne's bodyguard. He led an army against the Turks and discovered that the Turkish peace negotiator was a boyhood acquaintance from Scotland. After being Governor of Ukraine, he joined Frederick the great and died a field marshal in Prussian service. A statue of Keith was erected in Prussia and his eulogy in the *Scots Magazine* of the time (1758) is worth reading.
47. Captain John Fraser (c.1729-95) had brothers: Roderick and Donald in the Austrian army, Peter in the Spanish army, and Archibald, a fellow officer in the 78th.
48. A.V. Campbell, *The Royal American Regiment* (Oklahoma: University of Oklahoma Press, 2010), 69.
49. Steuart, *Papers Relating to the Scots in Poland, 1576-1793*, XXI.
50. T.C. Smout, "Foreword," in *Scottish Communities Abroad in the Early Modern Period*, A. Grosjean and S. Murdoch, eds. (Boston: Brill, 2005), XI.

Chapter 2: Explaining the Scots Highland and Mercenary Traditions

1. R.W. Munro, *Highland Clans and Tartans* (London: Octopus Books, 1977), 9, 11.
2. D. Turnock, *The Historical Geography of Scotland Since 1707* (Cambridge: Cambridge University Press, 2004), 33.
3. C. MacKinnon, *Scottish Highlanders* (New York: Barnes & Noble Books, 1992), 29.
4. H.G. Graham, *Social Life in Scotland in the Eighteenth Century*, 5th ed. (London: Black, 1969), 3.
5. Ibid., 3.
6. Munro, *Highland Clans and Tartans*, 36.
7. Turnock, *The Historical Geography of Scotland Since 1707*, 8.
8. MacKinnon, *Scottish Highlanders*, 34-35.
9. Munro, *Highland Clans and Tartans*, 34-35.
10. Duke of Argyll, *Scotland As It Was and As It Is*, vol. 1 (Edinburgh: David Douglas, 1887), 232.
11. M. MacGregor, "Clans of the Highlands and Islands" in *Oxford Companion to Scottish History*, Michael Lynch, ed., (Oxford: Oxford University Press), 94.

12. I.M. McCullough, *Sons of the Mountains: The Highland Regiments in the French & Indian War, 1756–1767* (Montreal: Robin Brass Studio, 2006), 96.
13. F.M. Fraser, *Clan Fraser: A History Celebrating Over 800 Years of the Family in Scotland* (Edinburgh: Scottish Cultural Press, 1997), 1–2.
14. Clyde, *From Rebel to Hero*, 17.
15. Ibid., 182.
16. A.H. Millar, *Scottish Forfeited Estate Papers, A Selection of Scottish Forfeited Estate Papers: 1715* (Edinburgh: T. and A. Constable for the Scottish History Society, 1909), 63.
17. Munro, *Highland Clans and Tartans*, 28.
18. Millar, "Introduction," in *Scottish Forfeited Estate Papers, A Selection of Scottish Forfeited Estate Papers: 1715*, XXXIX.
19. Millar, *Scottish Forfeited Estate Papers*, Lovat Estate Papers, 61–63.
20. Millar "The Jacobite Rising of 1745" ("Introduction") in *Scottish Forfeited Estate Papers*, XXXVII.
21. Clyde, *From Rebel to Hero*, 22.
22. Millar, *Scottish Forfeited Estate Papers*, 61, 71, 75.
23. Ibid., 83.
24. Ibid., 110, 130.
25. Ibid., 73.
26. Ibid., 101.
27. Clyde, *From Rebel to Hero*, 21.
28. G. Himmelfarb, *The Roads to Modernity: The British, French, and American Enlightenments* (Toronto: Random House of Canada, 2004), 5.
29. T. Pennant, *A Tour of Scotland* (Warrington: n.p., 1774), 226.
30. W.H. Murray, *Rob Roy MacGregor* (Edinburgh: Canongate Press, 1995), 39.
31. Ibid., 29–30.
32. Ibid., 47.
33. Ibid., 126.
34. Fraser, *Clan Fraser*, 39.
35. E. Hobsbawm, "Mass-Producing Traditions: Europe, 1870–1914," in *The Invention of Tradition*, E. Hobsbawm and T. Ranger, eds. (Cambridge: Cambridge University Press, 1995), 282.
36. H.T. Buckle, *On Scotland and the Scotch Intellect* (Chicago: University of Chicago Press, 1970), 25.
37. J. Wormald, *Lords and Men in Scotland: Bonds of Manrent (1442–1603)* (Edinburgh: John Donald Publishers, 1985), 18.
38. S. Wallace, *The Pedlars from Quebec and Other Papers on the Nor'Westers* (Toronto: The Ryerson Press, 1954), 49.
39. Ibid., 48–49.
40. Ibid., 49.
41. Duke of Argyll, *Scotland As It Was and As It Is, Volume 1*, 235.
42. Ibid., 233.

43. R.B. Sher and J.R. Smitten, eds., *Scotland and America in the Age of Enlightenment* (Princeton, NJ: Princeton University Press, 1990), 53–54.
44. T.A. Fischer, *The Scots in Sweden* (Edinburgh: Otto Schulze & Co., 1907), 63.
45. M. Brander, *The Scottish Highlanders and Their Regiments* (New York: Barnes & Noble Books, 1971), 74.
46. A. MacKillop, *"More Fruitful than the Soil": Army Empire and the Scottish Highlands 1715–1815* (East Linton, East Lothian: Tuckwell Press, 2000), 132.
47. T. Sowell, *Conquests and Cultures: An International History* (New York: Basic Books, 1998), 264.
48. A. Giddens, *The Consequences of Modernity* (Stanford, California: Stanford University Press, 1990), 36.
49. Ibid., 38.
50. Clyde, *From Rebel to Hero*, 12, 15.
51. *Statistical Account of Scotland 1791*, Kilmorack Parish, 405–06. See: *http://stat-acc-scot.edina.ac.uk/link/1791-99/Inverness/Kilmorack/*.
52. Giddens, *The Consequences of Modernity*, 11.
53. Ibid., 175.
54. Michael Bliss, *Northern Enterprise: Five Centuries of Canadian Business* (Toronto: McClelland & Stewart, 1987), 97.

Chapter 3: The Eighteenth-Century British Military Machine in America

1. S. Pargellis, ed., *Military Affairs in North America, 1748–1765. Selected documents from the Cumberland Papers* (New York: D. Appleton for the American Historical Association, 1936), 9.
2. A. Macdonald, *The Old Lords of Lovat and Beaufort* (Inverness: The Northern Counties Newspaper & Publishing Co., 1934), 135.
3. J.A. Houlding, *Fit for Service: The Training of the British Army, 1715–1795* (Oxford: Clarendon Press, 1981), 153.
4. Ibid.
5. LAC, J. Nairne and T. Nairne, "Standing Orders," R5991-0-3-E, MG23-GIII 23, September 1, 1762.
6. Ibid.
7. Ibid., December 27, 1762.
8. S. Brumwell, *Redcoats: The British Soldier and War in the Americas, 1755–1763* (Cambridge: Cambridge University Press, 2002), 302–03.
9. McCulloch, *Sons of the Mountains*, 93, 174.
10. Brumwell, *Redcoats*, 300.
11. Ibid., 299
12. LAC, Nairne and Nairne, May 11, 1762.
13. An old Scots word meaning "rustic."
14. LAC, Nairne and Nairne, June 19, 1762.
15. LAC, Nairne and Nairne, May 11, 1762.

16. B. Connell, *The Plains of Abraham* (London: Hodder & Stoughton, 1959), 157.
17. D.J. Beattie, "The Adaptation of the British Army to Wilderness Warfare, 1755–1763," in *Adapting to Conditions: War And Society in the Eighteenth Century*, M. Ultee, ed. (Tuscaloosa, AL: University of Alabama Press, 1986), 83.
18. J.R. Harper, *The Fraser Highlanders*, 2nd ed. (Bloomfield, ON: Museum Restoration Service, 1995), 48–49.
19. Brumwell, *Redcoats*, 25.
20. B. De Voto, *The Course of Empire* (Boston: Houghton Mifflin Sentry Edition, 1962), 226.
21. General J. Murray, *Journal of the Siege of Quebec*, Literary and Historical Society of Quebec, Historical Document Series 3, vol. 5 (February 28, March 11, and March 30, 1871): 12.
22. Harper, *The Fraser Highlanders*, 50.
23. Helen McMillan, "John Nairne," an unpublished biography written 1959–1979 (Old Fort, Montreal: David M. Stewart Museum), 13. The original is unpaginated. Much of McMillan's material appears to have come from the letters also found in the John and Thomas Nairne Fonds now held by LAC Fonds, R5991-0-3-E, MG23-GIII.
24. "Read the Articles of War; learn the words of Command and every duty of a Subaltern; go upon every military duty; learn the Adjutant's duty/to Exercise the Co.; make yourself fit for paying the Co.; Practise writing Courts-Martials, Returns and Reports; study military books."
25. McMillan, "John Nairne."
26. Connell, *The Plains of Abraham*, 130.
27. Devine, *Scotland's Empire 1600–1815*, 316–17.
28. Brumwell, *Redcoats*, 281–82.
29. Highland chiefs, or the sons and brothers of chiefs were: John MacDonald of Lochbuie; Donald MacDonald of Benbecula and his brothers, William and Norman; Ronald MacDonald of Keppoch; Alexander MacLeod of MacLeod; John MacPherson of Cluny; Roderick MacNeil of Barra; Archibald MacAllister of the Loup; and Archibald Campbell of Glen Lyon and Colonel Simon Fraser himself. The eldest son of the MacGregor chief enlisted under the name of Murray.
30. Devine, *Scotland's Empire, 1600–1815*, 12.
31. D.H. Henderson, "Highland Regiments, 1750–1830" in *Oxford Companion to Scottish History*, Michael Lynch, ed. (Oxford: Oxford University Press, 2007), 25.
32. Ibid.
33. MacKillop, *"More Fruitful than the Soil,"* 173.
34. Ibid., 188.
35. Ibid., 188–89.

36. John was the younger brother of Ewan MacPherson of Cluny, Colonel Simon Fraser's brother-in-law.
37. D. Currie, *The Lairds of Glenlyon* (Perth, Scotland: S. Cowan & Co., 1886), 282.
38. MacKillop, *"More Fruitful than the Soil,"* 173.
39. P. Paret, "Colonial Experience and Military Reform at the End of the Eighteenth Century," *Bulletin of the Institute of Historical Research* vol. 37 (Nov. 1965), 50.
40. Ibid., 52.
41. Ibid., 53.
42. Pargellis, *Military Affairs in North America, 1748–1765, Selected Documents from the Cumberland Papers*, 115–16.
43. Ibid., 82.
44. Beattie, "The Adaptation of the British Army to Wilderness Warfare, 1755–1763," 64–65.
45. Houlding, *Fit for Service: The Training of the British Army, 1715–1795*, 375.
46. Harper, *The Fraser Highlanders*, 26.
47. John Fraser became a judge in Montreal and was the uncle of Simon Fraser the explorer.
48. A soldier had to have "his Bonnet proper so as to reach his Brues [brow] Before, and as high as possible behind...." The red waistcoats had to "remain unbuttoned as far as the fifth button." See LAC, Nairne and Nairne, August 5, 1762.
49. McCulloch, *Sons of the Mountains*, 118.
50. LAC, Nairne and Nairne, May 13, 1762.
51. A sergeant wore a red sash over the left shoulder and down the centre, and white lace cords around the right shoulder to distinguish his rank, whereas a corporal wore only the white cords on the shoulder but no sash.
52. Harper, *The Fraser Highlanders*, 29.
53. McCulloch, *Sons of the Mountains*, 164–70.
54. Murray, "Journal of the Seige of Quebec."
55. LAC, Nairne and Nairne, August 12, 1762; May 28, 1762.
56. Ibid., August 16, 1762.
57. Ibid., October 12, 1762.
58. Murray, "Journal of the Seige of Quebec."
59. LAC, Nairne and Nairne, August 5, 1762.
60. Ibid., December 8, 1762.
61. Ibid., November 28, 1762.
62. Ibid., November 28, 1762.
63. Murray, "Journal of the Siege of Quebec."
64. Harper, *The Fraser Highlanders*, 101–02.
65. LAC, Nairne and Nairne, June 4, 1762.
66. Ibid., May 26, 1762.

67. Ibid., December 28, 1762.
68. MacKillop, *"More Fruitful than the Soil,"* 63.
69. Ibid.
70. LAC, Nairne and Nairne, August 10, 1762.
71. See Murray, "Journal of the Siege of Quebec," November 25, 1759.

Chapter 4: Raising the 78th Fraser's Highlanders

1. NAS, Papers of the Rose Family of Kilravock, Inverness-shire, GD125/22/16, page 6.
2. "Chronicles of the Families of Atholl and Tullibardine" (January 6, 1757), *The Manuscripts of the Duke of Atholl, K.T. and Earl of Home* (London: Printed for Her Majesty's Stationary Office by Eyre & Spottiswoode, 1901), 426.
3. Ibid., July 9, 1757, 428–29.
4. A. Grant, *General James Grant of Ballindalloch 1720–1806* (London: Published privately by A.M. Grant, 1930), 48.
5. Ibid., 33.
6. Hugh Rose and Lachlan Shaw, *A Genealogical Deduction of the Family of Rose of Kilravock*, Spalding Club Series 18 (Edinburgh: T. Constable, 1848), 462.
7. Wood, *The Auld Alliance*, 91.
8. NAS, Papers of the Rose Family of Kilravock, Inverness-shire, GD 125/22/16/17.
9. G. Bain, *History of Nairnshire* (Nairn: Telegraph Office, 1813), 402.
10. NAS, Papers of the Rose Family of Kilravock, EXGD 125/22/2.
11. Ibid.
12. Ibid.
13. Ibid., 125/22/24.
14. Bain, *History of Nairnshire*, 401.
15. Grant, *General James Grant of Ballindalloch, 1720–1806*, 50.
16. NAS, Papers of the Rose Family of Kilravock, FXGD 125/22/2.
17. "Chronicles of the Families of Atholl and Tullibardine" (February 19, 1757), 427.
18. NAS, Papers of the Rose Family of Kilravock, GD 125/22/16/11.
19. Harper, *The Fraser Highlanders*, 18.
20. Rose and Shaw, *A Genealogical Deduction of the Family of Rose of Kilravock*, 463–64.
21. Harper, *The Fraser Highlanders*, 16.
22. Ibid.
23. Grant, *General James Grant of Ballindalloch, 1720–1806*, 48–49.
24. Macdonald, *The Old Lords of Lovat and Beaufort*, 135.
25. J. Prebble, *Mutiny: Highland Regiments in Revolt, 1743–1804* (London: Penguin Books, 1977), 104.

26. S. Johnson and J. Boswell, *A Journey into the Western Island of Scotland and the Journal of a Tour to the Hebrides* (London: Penguin Books, 1984), 177.

Chapter Five: The Fighting Fraser's

1. P. Pouchot, *Memoirs on the Late War in North America Between France and England*, Michael Cardy, trans., Brian Dunnigan, ed. (Youngstown, New York: Old Fort Niagara Publications, 2004), 59.
2. P. Kennedy, *The Rise and Fall of the Great Powers* (New York: Random House, 1989), 111–14.
3. Britain was inferior to the Netherlands and Spain as a colonial power and to Austria, Prussia, and France as a land power. Britain was a financially-sound sea power able to spend far more on the North American war sector than France. British success was not inevitable in this war.
4. The huge British debt and high taxes in the postwar years created major problems. Military spending benefited the Scots and led to anti-Scots riots by the London mob under John Wilkes. Increased taxation without representation in Britain's Thirteen Colonies led to revolution.
5. French settlement, which entailed about sixty-five thousand people in 1759, was concentrated along the St. Lawrence River from Quebec City to Montreal.
6. The war began because the French continued their strategy of building forts and began to fortify strong points along the Ohio River, also claimed by Britain.
7. Pouchot, *Memoirs on the Late War in North America Between France and England*, 67.
8. Only about ten thousand people immigrated permanently to New France and it is probable that *more* French people immigrated to New England in colonial times. See J.R. Reich, *Colonial America* (Englewood Cliffs, New Jersey: Prentice Hall, 1994), 137–38.
9. The very different British North America was a scattered series of self-ruling maritime colonies along the coast that stretched from Newfoundland in the North down through New England, to Georgia in the South.
10. Militiamen from New France canoed to attack New England and inflicted far more damage on New England than vice versa until the last year of the war.
11. The Black Watch lost more men besieging Fort Ticonderoga than in any other battle up to the First World War.
12. Macdonald, *The Old Lords of Lovat and Beaufort*, 137.
13. Harper, *The Fraser Highlanders*, 48–50.
14. Ibid.
15. Macdonald, *The Old Lords of Lovat and Beaufort*, 138.

16. D. MacLeod, *Memoires of Sergeant Donald MacLeod* (London: Peterborough House Press, n. d.).

17. Harper, *The Fraser Highlanders*, 51.

18. Ibid., 53.

19. Ibid., 57.

20. Fraser's garrisoned the Albany region, Schenectady, Stratford, Fort Stanwix, and Fort Herkimer (New Rome) in the autumn of 1758.

21. William Wood, ed., *The Logs of The Conquest of Canada* (Toronto: Champlain Society, 1909), 26, 95, 110.

22. Captain James Cook's charts greatly facilitated later trade with Britain.

23. Pouchot, *Memoirs on the Late War in North America Between France and England*, 249.

24. Despite Montcalm's arguments to the contrary, the colony failed to construct a strong point at Lévis, south across the St. Lawrence from Quebec City.

25. On this date in 1690, the British defeated the French and Jacobites at the Battle of the Boyne.

26. C.P. Stacey, *Quebec, 1759* (London: Pan Books, 1973), 65.

27. The British efforts to land had alerted their enemy and the British Grenadiers charged prematurely, only to be cut down by the French defenders inside the entrenchments.

28. Stacey, *Quebec, 1759*, 81.

29. Ibid.

30. M. Fraser, "Extract from a Manuscript Journal Relating to the Siege of Quebec in 1759," Literary and Historical Society of Quebec, Historical Document Series 2, vol. 1 (1867): 10–11.

31. A. Doughty, *Historical Journal of the Campaign in North America,* vol. 11 (Toronto: Champlain Society, 1901), 4.

32. The Rangers were recruited from the frontier areas of the Thirteen Colonies, which had been subjected to vicious attacks from the French over the years.

33. Fraser, "Extract from a Manuscript Journal Relating to the Siege of Quebec in 1759," 4–6.

34. Captain Montgomery was held in great disrepute. Sergeant Thompson of the 78th, who helped to bury General Montgomery, identified him as the "errant captain." Modern historians in the United States claim him to be Captain Alexander Montgomery, the general's brother.

35. Fraser, "Extract from a Manuscript Journal Relating to the Siege of Quebec in 1759," 13–14.

36. W.T. Waugh, *James Wolfe, Man and Soldier* (Montreal and New York: Louis Carrier & Co., 1928), 246–47.

37. One version of the story has women and children and another version has a seigneur and his female lover as the prisoners in the boat.

38. Doughty, *Historical Journal of the Campaign in North America*, 440.
39. L. Antoine de Bougainville, Edward P. Hamilton, trans., Edward P. Hamilton, ed. *Adventure in the Wilderness: The American Journals of Louis Antoine de Bougainville* (Norman, Oklahoma: University of Oklahoma Press, 1964), 320.
40. Stobo knew that it was possible to sail above Quebec despite the supposed impassability of the river and was the one who informed Wolfe about the serious food shortages.
41. Harper, *The Fraser Highlanders*, 85.
42. His original force of three thousand was apparently reduced to two thousand by the day of the battle.
43. O. Warner, *With Wolfe to Quebec* (Toronto: Collins, 1972), 158–59.
44. Ibid., 152.
45. John Knox, *The Journal of Captain John Knox*, vol. 2 (New York: Greenwood Press, 1968), 95. According to Captain Knox, the names of the soldiers were Bell, Cameron, Fitzgerald, Robertson, Stewart, MacPherson, MacKenzie, and McAllester (MacAllister).
46. Pouchot, *Memoirs on the Late War in North America Between France and England*, 245.
47. Knox, *The Journal of Captain John Knox*, 96.
48. Fraser, "Extract from a Manuscript Journal Relating to the Siege of Quebec in 1759," 12.
49. Harper, *The Fraser Highlanders*, 88.
50. Pouchot, *Memoirs on the Late War in North America Between France and England*, 255.
51. Fraser, "Extract from a Manuscript Journal Relating to the Siege of Quebec in 1759," 19.
52. A nun of the General Hospital of Quebec, *The Siege of Quebec and Conquest of Canada in 1759* (Quebec City: *Quebec Mercury* Office, 1855), 6. An anonymous nun in the convent hospital wrote a diary of the events of 1759, a diary that was published much later.
53. De Bougainville, *Adventure in the Wilderness: The American Journals of Louis Antoine de Bougainville*, 320.
54. Ibid., 320–21.
55. Connell, *The Plains of Abraham*, 242.
56. Pouchot, *Memoirs on the Late War in North America Between France and England*, 256.
57. Warner, *With Wolfe to Quebec*, 166–67.
58. Harper, *The Fraser Highlanders*.
59. Fraser, "Extract from a Manuscript Journal Relating to the Siege of Quebec in 1759," 20.
60. MacLeod fought in the Royal Scots at Blenheim, Ramilles, and Sheriffmuir, and was one of the original members of the Black Watch. As

a colour guard he went back with Wolfe's body to Britain. A book ghost-written for him perhaps started the myth that Wolfe died in a Fraser plaid.

61. MacLeod, *Memoires of Sergeant Donald MacLeod*, n.p.
62. Literary and Historical Society of Quebec, "War," in *The Centenary Volume of the Literary and Historical Society of Quebec, 1824-1924* (Quebec: L'Événement Press, 1924), 60.
63. Harper, *The Fraser Highlanders*, 90.
64. Ibid.
65. Rose of Kilravock Municipens, *Papers relating to Major Clephane's service with the 63rd (later 78th) Foot (Col. Simon Fraser's Highlanders), 1757-1765*, NAS (formerly Scottish Records Office) GD1 25/22 (29), November 10, 1759.
66. Harper, *The Fraser Highlanders*, 90.
67. Knox, *The Journal of Captain John Knox*, 107.
68. Fraser, "Extract from a Manuscript Journal Relating to the Siege of Quebec in 1759," 21–22.
69. Lieutenant Roderick MacNeil, heir to the clan chief of the Barra MacNeils: Alexander MacDonnel.
70. Fraser, "Extract from a Manuscript Journal Relating to the Siege of Quebec in 1759," 22.
71. Chevalier de Johnstone, *Dialogue in Hades* (Quebec: Literary and Historical Society of Quebec, 1887), 48.
72. A nun of the General Hospital of Quebec, *Narrative of the Doings During the Siege of Quebec and the Conquest of Canada*, 9.
73. Harper, *The Fraser Highlanders*, 91.
74. Connell, *The Plains of Abraham*, 248.
75. Knox, *The Journal of Captain John Knox*, 99.
76. "Military Operations at or near Quebec," *The Scots Magazine* (James Boswell, ed.) vol. 21 (October 1759): 541–53. Easily the best contemporary account of the capture of Quebec using letters from Fraser's Highlanders. The quote appears on 553, written by James Calcraft.
77. R. Cole Harris, ed., *Historical Atlas of Canada*, vol. 1 (Toronto: University of Toronto Press, 1987), plate 43.
78. J. Thompson Sr., Quebec Archives, ZQ6601-4M00-4056, 73.
79. J.M. Lemoine, *Quebec Past and Present: A History of Quebec* (Quebec City: Augustine Coté, 1876), 182.
80. Harper, *The Fraser Highlanders*, 103–04.
81. Ibid., 108–09.
82. Ibid., 111.
83. Ibid., 112.
84. L. Colley, *Britons: Forging the Nation, 1707-1837* (New Haven, CT: Yale University Press, 1992), 126–45.

Chapter 6: Veterans Home from America

1. S. Johnson and J. Boswell, *A Journey into the Western Isles of Scotland* (London: Penguin Books, 1984), 104.
2. H. Trevor-Roper, *The Invention of Scotland: Myth and History* (New Haven and London: Yale University Press, 2008), 84.
3. Devine, *Scotland's Empire, 1600–1815*, 95.
4. MacNeil of Barra, *The Clan MacNeil: Clan Niall of Scotland* (New York: Caledonian Publishing, 1923), 133.
5. J.D.V. Loder, *Colonsay and Oronsay in the Isles of Argyll* (Edinburgh: Oliver Boyd, 1935), 160.
6. D. Hobson, *Scottish Emigration to Colonial America 1607–1785* (Athens, GA: University of Georgia Press, 1994), 154.
7. T. Pennant. *A Tour of Scotland* (N.P. Warrington, 1779), 198.
8. J. Schaw, E.W. Andrews, ed., *Journal of a Lady of Quality* (New Haven, CT: Yale University Press, 1921), 38.
9. Johnson and Boswell, *A Journey into the Western Isles of Scotland*, 101–02.
10. Ibid., 327.
11. Bailyn's numbers are in *Voyagers to the West*, 26, other estimates are in Eric Richard's *A History of the Highland Clearances*, vol. II (London: Croom Helm, 1985), 194.
12. W.R. Brock, *Scotus Americanus* (Edinburgh: Edinburgh University Press, 1982).
13. D.H. Fischer, *Albion's Seed: Four British Folkways in America* (Toronto: Oxford University Press, 1989), 818.
14. Bailyn, *Voyagers to the West*, 26.
15. Duke of Argyll, *Scotland As It Was and As It Is*, vol. 2: 132.
16. D.S. MacMillan, R.A. Cage, eds., "Scottish Enterprise and Influence in Canada: 1620–1900," in *The Scots Abroad: Labor, Capital, Enterprise 1750–1914* (London: Crum Helm, 1985), 1118–125.
17. J.P. MacLean, *An Historical Account of the Settlement of Scotch Highlanders in America Prior to the Peace of 1783* (Cleveland, OH: The Helman-Taylor Co., 1900), 283–85.
18. Duke of Argyll, *Scotland As It Was and As It Is*, 2: 131.
19. R. Mitchison, *A History of Scotland* (London: Methuen and Co., 1970), 183.
20. Mackillop, *"More Fruitful than the Soil,"* 189.
21. Devine, *Scotland's Empire, 1600–1815*, 138.
22. Ibid., 134.
23. Bailyn, *Voyagers to the West*, 137.
24. Ibid., 140–41.
25. Ibid., 133–34.
26. Ibid., 132.
27. Ibid., 142.

28. Ibid., 166.
29. Ibid., 199.
30. Ibid., 176.
31. Ibid., 210.
32. Duke of Argyll, *Scotland As It Was and As It Is,* 2: 129–30.
33. D.B. Horne and M. Ransome, eds., *English Historical Documents, 1714–1783* (London: Eyre & Spottiswoode, 1957), 667–68.
34. Duke of Argyll, *Scotland As It Was and As It Is,* 2: 133–34.
35. Meyer, *The Highland Scots of North Carolina, 1732–1776,* 31.
36. There were several John MacDonnels thus creating debates about the leader's history.
37. Bailyn, *Voyagers to the West,* 582–83.
38. D. MacKay, *Scotland Farewell* (Toronto: McGraw Hill Ryerson, 1980), XIX, 97.
39. E.R. Fingerhut, *From Scots to Americans: Ryegate's Immigrants in the 1770s* (Ryegate, VT: The Proceedings of the Vermont Historical Society, Vermont History: Autumn 1967): 207.
40. Ibid., 186.
41. Bailyn, *Voyagers to the West,* 604–37.
42. MacKillop, *"More Fruitful than the Soil,"* 148.
43. Ibid., 173.
44. Duke of Argyll, *Scotland As It Was and As It Is,* 2: 138–39.
45. John Prebble, *The Highland Clearances* (Toronto: Penguin Books, 1963), 191.
46. W. McGill, *Old Ross-shire and Scotland* (Inverness, Scotland: The Northern Counties Newspaper & Printing & Publishing Co., 1909), 47.
47. Ibid., 158.
48. Fischer, *Albion's Seed,* 611.
49. Annexed by the government after the 1745 rebellion.
50. L. Holcombe, *Ancient Animosity: The Appin Murder and the End of Scottish Rebellion* (Bloomington, IN: Author House, 2004), 508.
51. A.R. Newsome, ed., *Records of Emigrants from England and Scotland to North Carolina, 1774–1775,* reprinted from the *North Carolina Historical Review* 11 (January & April 1934, 1989), 25–29.
52. Will of Allan Stewart (Charlotte County, NB, 1798), Provincial Archives of New Brunswick. Microfilm F11589 Series RS63 (Charlotte County Probate Records).
53. *Calendar of Home Office Papers, 1760–1765* (London: Longman & Co., 1878), 1291.
54. NAS, Exchequer Records: Forfeited Estates, Reference E745/48/(1) and E745/24-15.
55. Ibid.
56. Johnson and Boswell, *A Journey into the Western Isles of Scotland,* 102.

Chapter 7: Choosing America

1. Approximately 170 stayed and facilitated the re-migration of about one hundred others.
2. *Calendar of Home Office Papers, 1760–1765*, 304.
3. Colonel Simon Fraser petitioned for free land on Prince Edward Island on behalf of the 78th officers. The French stored food and cattle there during the Seven Years' War, and the Frasers thought, mistakenly, that it was an agricultural wonderland.
4. Similar names and the same soldier claiming different plots make it difficult to know exactly how many Alexander Frasers, for instance, took up land in North America.
5. Captain John Nairne and Lieutenant Malcolm Fraser were allowed by General Murray to buy seigneurial land before the Treaty of Paris was signed in 1763, transactions that do *not* appear on official land lists. Some believe Murray claimed land as a field officer, then sold it to his fellow Scots. This may be an anti-Scots slur reflecting Scots-English rivalry during Murray's rule.
6. Bailyn, *Voyagers to the West*, 232.
7. Meyer, *The Highland Scots of North Carolina, 1732–1776*, 52–53.
8. E.B. O'Callaghan, compiler, *Calendar of N.Y. Colonial Manuscripts Indorsed Land Papers, 1643–1803*, revised reprint (Harrison, NY: Harbour Hill Books, 1987), 352–53, 364.
9. F.B. Richards, "The Black Watch at Ticonderoga and Major Duncan Campbell of Inverawe," an excerpt from vol. 10 of the proceedings of the New York State Historical Association (1911): 369–461.
10. Ibid., 89, 91.
11. Ibid., 87, 92.
12. O'Callaghan, *Calendar of N.Y. Colonial Manuscripts Indorsed Land Papers, 1643–1803*, 335.
13. Richards, "The Black Watch at Ticonderoga and Major Duncan Campbell of Inverawe," 75–78.
14. I.M. McCulloch and T.J. Todish, eds., *Through So Many Dangers: The Memoirs and Adventures of Robert Kirk, Late of the Royal Highland Regiment* (Fleischmanns, NY: Purple Mountain Press, 2004).
15. Beattie, "The Adaptation of the British Army to Wilderness Warfare," 73.
16. A. Grant, *Memoirs of an American Lady* (Albany, NY: Joel Munsell, 1876).
17. Ibid., 292–93.
18. Newsome, *Records of Emigrants from England and Scotland to North Carolina*.
19. W.A. McDougall, *Throes of Democracy: The American Civil War Era, 1829–1877* (New York: Perennial, HarperCollins, 2008), 21.

20. Richards, "The Black Watch at Ticonderoga and Major Duncan Campbell of Inverawe," 70–73.
21. It is difficult to count the thousands of names taking land between 1763 and 1774, but many of the Black Watch and Montgomerie's Highlanders re-migrated back to North America.
22. Bailyn, *Voyagers to the West*, 586.
23. Major Phillip Skene was a Scots soldier but not in the 78th. He was a Loyalist-Tory and organized possibly the most famous of the Scots military settlements in upstate New York/Vermont from 1763 to 1774.
24. Mary H. Bort, Vermont researcher, personal email correspondence, 1996.
25. Bailyn, *Voyagers to the West*, 604–37.
26. O'Callaghan, *Calendar of N.Y. Colonial Manuscripts Indorsed Land Papers, 1643–1803*, 440.
27. Ibid., 1,059–60.
28. H. Neatby, *The Administration of Justice Under the Quebec Act* (Minneapolis: University of Minnesota Press, 1949), 109.
29. Ibid., 57.
30. E. Arthur, "Adam Mabane and the French Party," unpublished Master's thesis (McGill University, 1947), 114–16.
31. *Statistical Account of Scotland*, 6: 145. http://stat-acc-scot.edina.ac.uk/link/1791-99/Aberdeen/Tyrie/6/145/.
32. Captain John Fraser had been educated in France as had several officers who spoke French well enough to be taken as French in the postwar years.
33. Bailyn, *Voyagers to the West*, 503.
34. Lieutenant Hugh Fraser, who had done so much to settle upstate New York, returned to Scotland and died there.
35. Private John MacMillan of the 78th, after being discharged in Scotland, re-migrated to New York, then, at government expense, went to Northern Ireland. Again at government expense, he finally settled in Glengarry, Ontario, with Treasury Loyalists, those financed by the British Treasury to claim land in British North America.
36. Private Donald MacKay returned to Scotland in 1763; re-migrated to upstate New York in the 1770s; fought in the Revolution; moved as an innkeeper to Three Rivers, Lower Canada; then relocated to Glengarry, Upper Canada. His two sons continued this restless tradition and explored both across and down the entire North American continent.
37. Ensign Malcolm Fraser of the 78th as quoted in Major R.M. Barnes, *The Uniforms and History of the Scottish Regiments* (London: Seeley Service & Co., 1956), 69.

Chapter 8: Redcoats, Revolution, and Re-Migration

1. France, the Netherlands, and Spain financed the rebels and attacked

British ships. France and Spain also sent troops.

2. M.A. Jones, *American Immigration* (Chicago: University of Chicago Press, 1960), 62.

3. W. Nelson, *The American Tory* (Boston: Beacon Press, 1964), V.

4. M. Stephenson, *Patriot Battles* (New York: HarperCollins Publishers, 2007), 54.

5. Ibid., 43.

6. This was a great propaganda victory for the Patriots. Ironically, Jane McCrea, engaged to a Loyalist, not a Patriot soldier, was probably a Loyalist herself.

7. M.O. Logusz, *With Musket and Tomahawk* (Havertown, PA: Casemate Publishers, 2010), 70.

8. The British threatened to hang Patriots Ethan Allen and General Henry Lee as traitors. In retaliation, the Patriots put Archibald Campbell and some Hessian officers into unheated, confined, and cramped quarters and held the threat of hanging over them.

9. Dobson, *Scottish Emigration to Colonial America, 1607–1785*, 166.

10. G.M. Wrong, *A Canadian Manor and Its Seigneurs* (Toronto: MacMillan, 1908), 78.

11. Jacqueline Roy, "John Nairne," *Dictionary of Canadian Biography*, vol. 5, *1801–1820*, 621.

12. W.A. McDougall, *Freedom Just Around the Corner: A New American History, 1585–1828* (New York: Perennial, HarperCollins Publishers, 2004), 281–82.

13. D.H. Fischer, *Washington's Crossing* (New York: Oxford University Press, 2004), 364.

14. Logusz, *With Musket and Tomahawk*, 271.

15. M. Beacock Fryer, *Allan Maclean: Jacobite General* (Toronto: Dundurn Press, 1987).

16. G. Murray Logan, *Scottish Highlanders and the American Revolution* (Halifax, NS: McCurdy Printing Co., 1976), 115.

17. P. Maier, *American Scripture* (New York: Vintage Books, 1998), 38–39.

18. N. Ferguson, *Empire* (London: Penguin Books, 2002), 95.

19. Himmelfarb, *The Roads to Modernity*, 69.

21. Colley, *Britons: Forging the Nation, 1707–1837*, 132.

22. The Stamp Act of 1765 imposed direct taxes on Britain's American colonists, and required revenue stamps on all newspapers, pamphlets, playing cards, dice, almanacs, and legal documents. The British were trying to raise about one-third of the total cost of the British army in the Thirteen Colonies through these taxes.

23. See Stephen M. Wise, *Though the Heavens May Fall* (Cambridge, MA: Da Capo Press, 2005).

24. G.B. Nash, *The Unknown American Revolution* (New York: Penguin Books, 2005), 120.

25. Ibid., 161.

26. Ibid., 160.

27. Ibid., 166.

28. R. Kagan, *Dangerous Nation: America's Foreign Policy from Its Earliest Days to the Dawn of the Twentieth Century* (New York: Vintage Books, 2007), 31.

29. Meyer, *The Highland Scots of North Carolina, 1732–1776*, 132.

30. The slogan "All men are created equal" certainly did not intend to include women, Aboriginal people, African Americans, and probably not Roman Catholics.

31. Dr. Elinor Kyte Sr., "Loyalist Regiments After the American Revolution," in *Canadian Geneologist* 2, no. 1 (1980): 31–46.

32. H. Zinn, *A People's History of the United States* (New York: HarperPerennial, 2003), 94–95.

33. Even prominent Scots who fought for the Patriots, such as General Arthur St. Clair (1734–1818), did badly economically. The Scots-born founder of the American navy, John Paul Jones, left the United States for financial reasons to enlist in the Russian navy.

34. Nash, *The Unknown American Revolution*, 307–10.

35. Taylor, *The Civil War of 1812*, 38.

36. *St. Croix Courier*, St. Stephen, NB (December 14, 1893), 37. Patrick Campbell was an ex-mercenary and forester who had served in Germany, travelled through New Brunswick, Quebec, and New York in 1791, meeting some of the people he knew.

38. P. Campbell, *Campbell's Travels in North America* (Edinburgh: John Guthrie, 1793), 154.

39. See Devine, *Scotland's Empire, 1600–1815*, and MacKillop, *"More Fruitful than the Soil."*

40. Sergeant William Ross was born and died a Protestant. Family lore ("William Ross 1734–1808, Pilote du St-Laurent," Clan Ross Quebec Inc., 407 Dufferin St., Granby, QC) has him buried just outside the local Catholic cemetery near his family.

41. Sergeant James Thompson constructed a wooden trellis to block a path leading to the lower town and helped fortify a house belonging to the merchant Simon Fraser. The Patriot General Montgomery smashed the trellis with a hammer and alerted the Scots defenders in Fraser's house. Sergeant Hugh MacQuarters then fired his pre-aimed cannon from the house, instantly killing Montgomery along with many of his staff. Thompson, kept Montgomery's sword, buried him but re-interred him years later for Montgomery's family.

42. Nash, *The Unknown American Revolution*, 1.

43. Colley, *Britons: Forging the Nation, 1707–1837*, 116.

44. K. Gutzman, *The Politically Incorrect Guide to the Constitution* (Washington: Regnery Publishing, 2007), 12.

45. John Stuart, a 78th drummer boy on the Plains of Abraham, stayed in North America at Miramichi, Nova Scotia (now part of New Brunswick) See W.D. Hamilton, *Dictionary of Miramichi Biography* (Saint John, NB: Private Printing, Box 2623, 1997), 371.
46. See G. Patterson, *History of the County of Pictou* (Montreal: Dawson Brothers, 1877).
47. Jones, *American Immigration*, 61–62.

Chapter 9: Modernizing America: The Highland Scots Heritage in the New World

1. J. Goody, *Capitalism and Modernity* (Cambridge, MA: Polity Press, 2004), 58, 65, 174.
2. *Statistical Account of Scotland, 1791–1799,* 5: 405–06.
3. *St. Croix Courier,* St. Stephen, NB, December 14, 1893.
4. F. Braudel, *Civilization and Capitalism, 15th–18th Century: The Structures of Everyday Life,* vol. 1 (New York: Harper and Row Publishers, 1981), 167–71.
5. On Île d'Orléans, near Quebec City (where Governor James Murray's potato experiments were conducted), over twenty-two thousand bushels were grown in 1770. H.A. Innis, *Select Documents in Canadian Economic History* (Toronto: The University of Toronto Press, 1929), 192–93, 572.
6. New Englanders drove many MacIntoshes out during the Revolution, but now claim on websites that "New England's apple was developed by a native son of New York." The apple reflects a "New Scotland" in Upper Canada more than a New England in the United States.
7. O'Callaghan, *Calendar of N.Y. Colonial Manuscripts Indorsed Land Papers,* 345, 615, 623.
8. AO, M. Fraser, "Malcolm Fraser Letters," *Old Miscellaneous Collection,* No. 1779.
9. James Ker sent a letter to Nairne's estate in 1805 saying that the cost of a plough with horse trees (likely whipple trees) had doubled since the one sent to Colonel Nairne some years before.
10. David Stewart Museum (Montreal), H. McMillan, "John Nairne," an unpublished biography written 1959–79, circa page 107.
11. New England and New France were land rich, and had far less incentive to improve the use of the land than Scotland, which was not land rich. A steady, deliberate flow of new crops, techniques, knowledge, and machinery enabled the Scots to produce more from the land.
12. Giddens, *The Consequences of Modernity,* 36, 38.
13. Samuel Neilson, William Brown's nephew, emigrated from Scotland and took over the business. The Neilson family had established a large publishing and bookselling business by 1800.

14. S. Neilson, *Papers and Letters on Agriculture Recommended to the Attention of the Canadian Farmers by the Agricultural Society in Canada* (Quebec City, QC: Samuel Neilson, 1790), 32.
15. Baltimore claims to have published the first farm journal in the United States, *The American Farmer*, in 1819. Many of the world's first journals for specialized intellectual fields started in Edinburgh. The Agricultural Society in Canada was partly an elite club where militia officers, seigneurs, gentlemen, merchants, and the colonial governor could meet.
16. Neilson, *Papers and Letters on Agriculture*, 1.
17. S. Zeller, *Land of Promise, Promised Land* (Ottawa: Canadian Historical Association Historical Booklet No. 56, 1996), 6–7.
18. Edinburgh University in Scotland was the first in the world to set up a professorship of Agriculture and Rural Economy. Lord Kames (1696–1782) was a prime mover of the Agricultural Revolution and a regular correspondent and (perhaps) friend of Major James Clephane, the ex-mercenary and letter writer of the 78th Fraser's Highlanders.
19. P. Campbell, *Campbell's Travels in North America*, n.p.
20. C.E. Carrington, *The British Overseas: Exploits of a Nation of Shopkeepers*, 2nd ed. (Cambridge,MA: Cambridge University Press, 1968), 263, 459.
21. Royal Commission on Historical Manuscripts, *Report on the Laing Manuscripts Preserved in the University of Edinburgh*, vol. 2, His Majesty's Stationery Office, 1925.
22. Francis and Samuel MacKay of the Royal American Regiment and Governor James Murray had served in the Scots Brigade in the Netherlands. Francis and Samuel were the sons of General Francis MacKay, a mercenary in Austrian service. They married French Canadians, and their descendants became French-speaking officers who fought loyally for the Crown in 1812, the 1837 Rebellion, the Riel Rebellion, the First World War, and the Second World War.
23. A. Campbell, *The Royal American Regiment: An Atlantic Microcosm, 1755–1772* (Norman, OK: University of Oklahoma Press, Publishing Division of the University, 2010), 204.
24. A. Lower, *Great Britain's Woodyard: British America and the Timber Trade, 1763–1867* (Montreal: McGill-Queen's University Press, 1973), 160.
25. Richards, *The Black Watch at Ticonderoga and Major Duncan Campbell of Inverawe*, 38,
26. Peter N. Moogk, "Young, John (d. 1819)," *Dictionary of Canadian Biography*, vol. 5, University of Toronto/Université Laval, 2003, accessed October 29, 2013, www.biographi.ca/en/bio/young_john_1819_5E.html.
27. T. Flannery, ed., *The Life and Adventures of John Nicol, Mariner* (New York: Atlantic Monthly Press, 1997), 34.
28. Lower, *Great Britain's Woodyard: British America and the Timber Trade, 1763–1867*, 187.

29. Braudel, *Civilization and Capitalism, 15th–18th Century*, 1: 362–67.

30. J.M. Lindsay, "Forestry and Agriculture in the Scottish Highlands, 1700–1850: A Problem in Estate Management," *Agricultural History Review* 25, Silver Jubilee Issue, Part I (1977): 34–35.

31. *Statistical Account of Scotland, 1791–1799*, 13: 523.

32. Ibid., 524.

33. Ibid., *Volume 5*, 298.

34. Ibid., *Volume 14*, 394–95.

35. E. Grant, *Memoirs of a Highland Lady* (Edinburgh: Canongate Classics, 2001), 268–79.

36. Lindsay, "Forestry and Agriculture in the Scottish Highlands, 1700–1850," 26–27.

37. Ibid., 26.

38. Napoleon did not have the ships to actually blockade European ports. He threatened those countries who continued to trade with Britain; hence the term "boycott" is more accurate.

39. Carrington, *The British Overseas: Exploits of a Nation of Shopkeepers*, 263.

40. Canadian historians Douglas Creighton and A.M. Lower say that timber subsidized migrants. British historian Terrence Coleman in *Passage to America* says migrants subsidized timber.

41. Many Irish and Highland Scots, caught up in the Potato Famine of the 1840s, came to North America via Canada.

42. D.S. MacMillan, "Gilmour, Allan (1775–1849)," *Dictionary of Canadian Biography*, vol. 7 (Toronto: University of Toronto Press, 1988), 343–44.

43. D.S. MacMillan, "The Scot as Businessman," in *The Scottish Tradition in Canada*, W. Stanford Reid, ed., (Toronto: McClelland & Stewart, 1976) 195.

44. Colcord dismisses the popular idea that the word *shanty* derives from *chanter*. The word was first used in print only in 1869. Joanna C. Colcord, *Songs of American Sailormen* (New York: Oak Publications, 1964), 29–30.

45. "Donkey Riding," derived from the music of "Highland Laddie," is a St. Lawrence Scots sea-shanty. The "donkey" of the title was a steam donkey engine used to load timber. The opening line runs "Were you ever in Quebec, stowing timber on the deck?"

46. Flannery, *The Life and Adventures of John Nicol, Mariner*, 34.

47. I.P. MacMillan, *An Account of The Emigration from Scotland to North America of John Ban McMillan and his Descendants* (privately printed, 1987), 64.

48. *The Scotsman*, Edinburgh (September 15, 1824): 3.

49. Robert Fulton used imported engines from Britain and did not build them locally.

50. Eileen Marcil, "Goudie, John," in *Dictionary of Canadian Biography*, vol. 6, University of Toronto/Université Laval, 2003, accessed October 29, 2013, www.biographi.ca/en/bio/goudie_john_6E.html.

51. Eileen Marcil, "Charles Wood" (1790–1847) *Dictionary of Canadian Biography,* vol. 7, 921–22.

52. Ibid.

53. There were several Donald MacKays in the 78th. The shipbuilder's grandfather *may* have fought in the Seven Years' War too.

54. According to Canadian historian Desmond Morton, the Germans apparently feared the Canadians more than any other troops in the First World War.

55. Much of early frontier life in Canada revolved around the Loyalist and British regiments that settled these areas. Later, local militia units evolved from such regiments.

56. The New England Yankees, the Dutch Americans, the English, Irish, and African-Canadians that made up the rest of the Loyalists were not conspicuous for controlling violence within their communities to the degree the Highland Scots did.

57. The French army's debts were written on playing cards. There were mutinies in the United States because its soldiers never received the full value of the money promised to them.

58. E.J. Chapman and I.M. McCulloch, eds., *A Bard of Wolfe's Army* (Montreal: Robin Brass Studio, 2010), 225.

59. As was said, during the first winter in Quebec, Murray borrowed two thousand pounds from the rank and file Highland soldiers and gave them interest on the money when he repaid them.

60. Giddens, *The Consequences of Modernity*, 25–26.

61. Chapman and McCulloch, eds., *A Bard of Wolfe's Army*, 224–25.

62. Glenn A. Steppler, "Green, James," in *Dictionary of Canadian Biography,* vol. 6, University of Toronto/Université Laval, 2003–, accessed October 28, 2013, www.biographi.ca/en/bio/green_james_6E.html.

63. Ibid.

64. James Green became paymaster of the British Army in Revolutionary New York, Colonel of the Cameronians, and headed the commissariat to buy supplies for the army in 1812.

65. The Quebec Savings Bank was intended for poor people, and it succeeded in its mission. The bank paid interest on their savings, another example of Scots transferring modernity to Canada.

66. E. Healey, *Coutts & Co. 1692–1992: The Portrait of a Private Bank* (London: Hodder & Stoughton, 1992), 87.

67. H. Bolitho and D. Peel, *The Drummonds of Charing Cross* (London: George Allen & Unwin, 1967), 55.

68. The Drummonds paid out approximately two million British pounds

during that war. Fur-trade exports at that time involved transactions of only a quarter of a million pounds.

69. Bills of exchange were written orders for the bank to pay a sum of money to the holder and were then the financial instruments of credit, debt, export, and import.

70. There was a huge shortage of cash in frontier Canada that severely hampered trade.

71. D. S. MacMillan and A.J.H. Richardson, "Dunlop, James," in *Dictionary of Canadian Biography,* vol. 5, University of Toronto/Université Laval, 2003, accessed October 28, 2013, www.biographi.ca/en/bio/dunlop_james_5E.html.

72. John Richardson read Adam Smith and probably the economic ideas of other Scots who played a major role in the economic theories of the Enlightenment.

73. According to Merrill Denison's *History of the Bank of Montreal,* vol. 1 (Montreal: McClelland & Stewart, 1966), 52–54, the Bank of America, established only in 1782, had a much bigger impact on Richardson's thinking than forty years of banking methods in Canada, Adam Smith, or centuries of banking had in Richardson's native Scotland.

74. D. Geddes, "How 'Habeas Corpus' Came to Canada: The Bills on Credit Scandal — Quebec 1783," *Three Banks Review* 112 (December 1976) and "John Cochran's Troubles," *Three Banks Review* 111 (September 1976).

75. Adam Mabane of the Scots "French Party" advised governor Sir Frederick Haldimand to use both medieval French law and English commercial law to sue John Cochrane, the bank's agent. Mabane sat as the judge of the case (there was no jury) and Haldimand won. However, as a consequence of the writs issued by Haldimand, goods owned by the completely innocent Fraser were seized. Fraser (not the guilty banker), went to prison and was ruined.

76. As we state elsewhere, black slaves used habeas corpus to win freedom in Lower Canada of the 1790s.

77. Giddens, *The Consequences of Modernity,* 24.

78. Ibid., 26, 34, 47.

79. Zeller, "Land of Promise, Promised Land," 6.

80. W. Irving, "Astoria," in *The Works of Washington Irving,* vol. 8 (New York and London: The Co-operative Publication Society, Inc., n.d.), 26.

81. For instance, at the Battle of Seven Oaks on June 19, 1816, Cuthbert Grant (1796–1854) led the NWC side. This famous Métis was the son of an NWC partner, also named Cuthbert Grant and an Aboriginal person, probably of mixed Cree and French origin. Leading the Hudson's Bay Company (HBC) side was Miles McDonell (1767–1828). However, his brother, John worked for the NWC. Both were sons of Spanish John McDonell, the ex-mercenary who had fought against King George for Bonnie Prince Charlie, then later for King George with the Loyalists in

the American Revolution.
82. Allen Johnson and Dumas Malone, eds., "William Dunbar" *Dictionary of American Biography* (New York: Charles Scribner's Sons, 1930), 507–08.
83. Irving, "Astoria," 28.
84. Giddens, *The Consequences of Modernity*, 47.

Chapter 10: The Scots March to Modernity

1. R. Porter, *Enlightenment* (London: Penguin Books, 2000), 243.
2. K. Mason, "The American Loyalist Problem of Identity in the Revolutionary Atlantic World," in *The Loyal Atlantic: Remaking the British Atlantic in the Revolutionary Era*, J. Bannister and L. Riordan, eds. (Toronto: University of Toronto Press, 2012), 55.
3. Bolitho and Peel, *The Drummonds of Charing Cross*, 56–58.
4. See "Innovation," (1750), www.rampantscotland.com/SCM/story.htm.
5. I. Gilmour, "Out of Bounds," *London Review of Books*, vol. 27, no. 2 (January 20, 2005): 26–28.
6. S.M. Wise, *Though The Heavens May Fall* (Cambridge, MA: Da Capo Press, Perseus Books Group, 2005), 71.
7. Ibid., 198.
8. Colonel H. Neilson, "Slavery in Old Canada," in *Transactions of the Literary and Historical Society of Quebec, Sessions of 1905, No. 6* (Quebec City: The Daily Telegraph Job Printing House, 1906), 40–41.
9. LAC, Journal of the House of Assembly of Lower Canada From 28th March to 3rd June 1798, http://eco.canadiana.ca/view/oocihm.9 00938_6.
10. Himmelfarb, *The Roads to Modernity*, 5.
11. McDougal, *Freedom Just Around the Corner*, 281–82.
12. E.J. Collins, "Dietary Change and Cereal Consumption in Britain in the Nineteenth Century," *Agricultural History Review* 23, Part 2 (1975): 94, 107.
13. Hunter, *Scottish Exodus*, 97.
14. McMillan, "John Nairne," 95.
15. D.S. MacMillan, *Scotland and Australia: 1788–1850* (Oxford: The Clarendon Press, 1967), 26.
16. Bailyn, *Voyagers to the West*, 175–85.

Chapter 11: Past Fiction: Sir Walter's Scott-Land

1. Hamilton James Eckenrode, "Sir Walter Scott and the South," in *The North American Review*, vol. 206, no. 743 (October 1917).
2. Holcombe, *Ancient Animosity*, 12.
3. Sir Walter Scott read and translated German, Italian, French, and Latin into English; married the daughter of a French émigré; travelled and researched in France; collected songs, stories, and folk tales in Italy; and travelled all over Britain and Ireland.

4. J. Brewer, *The Pleasures of the Imagination* (London: Harper Collins, 1997), 643.
5. Macdonald, *The Old Lords of Lovat and Beaufort*, 136.
6. Scott's imitators included: Russia with Pushkin, Balzac, and Tolstoy (*War and Peace*); France with Dumas (*The Count of Monte Cristo, The Three Musketeers*) and Hugo (*The Hunchback of Notre Dame*); Denmark with Hans Christian Andersen; the Caucasus with Lermontov (who was descended from a Scots mercenary); and Malta with Curmi's opera *Rob Roy*.
7. Mendelssohn, Beethoven, and Schubert are some of those inspired by Scott.
8. The "British Invasion" of North American pop music in the 1960s by The Beatles and The Rolling Stones was somewhat similar to the "Scottish Invasion" of music in the 1800s.
9. The second half of the eighteenth century saw a movement against the formal gardens of the French and a gradual change favouring the "natural" landscaped gardens of the British.
10. A. Welsh, *The Hero of the Waverly Novels* (New York: Atheneum, 1968), 22.
11. Sir Walter Scott, *Manners, Customs, and History of the Highlanders of Scotland* (New York: Barnes & Noble Books, 1993), 31.
12. MacKinnon, *Scottish Highlanders*, 36.
13. Trevor-Roper, *The Invention of Scotland*, 211.
14. Burton, *The Scot Abroad*, 23–24.
15. Ibid., 316.
16. John Nairne of the 78th was related to Lady Nairne who was married to his relative, another John Nairne. There are many John Nairnes, and it is difficult to know exactly how they were related. A third John Nairne of the same family was in the 71st Fraser's Highlanders.
17. M. MacMillan, *The Uses and Abuses of History* (Toronto: Viking Canada, 2008), 47.
18. Trevor-Roper, *The Invention of Scotland*, 217.
19. Ibid., 214.
20. Munro, *Highland Clans and Tartans*, 90.
21. Trevor-Roper, *The Invention of Scotland*, 84.
22. The author of this book, Sam Allison, gave a talk to British history teachers in 2003. Only a small minority of them knew that "Hail to the Chief" originally referred to clan chiefs.
23. See R. Lamont Brown, *John Brown: Queen Victoria's Highland Servant* (Stroud, Gloucestershire: Sutton Publishing, 2000).
24. Fischer, *Washington's Crossing*, 50.
25. Trevor-Roper, *The Invention of Scotland*, 212.
26. Ibid.
27. H. Trevor-Roper, "The Invention of Tradition: The Highland Tradition of Scotland," in *The Invention of Tradition*, Eric Hobsbaum and Terence Ranger, eds. (Cambridge, MA: Cambridge University Press, 1995), 35–41.

28. Trevor-Roper, "The Invention of Tradition: The Highland Tradition of Scotland," 31.
29. D.M. Henderson, *The Scottish Regiments* (Glasgow: HarperCollins Publishers, 1993), 38.
30. Ibid., 90.
31. Ibid., 43.
32. Colley, *Britons: Forging the Nation, 1707–1837*, 126–31.
33. Trevor-Roper "The Invention of Tradition: The Highland Tradition of Scotland," 31.
34. Welsh, *The Hero of the Waverly Novels*, 90.
35. W. Schivelbusch, *The Culture of Defeat* (New York: Picador, Henry Holt and Company, 2003), 48.
36. U.S. Geographic Names Information System (GNIS) http://geonames.usgs.gov/domestic/index.html.
37. W. Irving, "Abbotsford," in *The Work of Washington Irving*, vol. 3 (New York: The Co-operative Publication Society Inc., n. d.), 576.
38. Irving, "Astoria," 27.
39. Schivelbusch, *The Culture of Defeat*, 50.
40. Welsh, *The Hero of the Waverly Novels*, 22, 240.
41. Schivelbusch, *The Culture of Defeat*, 50.
42. *Burlington Times News*, Burlington, NC, Thursday, October 12, 2006.
43. Schivelbusch, *The Culture of Defeat*, 60.
44. Eckenrode, "Sir Walter Scott and the South," 595–603.
45. T. Dixon, Jr., *The Clansman: An Historical Romance of the Ku Klux Klan* (New York: Doubleday, Page & Co., 1905), electronic edition: Academic Affairs Library (Chapel Hill, NC: University of North Carolina, 1997), title page.
46. Dixon, *The Clansman*, To the Reader page.
47. The story involves a Northern family and a Southern family before and after the Civil War. The Northern Stonehams marry into the Southern Camerons, who, with the KKK, saved the day by attacking upstart African Americans.
48. Dixon, *The Clansman*, 324.
49. Schivelbusch, *The Culture of Defeat*, 317.
50. Ibid., 50, 51.
51. Douglass ended a speech by quoting Burns, saying "A man's a man for a' that."
52. In Canada, the 1837 Rebellion and the unification of British North America were major problems, as well as industrialization and urbanization. The ruling order in the United States were worried by the Civil War, the new immigrant masses crowding Northern cities, the Irish Catholics of the Great Famine years, and the perceived pushiness of African-American freedmen.
53. Hunter, *Scottish Exodus*, 103.
54. Quoted in Fischer, *Albion's Seed*, 818.
55. Eckinrode, "Sir Walter Scott and the South," 595–603.

56. Trevor-Roper, *The Invention of Scotland*, 207.

57. Ibid., 143.

58. Ibid., 119.

59. James MacPherson claimed that the Ossian was based on a real Scottish warrior-bard, not a fictitious Irish figure. Ossian had a massive impact on romantic literature throughout Europe. The Highland Society of London unknowingly promoted a forgery and Scottish history would have required rewriting to accommodate the idea that the hero of the poem actually lived.

60. Trevor-Rope, *The Invention of Scotland*, 141, 146.

61. Holcombe, *Ancient Animosity*, 257.

62. Ibid., 16.

63. Ibid., 359.

64. A Stewart of Appin helped to free the imprisoned Archibald Campbell, the ex-78th officer mistreated by American rebels. Unlike fiction, the mother of Allan Stewart of the 78th was a Campbell and so he had family on both sides of the Appin murder.

65. Prebble, *Mutiny* (London: Penguin Books, 1977), 104.

66. D. Stewart, *Sketches of the Character, Manners and Present State of the Highlanders of Scotland* (Edinburgh: Reprinted by John Donald Publishers, 1977), 19.

67. Prebble, *Mutiny*, 98.

68. Ibid., 104.

69. Ibid., 97.

70. Trevor-Roper, *The Invention of Scotland*, 71.

71. Holcombe, *Ancient Animosity*, 275.

72. T. Sowell, *Intellectuals and Society* (New York: Basic Books, Perseus Books Group, 2009), 138–40.

73. C.H. Enloe, *Ethnic Soldiers: State Security in Divided Societies* (Athens, GA: University of Georgia Press, 1980), 34–36.

74. Ibid., 1, 30.

75. Sowell, *Intellectuals and Society*, 140.

Chapter 12: The March of the Highland Men Through the History Books

1. Trevor-Roper, *The Invention of Scotland*, xx.

2. E. Hobsbawm and T. Ranger, eds., *The Invention of Tradition* (Cambridge: Cambridge University Press, 1995), 13.

3. MacMillan, *The Uses and Abuses of History* (Toronto: Viking Canada, 2008), 36.

4. Meyer, *The Highland Scots of North Carolina, 1732–1776*, Preface, vi.

5. The Highlands were brutally integrated into Britain; New France was battered into British America, and an aggressive Republic battled its way out of British America. A reinvigorated set of colonies emerged that

eventually became Canada. Ireland after the 1798 Rebellion was forced to join a triumphant, Protestant-dominated United Kingdom.

6. MacMillan, *The Uses and Abuses of History*, 87.
7. E. Foner, *Who Owns History?* (New York: Hill & Wang, A Division of Farrar, Straus, and Giroux, 2002), 151.
8. Pennant, *A Tour of Scotland* (1774), 346.
9. J. Vincent, *An Intelligent Person's Guide to History* (London: Duckworth Overlook, 2006), 147.
10. D. Lowenthal, *The Heritage Crusade and the Spoils of History* (Cambridge: Cambridge University Press, 1998), 132.
11. E. Hobsbawm, *On History* (London: Abacus, 1999), 357.
12. MacMillan, *The Uses and Abuses of History*, 39.
13. Hobsbawm and Ranger, eds., *The Invention of Tradition*, 303.
14. D.P. MacLeod, *Northern Armageddon* (Vancouver, BC: Douglas & McIntyre, 2008), 170.
15. Colley, *Britons: Forging the Nation, 1707–1837*, 131.
16. *The Scotsman*, Edinburgh, March 18, 1899.
17. Fischer, *Washington's Crossing*, 483.
18. McDougall, tells us that visitors to the new United States in the early 1800s "suspected that the glue holding the Union together was pretense," in *Throes of Democracy: The American Civil War Era, 1829–1877*, 40.
19. M. Kammen, *A Season of Youth: The American Revolution and the Historical Imagination* (New York: Alfred A. Knopf, 1978), 177.
20. A. Calder, *Revolutionary Empire: The Rise of the English-Speaking Empires from the Fifteenth Century to the 1780s* (New York: E.P. Dutton, 1981), 734.
21. Hector St. John Crèvecoeur's book played a role in the French Revolution of 1789. Frederick Turner (1861–1932) adapted Crèvecoeur's ideas in his much more famous thesis claiming that the frontier generated self-reliance, ingenuity, individualism, and resourcefulness. Thanks partly to Turner, "the new American man" is arguably part of the conventional historical wisdom.
22. Crèvecoeur fought for the French army in North America during the Seven Years' War. This author does not know whether he had any contact with the Scots during this military service. The large number of Scots soldier-settlers who flocked to New York State, where Crèvecoeur settled after the Seven Years' War, probably shaped his perspective.
23. Crèvecoeur had settled in Orange County on the New York State borderlands in 1769. This area had been made safe for settlement with the fall of New France in 1763.
24. Lieutenant Roderick MacNeil, the eldest son of the chief of the MacNeils of Barra in the Hebrides, recruited many of his clansmen for the 78th and some stayed in North America.

25. Modern historians have tried to trace Andrew, the Hebridean, and his family to determine how they fared in the New World. Andrew (possibly MacNeil?) was not traced.

26. F. Folsom, "North Carolina Scottish Loyalists Become the First Free Americans," in *Bicentennial/The Americans* (Los Angeles: Sky Delta Airlines, 1976).

27. Jones, *American Immigration*, 62.

28. Devine, *Scotland's Empire, 1600–1815*, 184.

29. Kammen, *A Season of Youth: The American Revolution and the Historical Imagination*, 178.

30. Women, for instance, won the vote after the First World War because of war service.

31. Political continuity in Canada overshadowed its radical economic and social change between 1783 and 1830. In the United States, progressive political innovations overshadowed the continuity of reactionary social policies. The American Revolution of 1776 inspired Europeans but inflicted slavery, genocide, or exile on African Americans, Aboriginal peoples, and Highland Scots.

32. J.J. Crow, *The Black Experience in Revolutionary North Carolina* (Raleigh, NC: Division of Archives & History, North Carolina Department of Cultural Resources, 1977), 82.

33. S. Orwell and I. Angus, eds., "Notes on Nationalism," in *The Collected Essays, Journalism and Letters of George Orwell*, vol. 3: *As I Please. 1943–1945* (London: Penguin Books, 1978), 420.

34. R.M. Morris, *Encyclopedia of American History* (New York: Harper and Row, 1965), 192.

35. Quoted in Lowenthal, *The Heritage Crusade and the Spoils of History*, 157.

36. M. Denison, *Canada's First Bank: A History of the Bank of Montreal*, vol. 1 (Montreal: McClelland & Stewart, 1966), 53.

37. Ibid., 59.

38. John Richardson was in the North West Company and helped found Canada's first canal, the Montreal General Hospital and McGill University. He ran the secret service against French Revolutionary and Yankee spies and is labelled by Canadian historians as a reactionary because he opposed the French Canadian nationalists of the time.

39. Richardson vehemently opposed slavery as economically inefficient and immoral.

40. Richardson's role in Female Suffrage in Lower Canada 1791–1830s is unknown. He sponsored what became the Female Benevolent Society. Papineau the younger removed the right of women to vote in the 1830s (See John Garner, *The Franchise and Politics in British North America, 1755–1867* (Toronto: Toronto Univ. Press, 1969), 158.

41. The British, under the Constitutional Act of 1791, gave Catholics in Lower Canada the right to vote and sit in Parliament, but denied these rights to their citizens elsewhere.

42. Garner, *The Franchise and Politics in British North America, 1755–1867*, 148–50.

43. Ezekiel Hart was elected but was barred by the Catholic Canadiens who controlled the Assembly because he was Jewish. Although he was re-elected, he was again rejected by the Assembly.

44. The hypocrisy of Papineau's Patriotes mirrors Samuel Johnson's criticism of American Patriots who demanded freedom from Britain for themselves, but black slavery for others.

45. Garner, *The Franchise and Politics in British North America, 1755–1867*, 150.

46. Few Canadian historians accept that the Scots initiated the timber trade.

47. Baylin, *Voyagers to the West* (New York: Alfred A. Knopf, 1986), 393.

48. Cole Harris, *Historical Atlas of Canada Vol.1: From the Beginning to 1800*, 173.

49. J. Ross (1831–1901) was premier of Quebec (1884–87); General Armand Ross was the first Canadian soldier to march into Germany in the Second World War, and Mgr. Francois-Xavier Ross was the first bishop of Gaspe. All three are descended from Highland soldiers.

50. The false assumption that there were no changes in the Highlands led to the idea that Highlanders remained medieval in outlook. Opposition to the American Revolution was then said to spring from this medieval outlook, rather than from progressive ideals or self interest.

51. Foner, *Who Owns History?*, xv.

52. Campbelltown was a centre of Loyalist activity and so the name was changed after the Revolution. In Quebec, French nationalism has changed many historical names associated with non-French groups such as Aboriginal peoples, the Irish, English, and of course the Scots.

53. B. Baylin, *The Ideological Origins of the American Revolution* (Cambridge: The Belknap Press of Harvard University Press, 1992), 123.

54. *The Sir William Johnson Papers*, vol. 11 (Albany, New York: The University of the State of New York, 1953), 742–44.

55. Orwell and Angus., "Notes on Nationalism," 418–19.

56. Foner, *Who Owns History?*, 165.

57. Crow, *The Black Experience in Revolutionary North Carolina*, 55.

58. Slavery and genocide were as much children of the American Revolution as were independence and liberty. It is time to legitimize those children, and to recognize that the Revolutionary War was not an ideological victory for all.

Epilogue

1. Bailyn, *Voyagers to the West*, 26.
2. N. Ascherson, "The money's still out there," *London Review of Books*, vol. 33, no. 19 (October 6, 2011): 8–12.
3. By the time of the 1812 war, there were approximately fifty thousand Highlanders in the British Army. See Ascherson, "The money's still out there," 8–12.
4. Porter, *Enlightenment*, 483.
5. Controlling illegal violence without repressing legitimate opposition is difficult as is promoting reform without harm. Promoting reform was often confused with rebellion.
6. A. Foreman, *A World on Fire: Britain's Crucial Role in the American Civil War* (New York: Random House, 2010), 35, 92–93, 163, 283, 462.
7. Porter, *Enlightenment*, 3.
8. Ian Anderson, *Sitting Bull and the Mounties* (The History Net) http://www.historynet.com/culture/native_american_history/3030091.html?page=1&c=y.

Selected Bibliography

Adam, Frank. *The Clan Septs and Regiments of the Scottish Highlands*. 4th ed. Edinburgh: W.K. Johnston, 1952.

Adam, M.I. "The Causes of the Highland Emigrations of 1783–1803." *The Scottish Historical Review* 17. (1920).

_____. "The Highland Emigration of 1770." *The Scottish Historical Review* 16. (1919).

_____. "The Eighteenth-Century Highland Landlords and the Poverty Problem." *The Scottish Historical Review* 19. (1922).

Anderson, Ian G. *Scotsmen in the Service of the Czars*. Edinburgh: Pentland Press, 1990.

Argyll, Duke of. *Scotland As It Was and As It Is*. Vol. 2. Edinburgh: David Douglas, MDCCCLXXXVII.

Arthur, Elizabeth. "Adam Mabane and the French Party." Master's thesis. McGill University, 1947.

Bailyn, Bernard. *The Ideological Origins of the American Revolution*. Cambridge, MA: The Belknap Press of Harvard University Press, 1992.

_____. *Voyagers to the West*. New York: Alfred A. Knopf, 1986.

Barnes, Major R.M. *The Uniforms and History of the Scottish Regiments*. London: Seeley Service & Company, 1956.

Beattie, Daniel J. "The Adaptation of the British Army to Wilderness Warfare, 1755–1763." In *Adapting to Conditions*. Edited by Maarten Ultee. Alabama: University of Alabama Press, 1986.

Blanning, Tim. *The Pursuit of Glory: Europe, 1648–1815*. London: Penguin Books, 2008.

Bliss, Michael. *Northern Enterprise: Five Centuries of Canadian Business*. Toronto: McClelland & Stewart, 1987.

Bolitho, Hector, and Derek Peel. *The Drummonds of Charing Cross*. London: George Allen and Unwin, 1967.

Braudel, Fernand. *Civilization and Capitalism, 15th–18th Century*. Vols. I, II, III. New York: Harper and Row Publishers, 1981.

_____. *The Perspective of the World*. New York: Harper and Row, 1986.

_____. *The Structures of Everyday Life*. Vol. I. New York: Harper and Row Publishers, 1981.

Brewer, John. *The Pleasures of the Imagination*. London: HarperCollins, 1997.

Brock, William. *Scotus Americanus*. Edinburgh: Edinburgh University Press, 1982.

Brockington, William S. Jr., ed. *Munro: His Expedition with the Worthy Scots Regiment Called Mac-Keys*. Westport, CT: Praeger, 1999.

Brown, Michael. "Franco-Scottish Relations to 1513." In *Oxford Companion to Scottish History*. Edited by Michael Lynch. Oxford: Oxford University Press, 2007.

Brumwell, Stephen. *Redcoats: The British Soldier and War in the Americas, 1755–1763*. Cambridge: Cambridge University Press, 2002.

Bumstead, J.M. *Land, Settlement and Politics on 18th-Century Prince Edward Island*. Montreal: McGill-Queen's University Press, 1987.

_____. *The People's Clearance: 1770–1815*. Edinburgh: Edinburgh University Press, 1982.

Burton, John H. *The Scot Abroad*. Edinburgh: William Blackwood and Sons, MDCCCLXXXIII (1883).

Calendar of Home Office Papers, 1760–1765. London: Longman and Company, 1878.

Campbell, Alexander V. *The Royal American Regiment: An Atlantic Microcosm, 1755–1772*. Norman Publishing Division: University of Oklahoma Press, 2010.

Campbell, M.W. *McGillivray: Lord of the Northwest*. Toronto: Clarke, Irwin and Company, 1962.

_____. *The North West Company*. Toronto: MacMillan Company of Canada, 1957.

_____. *Northwest to the Sea*. Toronto: Clarke, Irwin and Company, 1975.

Cannadine, David. *The Undivided Past*. New York: Alfred A. Knopf, 2013.

Canny, Nicholas, ed. *Europeans on the Move: Studies on European Migration, 1500–1800*. Oxford: Clarendon Press, 1994.

Chapman, Earl John, and Ian Macpherson McCulloch, eds. *A Bard of Wolfe's Army: James Thompson, Gentleman Volunteer, 1733–1830*. Montreal: Robin Brass Studio, 2010.

Clan Ross Quebec Inc. *William Ross 1734–1808 Pilote du St-Laurent.* 407 rue Dufferin, Granby, QC: Clan Ross Quebec, [n.d.]

Clyde, Robert. *From Rebel to Hero: The Image of the Highlander, 1745–1830.* East Linton, Scotland: Tuckwell Press, 1998.

Colley, Linda. *Britons: Forging the Nation, 1707–1837.* New Haven, CT: Yale University Press, 1992.

Collins, E. J. "Dietary Change and Cereal Consumption in Britain in the Nineteenth Century." *Agricultural History Review* 23, Part II. Exeter: British Agricultural History Society, 1975.

Connell, Brian. *The Plains of Abraham.* London: Hodder & Stoughton, 1959.

Crow, Jeffrey J. *The Black Experience in Revolutionary North Carolina.* Raleigh: Division of Archives & History, North Carolina Department of Cultural Resources, 1977.

David, James Corbett. *Dunmore's New World: The Extraordinary Life of a Royal Governor in Revolutionary America.* Charlottesville: University of Virginia Press, 2013.

Denison, Merrill. *Canada's First Bank: A History of the Bank of Montreal, Vol. I.* Montreal: McClelland & Stewart, 1966.

Devine, Tom M. *Scotland's Empire 1600–1815.* London: Penguin Books, 2003.

Dictionary of American History, Vol. VI. New York: Charles Scribner, 1967.

Dictionary of Canadian Biography, Vols. III–VIII. Toronto: University of Toronto Press, 1974–85.

Doughty, A. *Historical Journal of the Campaign in North America.* Vols. I, II. Toronto: Champlain Society, 1901.

Ferguson, James, ed. *Papers Illustrating the Scots Brigade in the Service of the United Netherlands, 1572–1782.* Edinburgh: Printed at the University Press by T. & A. Constable for the Scottish Historical Society, 1899–1901.

Fingerhut, Eugene. "From Scots to Americans: Ryegate's Immigrants in the 1770s." *Vermont History: The Proceedings of the Vermont History Society.* (Autumn 1967).

Fischer, David H. *Albion's Seed.* Toronto: Oxford University Press, 1989.

———. *Washington's Crossing.* New York: Oxford University Press, 2004.

Fischer, Thomas A. *The Scots in Sweden.* Edinburgh: Otto Schulze and Company, 1907.

———. *The Scots in Germany.* Edinburgh: Otto Schulze and Company, 1902.

Folsom, Franklin. "North Carolina Scottish Loyalists Become the First Free Americans." *Bicentennial/The Americans.* Los Angeles: Sky Delta Airlines, 1976.

Foner, Eric. *Who Owns History?* New York: Hill and Wang, A Division of Farrar, Straus, and Giroux, 2002.

Foreman, Amanda. *A World on Fire: Britain's Crucial Role in the American Civil War.* New York: Random House, 2010.

Fraser, Duncan. *The 1774 Ledger at Johnson Hall, Johnstown, New York: Biographical Notes on 125 Names*. New York: Private Printing, St. Andrew's Society, 1959.

Fraser, Flora Marjory. *Clan Fraser: A History Celebrating Over 800 Years of the Family in Scotland*. Edinburgh: Scottish Cultural Press, 1997.

Fraser, Malcolm. "Extract From a Manuscript. Journal Relating to the Siege of Quebec in 1759." Literary and Historical Society of Quebec, [n. d.].

————. "Malcolm Fraser Letters" *Old Miscellaneous Collection No. 1779*. Ontario Archives, Mu 2098.

Frey, Sylvia R. *Water from the Rock: Black Resistance in a Revolutionary Age*. Princeton, NJ: Princeton University Press, 1991.

Fryer, M. Beacock. *Allan Maclean: Jacobite General*. Toronto: Dundurn Press, 1987.

Garner, John. *The Franchise and Politics in British North America, 1755–1867*. Toronto: Toronto University Press, 1969.

Geddes, David. "How 'Habeas Corpus' Came to Canada: The Bills on Credit Scandal—Quebec 1783." *The Three Banks Review* No. 112. Edinburgh: Royal Bank of Scotland. (Dec. 1976).

————. "John Cochran's Troubles" *The Three Banks Review* No. 111. Edinburgh: Royal Bank of Scotland (Sept. 1976).

Giddens, Anthony. *The Consequences of Modernity*. Malden, MA: Polity Press, 2009.

Glozier, Matthew. "Scots in the French and Dutch Armies." *Scotland and the Thirty Years' War*. Edited by Steve Murdoch. Boston: Brill, 2001.

Goody, Jack. *Capitalism and Modernity: The Great Debate*. Cambridge: Polity Press, 2004.

Grant, Anne. *Memoirs of an American Lady*. Albany: Joel Munsell, 1876.

Grant, Elizabeth. *Memoirs of a Highland Lady*. Edinburgh: Canongate Classics, 2001.

Grever, Maria, and Stuurman, Siep, eds. *Beyond the Canon: History for the 21st Century*. Houndmills, Basingstoke, Hampshire: Palgrave Macmillan, 2007.

Grosjean, Alexia, and Steve Murdoch, eds. *Scottish Communities Abroad in the Early Modern Period*. Boston: Brill, 2005.

Harper, J. Ralph. *The Fraser Highlanders*. 2nd ed. Bloomfield, ON: Museum Restoration Service, 1995.

Healey, Edna. *Coutts & Co. 1692–1992: The Portrait of a Private Bank*. London: Hodder & Stoughton, 1992.

Henderson, Diana H. "Highland Regiments, 1750–1830." In *Oxford Companion to Scottish History*. Edited by Michael Lynch. Oxford: Oxford University Press, 2007.

————. *Highland Soldier, 1820–1920*. Edinburgh: John Donald Publishers, 1989.

————. *The Scottish Regiments*. Glasgow: HarperCollins, 1993.

Himmelfarb, Gertrude. *The Roads to Modernity*. Toronto: Random House of Canada, 2004.

Hobsbawm, Eric. *On History*. London: Abacus, 1999.

Hobsbawm, Eric, and Terence Ranger, eds. *The Invention of Tradition*. Cambridge: Cambridge University Press, 1995.

Holcombe, Lee. *Ancient Animosity: The Appin Murder and The End of Scottish Rebellion*. Bloomington, Indiana: Author House, 2004.

Hortling, Carl-Erik. "The Stuarts in Sweden and the Royal House of Scotland." *The Stewarts*, Vol. XVI, No. 4 (1983).

Houlding, J. A. *Fit for Service: The Training of the British Army, 1715-1795*. Oxford: Clarendon Press, 1981.

Johnson, Allen, and Dumas Malone, eds. *Dictionary of American Biography*. New York: Charles Scribner's Sons, 1930.

Johnson, Sir William. *The Sir William Johnson Papers* 14 vols. Albany, NY: The University of the State of New York, 1921-65.

Johnstone, Chevalier. *Dialogue in Hades*. Quebec: Literary and Historical Society of Quebec, 1887.

Kammen, Michael. *A Season of Youth: The American Revolution and the Historical Imagination*. New York: Alfred A. Knopf, 1978.

Kennedy, Paul. *The Rise and Fall of the Great Powers*. New York: Random House, 1989.

Knox, John. *The Journal of Captain John Knox*. Vol. II. New York: Greenwood Press, 1968.

Lindsay, J.M. "Forestry and Agriculture in the Scottish Highlands 1700-1850: A Problem in Estate Management (Part I)" *The Agricultural History Review* 25. Exeter: (British Agricultural History Society, 1977).

Literary and Historical Society of Quebec. *War: The Centenary Volume of the Literary and Historical Society of Quebec 1824-1924*. Quebec: L'Événement Press, 1924.

Livingstone, Alastair of Bachuil, Christian W. H. Aikman, and Betty Stuart Hart, eds. *No Quarter Given: The Muster Roll of Prince Charles Edward Stuart's Army, 1745-46*. Glasgow: Neil Wilson Publishing, 2009.

Loder, J. D. V. *Colonsay and Oronsay in the Isles of Argyll*. Edinburgh: Oliver Boyd, 1935.

Lowenthal, David. *The Heritage Crusade and the Spoils of History*. Cambridge: Cambridge University Press, 1998.

Lower, Arthur. *Great Britain's Woodyard: British America and the Timber Trade, 1763-1867*. Montreal: McGill Queen's Press, 1973.

Lynch, Michael, ed. *Oxford Companion to Scottish History*. Oxford: Oxford University Press, 2007.

MacKay, Donald. *Scotland Farewell: The People of the* Hector. Toronto: McGraw-Hill Ryerson, 1980.

MacKillop, Andrew. *More Fruitful than the Soil: Army Empire and the Scottish Highlands, 1715–1815*. East Linton, East Lothian: Tuckwell Press, 2000.

MacLean, John P. *An Historical Account of the Settlements of Scotch Highlanders in America Prior to the Peace of 1783*. Cleveland: The Helman-Taylor Company 1900; Glasgow: John MacKay, 1900.

MacLeod, Ada. "The Glenaladale Pioneers." *The Dalhousie Review* 2. Halifax (1931–32).

MacLeod, Donald. *Memoirs of Sergeant Donald MacLeod*. London: Peterborough House Press, [n. d.]

MacMillan, Ian. P. *An Account of the Emigration from Scotland to North America of John Ban MacMillan and His Descendants*. Minneapolis, MN: Privately printed for Cargill-MacMillan, 1987.

MacMillan, Margaret. *The Uses and Abuses of History*. Toronto: Viking Canada, 2008.

MacNeil of Barra. *The Clan MacNeil: Clan Niall of Scotland*. New York: Caledonian Publishing Co., 1923.

Maskill, Craig. "Where One Scot Comes Others Soon Follow." Unpublished Master's thesis. University of New Brunswick, 1995.

Mason, Keith. "The American Loyalist Problem of Identity in the Revolutionary Atlantic World." In *The Loyal Atlantic: Remaking the British Atlantic in the Revolutionary Era*. Edited by J. Bannister and L. Riordan. Toronto: University of Toronto Press, 2012.

McCulloch, Ian M. *Sons of the Mountains: The Highland Regiments in the French and Indian War, 1756–1767, Vols. I, II*. Fleischmanns, NY: Purple Mountain Press, 2006.

McDougall, W.A. *Freedom Just Around the Corner: A New American History, 1585–1828*. New York: Perennial, HarperCollins, 2004.

McLennan, William. *Spanish John*. Toronto: The Copp Clark Company, 1898.

McMillan, Helen. "John Nairne." *Unpublished Biography*. Old Fort, Montreal: David M. Stewart Museum (1959–79).

Meyer, Duane. *The Highland Scots of North Carolina*. Chapel Hill, NC: University of North Carolina, 1957.

Morgan, Philip, and Andrew O'Shaughnessy. "Arming Slaves in the American Revolution." In *Arming Slaves*. Edited by Christopher Brown and Philip Morgan. New Haven: Yale University Press, 2006.

Murdoch, Steve, and Andrew MacKillop, eds. *Fighting for Identity: The Scottish Military Experience c. 1550–1900*. Leiden: Brill, 2002.

Murray, General James. *Journal of the Seige of Quebec*. Literary and Historical Society of Quebec: The Gazette General Printing Establishment, [n. d.]

Nairne, John, and Thomas Nairne. Fonds, Archives Canada. R5991-0-3-E, MG23-GIII 23.

Nash, Gary B. *The Unknown American Revolution*. New York: Penguin Books, 2005.

Neilson, Colonel Hubert. "Slavery in Old Canada." *Transactions of the Literary and Historical Society of Quebec. Sessions of 1905. No. 6.* Quebec: The Daily Telegraph Job Printing House, 1906.

Neilson, Samuel. *Papers and Letters on Agriculture Recommended to the Attention of the Canadian Farmers by the Agricultural Society in Canada.* Quebec: Samuel Neilson, 1790.

Nun of the General Hospital of Quebec. *Narrative of the Doings During the Siege of Quebec and the Conquest of Canada in 1759.* Quebec City: Quebec Mercury Office, 1855 [?].

O'Callaghan, E.B., compiler. *Calendar of N.Y. Colonial Manuscripts Indorsed Land Papers, 1643–1803.* Revised reprint. Harrison, NY: Harbour Hill Books, 1987.

Orwell, Sonia, and Ian Angus, eds. "Notes on Nationalism," *As I Please, 1943–1945: The Collected Essays, Journalism and Letters of George Orwell.* Vol. III, London: Penguin Books, 1978.

Parkman, Francis. *Montcalm and Wolfe.* 3 vols. Toronto: George N. Morang, 1900.

Porter, Roy. *Enlightenment.* Toronto: Penguin Books Canada, 2000.

Poser, Norman. *Lord Mansfield: Justice in the Age of Reason.* Montreal: McGill-Queen's University Press, 2013.

Pouchot, Pierre. *Memoirs on the Late War in North America Between France and England.* Rev. ed. translated by Michael Cardy. Edited by Brian Dunnigan. Youngstown, NY: Old Fort Niagara Publications, 2004.

Prebble, John. *The Highland Clearances.* Harmondsworth, Middlesex, England: Penguin Books, 1963.

Reid, W., ed. *The Scottish Tradition in Canada.* Toronto: McClelland & Stewart, 1976.

Richards, F.B. "The Black Watch at Ticonderoga and Major Duncan Campbell of Inverawe." An excerpt from Volume X of the proceedings of the New York State Historical Association [n.p.] [n.d.]

Richards, Stewart. "Agricultural Science in Higher Education: Problems of Identity in Britain's First Chair of Agriculture, Edinburgh, 1790–c.1831 (Part I)" *The Agricultural History Review* 33. Exeter: British Agricultural History Society, 1985.

Rose of Kilravock Municipens. "Papers Relating to Major Clephane's Service with the 63rd (later 78th) Foot (Col. Simon Fraser's Highlanders) 1757–1765." Scottish Records Office, GD1 25/22 (29) November 10, 1759.

Schivelbusch, Wolfgang. *The Culture of Defeat.* New York: Picador, Henry Holt and Company, 2003.

Smout, Christopher T., Ned Landsman, and Tom Devine. "Scottish Emigration." In *Europeans on the Move: Studies on European Migration, 1500–1800.* Edited by Nicholas Canny. Oxford: Clarendon Press, 1994.

Sowell, Thomas. *Conquests and Cultures: An International History.* New York: Basic Books, 1998.

Stacey, C. P. *Quebec, 1759*. London: Pan Books, 1973.

Stanley, George. *Canada Invaded, 1775–1776*. Toronto and Sarasota: Samuel Stevens Hakkert and Company, 1977.

Taylor, Alan. *The Civil War of 1812: American Citizens, British Subjects, Irish Rebels, & Indian Allies*. New York: Alfred A. Knopf, 2010.

_____. *The Internal Enemy*. New York: W.W. Norton & Company, 2013.

The Sir William Johnson Papers. Vol. XI. The University of the State of New York, 1953.

Thompson, Stanbury, ed. *The Journal of John Gabriel Stedman, 1744–1797*. London: Mitre Press, 1962.

Trevor-Roper, Hugh. *The Invention of Scotland: Myth and History*. New Haven and London: Yale University Press, 2008.

Wallace, Stewart, ed. *The MacMillan Dictionary of Canadian Biography*, 3rd edition. Toronto: MacMillan, 1963.

_____. "Some Notes on Fraser's Highlanders." In *Canadian Historical Review* 18. No. 2. University of Toronto Press, 1937.

_____. *The Pedlars from Quebec and Other Papers on the Nor'Westers*. Toronto: The Ryerson Press, 1954.

Walton, Kristen P. "Scottish Nationalism Before 1789." *International Social Science Review* (September 22, 2006).

Winchester, Charles. *Memoires of the Chevalier De Johnstone*. Vol. III. Aberdeen: D. Wylie and Son, 1871.

Wise, Stephen M. *Though the Heavens May Fall*. Cambridge, MA: Da Capo Press, 2005.

Wormald, Jenny. *Lords and Men in Scotland: Bonds of Manrent, 1442–1603*. Edinburgh: John Donald Publishers, 1985.

Wrong, George M. *A Canadian Manor and Its Seigneurs*. Toronto: MacMillan and Company, 1908.

Zeller, Suzanne. *Land of Promise, Promised Land*. Ottawa: Canadian Historical Association Historical Booklet No. 56, 1996.

Websites:

Eckenrode, Hamilton James. *North American Review*. Boston, MA (October 1917): www.boondocksnet.com/twaintexts/scott_south.html.

Statistical Account of Scotland, 1791–1799. Vols. V, VI: http://stat-acc-scot.edina. ac.uk/link/1791-99/Aberdeen/Tyrie/6/145/.

Index

www.ingramcontent.com/pod-product-compliance
Lightning Source LLC
Chambersburg PA
CBHW070553270326
41926CB00013B/2294